Modeling and Visualization with AutoCAD®

Suining Ding

Indiana University Purdue University
Fort Wayne, Indiana

FAIRCHILD BOOKS, INC.   NEW YORK

Director of Sales and Acquisitions: Dana Meltzer-Berkowitz
Executive Editor: Olga T. Kontzias
Senior Development Editor: Jennifer Crane
Development Editor: Joseph Miranda
Assistant Development Editor: Blake Royer
Art Director: Adam B. Bohannon
Production Director: Ginger Hillman
Production Editor: Jessica Rozler
Associate Art Director: Erin Fitzsimmons
Copyeditor: Jennifer Sammartino
Cover Design: Adam B. Bohannon
Text Design and Composition: Dutton & Sherman Design

Library of Congress Catalog Card Number: 2007938128
ISBN: 978-1-56367-501-0
GST R 133004424
Printed in China
TP16

CONTENTS

EXTENDED CONTENTS

Chapter 3 | DesignCenter and Hatch Patterns 29

Chapter 4 | Putting Text on a Drawing 41

Chapter 11 | Perspectives and Rendering Interiors 139

Chapter 12 | Lighting Design 153

Chapter 13 | Solid Modeling 172

Chapter 14 | Development of Architectural Components 213

Chapter 15 | Apply and Modify Materials 251

Chapter 16 | Solid Editing and Form Transformation 269

THE INTENT OF THE BOOK

Although there are plenty of AutoCAD books available for architects, interior designers, and engineers, it has been difficult for me to find an appropriate textbook for students who major in interior design, while teaching AutoCAD, especially 3-D AutoCAD. Most existing 3-D AutoCAD textbooks are more engineering oriented with technical terminologies. Industrial machine components such as bolts and nuts are commonly used as tutorial or demonstration examples. I also found that existing 3-D AutoCAD textbooks lack art and design subjects, particularly subject matters of interior design and visual presentations. Therefore, this textbook has been created using tutorial examples that are relevant to interior design and architectural design with graphic images. Currently, limited generic procedures were found in the textbook to guide students to create 3-D architectural components and interior space models with 3-D AutoCAD. Thus, creating appropriate tutorial examples is important in this book.

I have more than a decade commercial architectural design and interior design practice experience of using AutoCAD. As a result of my teaching experience at Indiana University—Purdue University Fort Wayne, I wrote this book with an emphasis on an easy practical approach to instruction and visualization. It is my intent to summarize complicated concepts and procedures and transform them into a simple, straightforward and easy-to-understand format. The outcomes of the project look complex, but the procedure is very simple. During the book-writing process, I used some of the chapters and demonstration projects in class when I taught AutoCAD. I was pleased to find that my students liked the materials I handed out and worked through the demonstration projects and assignments well. I have to acknowledge my students for their very constructive feedback.

PREREQUISITE KNOWLEDGE FOR THE BOOK

This book covers both 2-D and 3-D AutoCAD. The 3-D AutoCAD is the focus of this book. This book targets an audience who has used basic 2-D AutoCAD and wants to explore advanced 2-D

AutoCAD and learn 3-D AutoCAD. There are two parts in the book: Part I covers 2-D AutoCAD and provides an overview of basic concepts. It also introduces advanced 2-D AutoCAD concepts in an easy to understand way. Part II covers 3-D AutoCAD by providing generic procedures of creating 3-D models with visual images. The book provides step-by-step tutorials, which are very easy to follow for different levels of learners.

DIFFERENT AUTOCAD VERSIONS

AutoCAD has been upgraded from Version 10 to Version 2008 during the past decades. It is my intention that instead of locking this book to a specific version, it provides a more generic procedure that could be adapted to different versions. Changes in AutoCAD from one version to another are relatively insignificant. It is not very hard for designers to master a new version if they have used the older version. I hope that this book will be suitable for future versions of AutoCAD.

AutoCAD and Other Software

It is true that many other 3-D software are available for creating three-dimensional models, such as 3-D Studio, Form Z, and Chief Architect. However, AutoCAD can be taught as a fundamental skill. Students can learn how to use other software when it is necessary. AutoCAD also has the function of inserting files from 3-D Studio. Maya from Autodesk is powerful 3-D software. Maya's powerful suite of animation tools makes it easy for users to produce animations for design reviews and client presentations. Maya allows users to import CAD data, such as dwg/DXF files to create dramatic photo real images, animations, and effects for print, web, multimedia, and television commercials. Therefore, learning 3-D AutoCAD is essential. It will prepare students for their advanced learning and professional practice.

SCOPE OF THE BOOK

This book is written for college level AutoCAD courses, especially for 3-D design. It provides students with more systematic and comprehensive tutorials and case studies. It provides objectives at the beginning of each chapter. It also provides summary, key terms, and projects at the end of each chapter. I integrated two case studies of an architectural masterpiece reconstruction in this book because it is a research topic that many researchers and scholars are exploring. It provides the three-dimensional visualizations for these scholars to explore the hidden treasures in the past and to get inspirations for today's design. These two case studies also presented typical architectural components, such as, triangular pediments, domes, and barrel vaults in the application of Boolean Operations in 3-D AutoCAD. Therefore, the book provides more relevant interior design and architectural design tutorials and case studies with generic procedures, as well as visual presentations.

The book provides two tutorials. One is for modeling and the other is for solid modeling. These two tutorials are designed for students to have a continued tutorial frame of reference. Students have the flexibility of saving the drawings, reopening the drawings, and continuing to work on the drawings. The tutorials provide students with step-by-step procedures and instructions and basic commands and procedures are demonstrated.

In addition to these two tutorials, four case studies were incorporated into the course material. Famous great buildings or masterpieces are chosen for these case studies. These case studies are 3-D models of reconstructions of the past—the Baths of Caracals; a 3-D model of a Florence Cathedral, which was created by solid modeling with geometric analysis, especially the application of Golden Ratio; 3-D model of the Falling

Water House designed by Frank Lloyd Wright, which is the application of solid modeling with Boolean Operations, and digitized materials application. The last one is a 3-D model of the Cooper Residence designed by Gwathmey-Siegel, which focuses on solid editing commands and procedures.

In general, this book covers almost every concept in both 2-D and 3-D AutoCAD with an emphasis on 3-D AutoCAD. It is also my intention to keep the project continuity from 2-D section to 3-D section. I hope that the approach of this book will help you to become a better designer with proficient skills of mastering AutoCAD. I believe that a good designer should have both productive drafting skills and creative modeling skills.

Suining Ding, ASID, IDEC

ACKNOWLEDGMENTS

This book is the result of my teaching, research, and practice.

I would like to acknowledge the Purdue Research Foundation (PRF) summer faculty research grant for its support for developing 3-D models. I was awarded a faculty research grant during the summer of 2006 to explore innovative design methods by using 3-D AutoCAD to achieve form transformation and space interlocking in design process. Most of the 3-D models in this book were created with the support of the PRF grant.

I would also like to thank all of my students whose very first critical feedback and project outcomes helped confirm and improve the pedagogical approach of the tutorial and demonstration projects and assignments. The positive student evaluations encouraged me to continue to develop an easy-to-understand textbook during the book-writing process. Special thanks are due to my students Tami Greene, Terri Glaze, Ben Wright, and Patricia Harmon for contributing their drawings to this book.

I greatly appreciate the team efforts of Fairchild Publications. I extend a heartfelt appreciation to Olga Kontzias, Executive Editor, for her belief, enthusiasm, and guidance. I also extend heartfelt thanks to Joseph Miranda, Acquisitions Editor and Development Editor for his trust, encouragement, and help. I am very grateful for their vision in understanding the importance of digital modeling and visualization of AutoCAD in interior design education. I also appreciate Jennifer Crane, Senior Development Editor, for her guidance, patience, and help. This book will not have become a reality without her belief in it and her enthusiasm, guidance, and collaboration. I also appreciate Jessica Rozler, Associate Production Editor, for her help and diligent collaborative work. Many thanks are due to Adam Bohannon, Art Director, for his talent. I extend my gratitude to the external reviewers and staff members at Fairchild who worked collaboratively to complete the project in a timely manner.

I am grateful to my family and friends who remain loyal, supportive and understanding of my absences from their lives while I spent many, many hours writing this book. I am grateful to my parents, both scientists and professors, for their inspiration of writing a book. I would not have been able to write this book without the unconditional support of my husband, Fanyu, and my lovely daughter, Laura. I dedicate this book to them and share all recognition with them.

Modeling and Visualization
with AutoCAD®

PART ONE

Two-Dimensional AutoCAD

Chapter One

Starting Drawings with AutoCAD

Objectives

This chapter presents an overview of AutoCAD features. The critical features of AutoCAD will be introduced in detail in subsequent chapters. After finishing this chapter, you will be able to:

- Switch to AutoCAD Classic workspace or 2-D Drafting & Annotation workspace for 2-D drafting.

- Understand basic AutoCAD settings, such as UCS, Limits, and Units.

- Understand Layers, Grid, Model Space, and Paper Space.

- After finishing Chapter 1, you will be able to set up a drawing with the appropriate settings.

OVERVIEW OF AUTOCAD

This book is written for interior designers, space planners and architects who already know how to use basic AutoCAD software and want to become more proficient in both 2-D and 3-D AutoCAD effectively and efficiently. There are two parts in this book: Part One introduces 2-D AutoCAD and Part Two focuses on 3-D AutoCAD. The emphasis has been put on the 3-D modeling in Part Two. Part One provides an overview of basic commands and settings in 2-D AutoCAD. Part I also introduces the drawing set up procedures. It is the intent of this book to present and introduce AutoCAD commands and features in a generic way other than lock it to a specific version of AutoCAD. AutoCAD commands and procedures are shown by using a project approach. The projects will be carried through from Part One to Part Two.

Most design firms are using AutoCAD to produce drawings and 3-D models. The benefits of using AutoCAD can be summarized as the following:

- Be able to change your drawing easily and quickly.

- Be able to produce more precise and clear drawings.

- Be able to save or store your drawings on CDs or post it on the web.

- Be able to exchange and share the drawings with other professionals, such as engineering consultants quickly and effectively.

- Be able to use other programs in combination with AutoCAD, such as, Excel, 3-D Studio Max and Photoshop.

DRAWING SHEET SET UP

Before the procedure of drawing sheet set up is introduced, it is important to understand the following concepts.

AutoCAD Workspaces

The AutoCAD system provides three different workspaces for 2-D drafting and 3-D modeling. AutoCAD Classic Workspace and 2-D Drafting & Annotation Workspace are designed for 2-D drafting, and 3-D Modeling Workspace is for 3-D modeling. It is very easy to switch between workspaces. To activate the AutoCAD Classic Workspace, move your mouse across the menu bar and click Tools, then Workspaces, AutoCAD Classic. You also can go to the upper left corner of your screen. There, you will see AutoCAD Classic shown in a small drop-down menu (Figure 1.1).

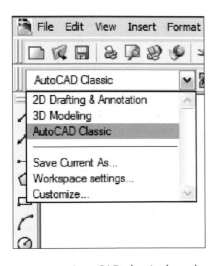

FIGURE 1.1 AutoCAD classic drop down menu

User Coordinate System

The **User Coordinate System (UCS)** icon is located at the lower left corner of the screen. It shows the orientation of the X, Y, and Z axis of the current coordinate system. In the World Coordinate System (WCS), the X axis is horizontal, the Y axis is vertical, and Z axis is perpendicular to the XY plane. The origin is where the X and Y axes intersected (0,0) in the lower left corner of the drawing. You define a UCS in terms of the WCS. The UCS icon appears as arrows that show the orientation of the X, Y, and Z axes of current UCS. It appears as a triangle in Paper Space.

There are two critical settings in AutoCAD that you have to set up correctly when you start a new drawing: Units and Limits.

Units

Units is an important setting in AutoCAD. It has to be set up correctly when you start your drawing. The Units dialog box enables you to set the way linear units are displayed in your drawing. For example, an inch is a drawing unit. In this book architectural units, which provide feet and fractional inches are used. You may set up the Architectural Units by typing Units at the command line, and then you will be prompted by the Drawing Units dialog box. (Figure 1.2). You also can access the Drawing Units dialog box by clicking on the Format pull down menu (Figure 1.3).

Limits

In AutoCAD, everything is drawn in model space 1:1. That means the object you draw is the actual size. For instance, if the opening to a door is three feet wide, you draw it in AutoCAD as three feet wide, too. You may draw a piece of furniture or you may draw the entire city in the Model Space. Therefore, it is curial to set up appropriate limits for your drawing. The limits define the lower left corner at 0, 0 as a default and the upper right corner, which defines the actual size of the model space, such as 500' × 500'. If you are going

FIGURE 1.2 Drawing units dialog box

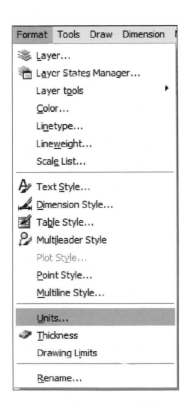

FIGURE 1.3 "Format" pull-down menu

to draw a floor plan which is 36' × 24', the limits could be set up to 50' × 40'. You may change the limits any time you need more or less space. The limits are determined based on your estimation. You just need to use command "limits" and respond to the prompt: Specify lower left corner 0, 0 and specify the upper right corner as 50', 40'. In AutoCAD that value is entered as 50', 40', using a comma with no spaces to separate the X and Y axes. AutoCAD defaults to inches, so the inch symbol is not required.

To set drawing limits:

Prompt	Response
Command	Highlight Drawing Limits on the Format pull-down menu (or TYPE: Limits)
Specify lower left corner or [ON/OFF] <0'-0", 0'-0">	
Specify upper right corner <1'-0", 0'-9">:	TYPE: 50', 40'

LAYER MANAGEMENT

Layers are the primary organizational tools used in drawing. You use layers to group information by function and to ensure linetype, color, and other standards. By creating layers, you can associate similar types of objects by assigning them to the same layer. For example, you can put construction lines, text, dimensions, and title blocks on separate layers. You can then control:

- Whether objects on a layer are visible in any viewports

- Whether color is assigned to all objects on a layer

- What default linetype and lineweight are assigned to all objects on a layer

- Whether objects on a layer can be modified

Every drawing includes a layer named 0. Layer 0 cannot be deleted or renamed. It is recommended that you create several new layers with which to organize your drawing rather than create your entire drawing on layer 0. In order to create new layers, you have to get into Layer Properties Manger dialog box (Figure 1.4).

Creating Layers

You also can access the Layer Properties Manger dialog box by clicking on Format on the pull down menu and highlighting Layers (Figure 1.3). You can create as many layers as you want. Different components of a project can be placed on separate layers. The exterior wall may be on one layer, the interior walls on another, the furniture can be on the Furniture Layer and Windows can be put on Window Layer. Usually, the layer names can be organized by different categories such as architecture, structure, electrical, and civil. For example, the layers for architectural components can be A-door, A-window, A-furniture, and A-ceiling, and so on. Layers for structural components can be S-beam and S-column. Layers for electrical and civil can be E-outlet and C-site.

It is critical to create separate layers for different components so that the components can be turned on or off as necessary.

Layer Properties

The layer options in Layer Properties Manger dialog box reading from left to right are:

- **On or Off:** On or Off controls the visibility of layers. When a layer is turned OFF, it is still part of the drawing, but any object drawn on that layer is not visible on the screen and cannot be printed.

- **Frozen or Thawed in All Viewport:** Frozen or Thawed also controls the visibility of layers. The difference between On/Off and Freeze/Thaw is a matter of how quickly the drawing regenerates on the display screen. If a layer is frozen, it is not visible and cannot be plotted, and AutoCAD spends no time regenerating it. If a layer is turned Off, it is not visible and cannot be plotted, but AutoCAD does regenerate it.

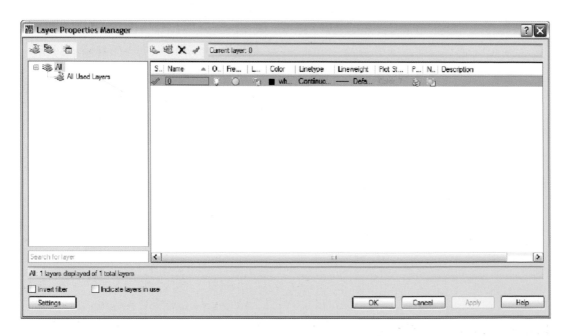

FIGURE 1.4 Layer Properties Manager dialog box

- **Frozen or Thawed in Current Viewport:** When you are working in Paper Space with more than one Viewport, you may free or thaw a layer only in the current viewport. The same layer in other viewports remains unaffected.

- **Locked or Unlocked:** When a layer is locked, it is visible and you can draw on it. But you can not use any command to edit or modify the entities on that layer.

OTHER SETTINGS IN AUTOCAD

The status bar at the bottom of your screen contains various drawing settings. These settings can be turned On or Off by clicking on the tab with your mouse.

- **Snap:** To enhance your drawing speed and efficiency, you can display and snap to a rectangular of grid points. You can also control its spacing, angle, and alignment. Snap mode restricts the movement of the crosshairs to intervals that you define. When the **Snap** mode is on, the cursor seems to adhere, or "snap" to an invisible rectangular grid. Snap is useful to specify precise points with the arrow keys on the pointing device.

- **Grid:** The **grid** is a rectangular pattern of dots that extends over the area you specify as the grid limits. The grid helps you align objects and visualize the distances between them. The grid is not plotted.

- **Model:** There are several benefits to switching between Model Space and Paper Space to perform certain tasks. Use Model Space for creating and editing your objects. Use Paper Space for composing your drawing sheet with multiple scales.

- **Ortho:** You can restrict cursor movement to horizontal and vertical for convenience and precision when creating and modifying objects. As you create or move objects, you can use the **Ortho** mode to restrict the cursor to horizontal or vertical axis.

- **Polar:** Shows temporary alignment paths along polar angles when on.

- **Osnap:** Use object snaps to specify precision locations on objects. For example, you can use an object snap to draw a line to the center of a circle or to the midpoint of a polyline segment.

- **Otrack:** Show temporary alignment paths along object snap points when on.

- **DYN:** Dynamic input – gives you information attached to the cursor regarding commands, dimensions, and tooltips.

- **LWT:** Assign varying lineweights (widths) to different parts of your drawing. When this button is on, the lineweights are displayed on the screen.

There are three different tabs at the bottom of your screen: Model, Layout1, and Layout2. By clicking on each of these tabs, you can switch back and forth between Model Space and Paper Space.

- **Model tab** – The **Model tab** accesses a limitless drawing area called Model Space. In Model Space, you draw, view, and edit your objects.

- **Layout tab** – **Layout tabs** access an area called Paper Space. In Paper Space, you place your titleblock, create layout Viewports to display views, dimension your drawing, and add notes.

DRAWING SET UP STANDARDS AND PROCEDURES

The following is a summary of the drawing set up standards and procedures. When you start a new drawing, you always have to set up correct drawing Units and Limits.

1. Switch to AutoCAD Classic or 2-D drafting & Annotation Workspace.

2. Set up appropriate drawing Units, which is architectural.

3. Set up appropriate drawing Limits, which should be big enough for the entire drawing.

4. Create separate layers for each component, such as exterior walls, interior walls, furniture, and ceilings.

Tutorial Project 1-1

SHEET SET UP FOR BEACH HOUSE FLOOR PLAN

Let's set up a new drawing for creating a floor plan of a beach house shown as Figure 1.5a. Figure 1.5b is the same floor plan with gradient hatches. It is an effective way to prepare drawing presentations especially during the schematic design phase. The gradient hatch command will be introduced in Chapter 3.

1. Open up a new drawing in AutoCAD.

2. Make sure that you are in AutoCAD Classic Workspace.

3. Click on the Format pull-down menu and highlight Unit.

4. You will be prompted with a Drawing Unit Dialog box (Figure 1.2).

5. Choose Architectural Unit in the dialog box. You also can choose precision as 1/8" and click on OK.

6. Type "Limits" at the command line; you will be prompted as follows:

Prompt	Response
Command line:	LIMITS <enter>
Reset Model Space limits: Specify lower left corner or [ON/OFF] <0'-0", 0'-0">:	ENTER
Specify upper right corner <1'-0", 0'-9">:	200', 200'
ENTER	

7. Set up new layers for the drawing, such as Furniture, Wall, Table, and Lamps. Click on the Layer command button and you will be prompted with Layer Manager dialog box shown as Figure 1.4. You may set up more layers later. For now, create several new layers as Figure 1.6.

8. Save the changes and name the drawing **Beach-House.dwg**. You will continue to work on this drawing when you move to through following chapters.

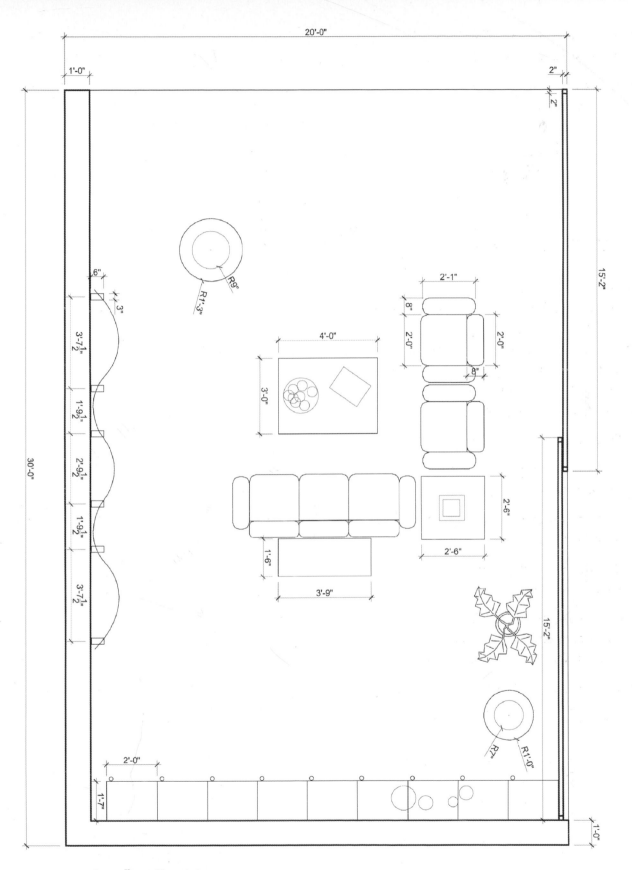

FIGURE 1.5A Floor plan of beach house

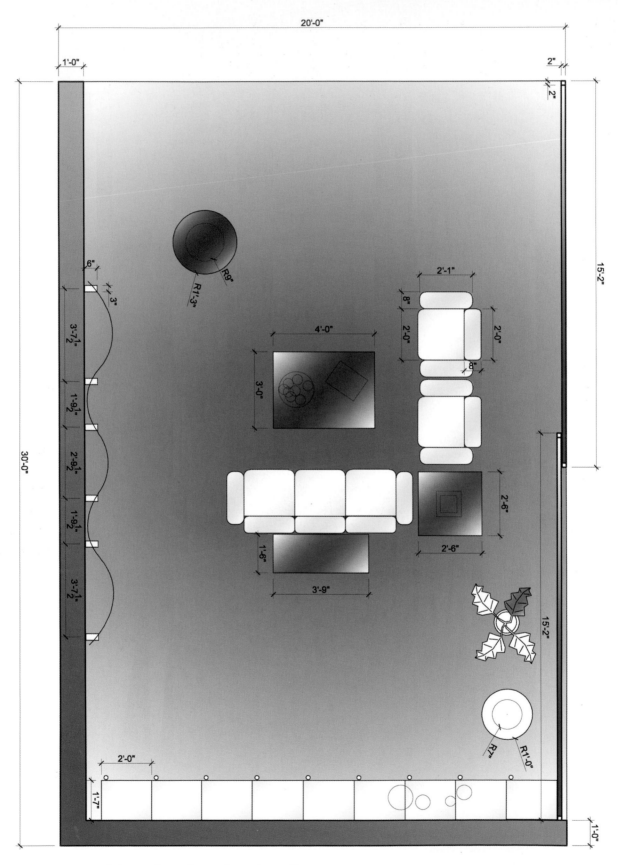

FIGURE 1.5B Beach house floor plan with gradient fill

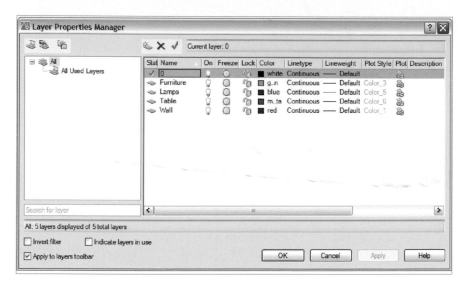

FIGURE 1.6 Layer properties manager dialog box

Tutorial Project 1-2

SHEET SET UP FOR GALLERY LOBBY FLOOR PLAN

The second tutorial project is to set up a new drawing for Gallery Lobby floor plan shown as Figure 1.7a. Same as Figure 1.5b, Figure 1.7b is the gallery lobby floor plan with gradient hatch, which is used often in presentation portfolio. Refer to Chapter 3 for detailed information about the gradient hatch command. By using Auto-CAD, you can produce technical drawings, such as construction documents with dimensions and annotations, and prepare renderings with color for presentation in schematic design. You may follow the procedures in Tutorial Project 1-1 to set up the drawing sheet and save your drawing as Gallery-Lobby.dwg. You may use this drawing in the following chapter tutorials.

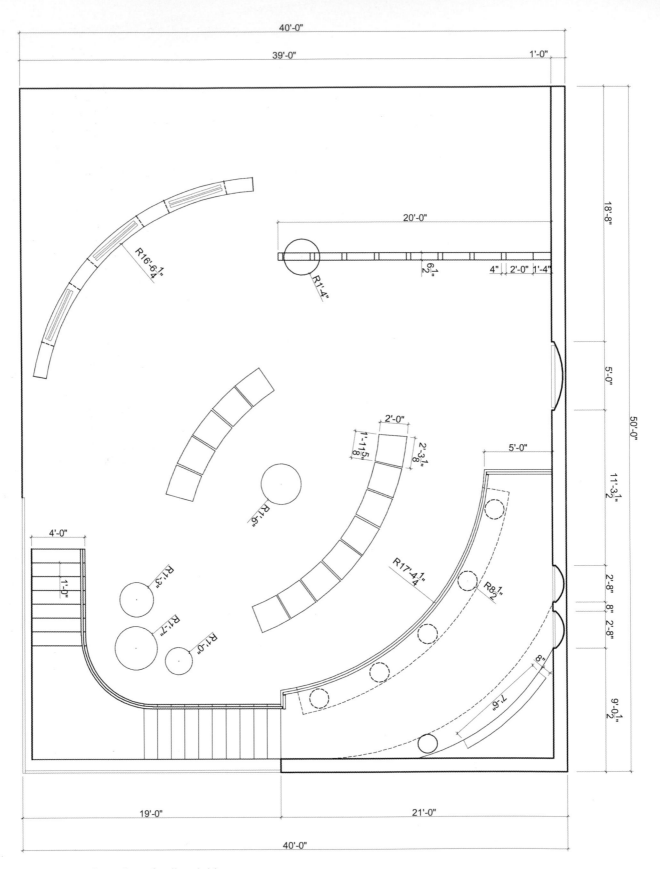

FIGURE 1.7A Floor plan of gallery lobby

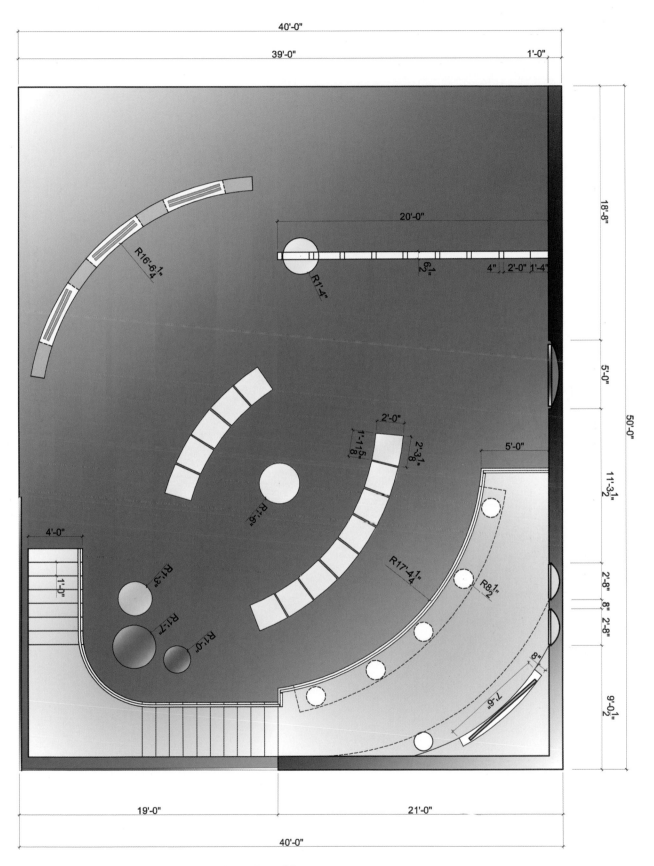

FIGURE 1.7B Gallery lobby floor plan with gradient fill

SUMMARY

Several new concepts were introduced in this chapter. When you start creating a new drawing, it is recommended to follow this procedure:

- Switch to AutoCAD Classic or 2-D Drafting & Annotation Workspace.

- Set up the correct Unit, which is architectural.

- Set up appropriate Limits.

- Set up appropriate Layers with different colors.

Turn on your Osnap when you are drawing lines. It enables you to snap to the end point, midpoint, and intersection of lines. When you draw horizontal lines and vertical lines, turn on Ortho. The Ortho model enables you to draw straight and perfect vertical and horizontal lines.

KEY TERMS

AutoCAD Workspaces	Model Tab
Grid	Ortho
Layer	Snap/Osnap
Layout Tab	UCS
Limits	Units

PROJECTS

1. Finish setting up the sheet for the beach house drawing. Create appropriate layers for this project and sign different color to each layer.

2. Finish setting up the sheet for the gallery lobby drawing. Create appropriate layers for this project and assign a different color to each layer.

3. Set up a new drawing sheet and start to draw your kitchen or bathroom floor plan at your house or apartment. Create appropriate layers and assign different colors to each layer.

Chapter Two

An Overview of 2-D AutoCAD Commands

Objectives

This chapter presents an overview of 2-D AutoCAD commands. Several Tutorial examples will be presented to demonstrate the command procedures. After finishing this chapter, you will be able to:

- Understand basic AutoCAD command and be familiar with how to access these commands.

- Recap the command access by using pull-down menu and toolbars.

- Move forward to advanced edit commands as this chapter serves as a warm-up exercise.

PULL-DOWN MENUS

In AutoCAD, **Pull-down menus** provide access to many of the same commands that are included on the toolbars. You may access these commands through pull-down menus or floating toolbars. You can move your mouse and point to the pull-down menu and hit enter; you will get a specific pull-down menu. The following are brief descriptions of the general content of the menu bar.

File

This pull-down menu includes the commands needed to start a new drawing, open an existing one, save drawings, and print or plot a drawing. It also includes export data and exit from AutoCAD. You may also click on the most recently active drawings and open these drawings (Figure 2.1).

Edit

This pull-down menu includes the Undo command (allows you to undo or reverse the most recent command) and the Redo command. It also contains the commands of Cut, Copy, and Paste (Figure 2.2).

View

This pull-down menu includes the commands that control the display of your drawing. The **Redraw** command redraws the display screen to remove blips. The **Regen** command is similar to the Redraw command, but regenerates the drawing. The Zoom command allows you to zoom in or zoom out of your drawing. The Pan command allows you to move the drawing up and down or from left to right. Viewports allows you to create several viewports for your drawing when you are working with 3-D AutoCAD. Named Views is another setting in 3-D AutoCAD. It restores the perspective views you just created. 3-D Views allow you to see your 3-D model in different views, such as isometric views, plan view, and elevations. 3-D Orbit is used to see a 3-D model from different angles and be able to rotate the 3-D model. The Hide, Shade, and Render commands are used to render the 3-D model (Figure 2.3).

Insert

This pull-down menu allows you to insert WBLOCKS and attach External references. You also can insert a drawing from previous AutoCAD drawings or other drawing programs (Figure 2.4).

Format

This pull-down menu allows you to create layers for your drawing. You may assign different colors, linetypes and lineweights to layers. You also can change the text style and dimension style from this pull-down menu. One of the most important settings is that you can set up the correct drawing units and drawing limits and prepare to draw with AutoCAD (Figure 2.5).

Tools

The workspaces and tool palettes are in the Tools pull-down menu. They are very useful when you are working in 3-D modeling. You can switch workspaces by going to Tools – Workspaces – 3–D Modeling. You also can get Dashboard on screen by going to Tools – Palette – Dashboard. This

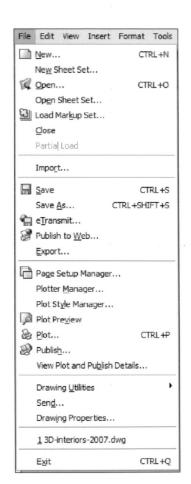

FIGURE 2.1 File pull-down menu

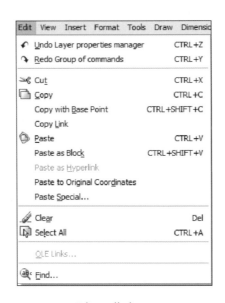

FIGURE 2.2 Edit pull-down menu

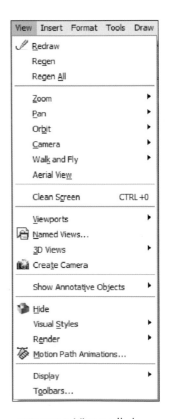

FIGURE 2.3 View pull-down menu

FIGURE 2.4 Insert pull-down menu

pull-down menu contains a spell checker and a Draw Order command that allows you to place images on top of one another. The Tool menu also has a command for customizing menus and toolbars, and activating the Options (Figure 2.6).

Draw

The **Draw** pull-down menu has all of the commands used to draw objects in AutoCAD. You also can access these commands from floating toolbars (Figure 2.7). You can access both solid and meshes 3-D modeling commands from the Draw – Modeling pull-down menu.

FIGURE 2.5 Format pull-down menu

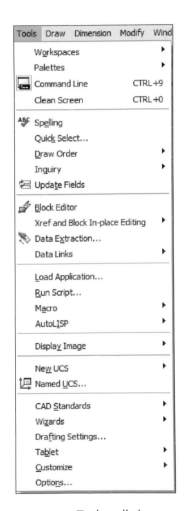

FIGURE 2.6 Tools pull-down menu

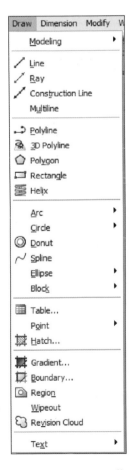

FIGURE 2.7 Draw pull-down menu

Dimension

This pull-down menu includes the commands used to place dimensions or modify dimensions on drawings. You also can access these commands from floating toolbars. All these commands are described in details in Chapter 5 (Figure 2.8).

Modify

This pull-down menu allows you to change the position, shape, or number of objects after they have been created. The commands to change the text and dimensions are also included in this pull-down menu. 3-D Operations, Solid Editing and Boolean Operations are found in the Modify Pull-down menu (Figure 2.9).

Window

This pull-down menu is used to arrange multiple drawings when you are working on more than one drawing at the same time (Figure 2.10). You also can lock or unlock your floating toolbar and floating window's location

Help

The AutoCAD Help menu provides information about all the concepts, commands, and procedures. It is a very helpful and powerful tool (Figure 2.11). When highlighting "Help" in the pull-down menu, a dialog box will pop up. Type a keyword such as "Paper Space" in the search line and a dialog box will appear and give you the descriptions about that concept.

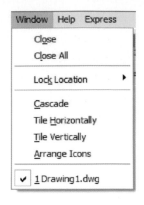

FIGURE 2.10 Window pull-down menu

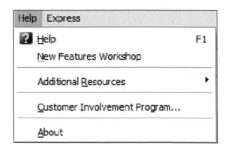

FIGURE 2.11 Help pull-down menu

FLOATING TOOLBARS

You can access all the commands by using both the pull-down menu and floating toolbars. It is a personal preference. Floating toolbars are very handy and easy to access. You just need to click on the command button and you will be prompted with that command. AutoCAD provides five different toolbars. They are shown as the following.

Figure 2.12 shows the Draw floating toolbar. In this toolbar, it contains a command line, Construction line, Polyline, Polygon, Retangle, Arc, Circle, Revision Cloud, Spline, Ellipse, Ellipse Arc, Insert Block, Make Block, Point, Hatch, Gradient, Region, Table, and Multiline Text.

FIGURE 2.8 Dimension pull-down menu

FIGURE 2.9 Modify pull-down menu

Figure 2.13 shows the Modify floating toolbar. In this toolbar, it contains the commands, Erase, Copy, Mirror, Array, Rotate, Scale, Stretch, Trim, Extend, Break at Point, Break, Join, Chamfer, Fillet, and Explode.

Figure 2.14 shows the Standard floating toolbar. In this toolbar, it contains many commands. The following are the commands that are used very often, such as Save, Print/Plot, Cut, Match Properties, Undo/Redo, Pan Realtime, Zoom Realtime, Zoom Window, Zoom Previous, DesignCenter, and Help.

Figure 2.15 is a floating toolbar that allows you to access the Layer dialog box. By clicking on the Layer icon, it will bring you the Layer Manager dialog box. You also can click on the dropdown and make the layer current.

BASIC 2-D AUTOCAD COMMAND

The followings are basic 2-D AutoCAD commands that are used extensively in AutoCAD drafting. Since this book is written for intermediate to advanced level readers, some basic commands such as LINE, ERASE, and so on will not be repeated in the following paragraph. The review of the following basic 2-D AutoCAD commands is to reinforce your knowledge.

Redraw, Regen Command

When you click on the Redraw button on the View menu or type "R" and "enter" at the command line, AutoCAD redraws and cleans up your drawing. Any plus-shaped markers on the screen disappear and drawing entities are redrawn.

When you click on the Regen button on the View menu, AutoCAD regenerates the entire drawing and recomputes the screen coordinates for all objects in the current viewport. It also reprograms the drawing databases for optimum display and object selection performance.

Blipmode Command

When a point is entered on a drawing, AutoCAD generates small plus-shaped markers on the screen. Commands such as Redraw or Regen will remove these Blip markers. When you Type BLIPMODE at the command line, you will be prompted with two responses: ON and OFF. When the Blipmode command is off, no plus-shaped markers are displayed. When the Blipmode command is on, the plus-shaped markers appear.

Array Command

You can create copies of objects in a rectangular or polar (circle) pattern called an **array**. For rectangular arrays, you control the number of

FIGURE 2.12 Draw floating tool bar

FIGURE 2.13 Modify floating tool bar

FIGURE 2.14 Standard floating tool bar

FIGURE 2.15 Layers floating tool bar

the rows and columns and the distance between each. For polar arrays, you control the number of copies of the object and whether the copies are rotated. To create many regularly-spaced objects, arraying is faster than copying.

You can access the Array command by clicking on the command button on the Modify pulldown menu (Figure 2.9) or the Modify floating tool bar (Figure 2.13). You will be prompted with the Array dialog box shown as Figure 2.16a.

- **The procedure of creating a rectangular array is as follows:**

1. Click on the Array command button on the Modify menu.

2. In the Array dialog box (Figure 2.16a), select Rectangular Array.

3. Click Select Objects. The Array dialog box closes. You are prompted for object selection.

4. Select the objects to be arrayed and press ENTER.

5. In the Rows and Columns boxes, enter the number of rows and columns in the array.

6. Specify the horizontal and vertical spacing (offsets) between the objects.

7. To change the rotation angle of the array, enter the new angle next to Angle of Array.

8. Click OK to create the array.

- **The procedure of creating a polar array is as follows:**

1. Click on the Array command button on the Modify menu.

2. In the Array dialog box (Figure 2.16b), select Polar Array.

3. Next to Center Point, do one of the following:
   a. Enter an X value and a Y value for the Center Point of the Polar Array.

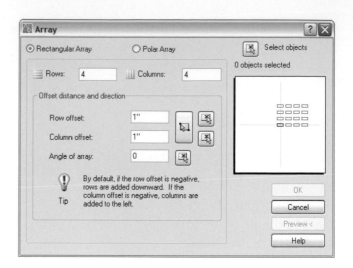

FIGURE 2.16A Array dialog box (Rectangular Array)

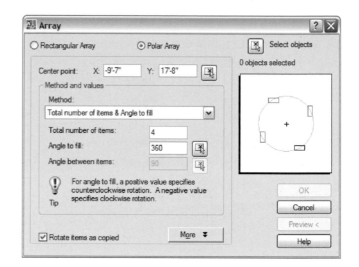

FIGURE 2.16B Array dialog box (Polar Array)

   b. Click the Pick Center Point button. The Array dialog box closes and you are prompted for specifying the center point for Polar Array on the screen. Use the pointing device to specify the center point of the Polar Array.

4. Click Select Objects. The Array dialog box closes and you are prompted for object selection.

5. Select the object to be arrayed.

6. In the Method box, select one of the following methods:

a. Total number of items and Angle to Fill. (This is the default setting and normally it is the one to select.)

b. Total number of items and Angle between items.

c. Angle to Fill and Angle between items.

7. Enter the number of items (including the original object), if available.

8. In "angle to fill," fill in "360."

TRIM and EXTEND Commands

Trim and Extend are paired commands. You can learn and memorize them together. You can shorten or lengthen objects to meet the edges of other objects by using the Trim or Extend commands. This means you can first create an object such as a line and then later adjust it to fit exactly between other objects.

- **The procedure to Trim an object:**

1. Click on the Trim command button on Modify menu.

2. Select the object to serve as cutting edges. To select all displayed objects as potential cutting edges, press ENTER without selecting any objects.

3. Select the object to trim.

- **The procedure to Extend an object:**

1. Click on the Extend command button on the Modify menu.

2. Select the objects to serve as boundary edges. To select all displayed objects as potential boundary edges, Press ENTER without selecting any objects.

3. Select the object to extend.

PLINE Command

A polyline is a connected sequence of line segments created as a single entity. You can create straight line segments, arc segments, or a combination of the two. Polyline is used widely in 2-D and 3-D AutoCAD. When you create a hatch pattern, it is recommended to use polyline to create boundaries. In 3-D AutoCAD, you will have to use polyline when you use solid modeling.

- **The procedure of drawing a polyline with straight segments:**

1. Click on the Polyline command button on the Draw menu.

2. Specify the first point of the polyline.

3. Specify the endpoint of the first polyline segment.

4. Continue specifying segment endpoints as needed.

5. Press ENTER to end, or enter C to close the polyline. To start a new polyline at the endpoint of the last polyline drawn, start the PLINE command again and press ENTER at the specifying start point prompt.

- **The procedure of creating a wide polyline:**

1. Click on the Polyline command button on the Draw menu.

2. Specify the start point of the line segment.

3. Enter W (Width).

4. Enter the starting width of the line segment.

5. Specify the ending width of the line segment using one of the following methods:
    a. To create a line segment of equal width, press ENTER.
    b. To create a tapering line segment, enter a different width.

6. Specify the endpoint of the polyline segment.

7. Continue specifying segment endpoints as needed.

8. Press ENTER to end or enter C to close the polyline.

OSNAP Command

It is very important that you become familiar with and use Object Snap modes when you are working on your drawing. Object Snap modes are used in combination with other commands to connect exactly to specific points, such as intersection, midpoint or the endpoint of a line. You can specify precise locations on objects by using object snaps. To turn on the object snap, you just need to right click on the toolbar on top of your screen and you will have a pull-down menu shown as in Figure 2.17. Highlight Object Snap; you will have a floating toolbar shown as in Figure 2.18. In this floating toolbar, you can click on each of these command buttons to get intersection, endpoint, midpoint, snap to center, snap to perpendicular and so on.

You also can set a running Osnap mode using Drafting Settings from the Tools menu (Figure 2.19). Highlight Drafting Settings and a Drafting Settings dialog box will appear (Figure 2.20). Make sure the Object Snap tab is active. Click a check mark beside the desired Osnap mode or modes.

OFFSET Command

Offset creates a new object whose shape parallels the shape of a selected object. Offsetting a circle or an arc creates a larger or smaller circle or arc depending on which side you specify for the offset. A highly effective drawing technique is to offset objects and then trim or extend their ends. You can offset lines, arcs, circles, ellipses, and so on. You may access the Offset command button at the Modify floating toolbar (Figure 2.13).

- **The procedure of offsetting an object by specifying a distance is:**

1. Click on the Offset command button on the Modify floating toolbar.

FIGURE 2.19 Tools pull-down menu (drafting settings)

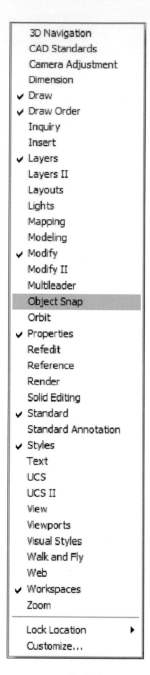

FIGURE 2.17 Pull-down menu (right click)

FIGURE 2.18 Object Snap floating tool bar

FIGURE 2.20 Drafting settings dialog box

2. Specify the offset distance. You can enter a value or use the pointing device.

3. Select the object to offset.

4. Specify a point on the side where you want to place the new object.

5. Select another object to offset or press ENTER to end the command.

HATCH, BHATCH Command

You can hatch an area using a predefined hatch pattern or create more complex hatch patterns. One type of pattern is called solid, which fills an area with a solid color. The **BHATCH** command has been renamed "**HATCH**" in the newest version of AutoCAD. If you enter "bhatch," HATCH and Gradient dialog box is displayed. The HATCH command will be discussed in detail in Chapter 3.

FILLET and CHAMFER Command

Fillet and **Chamfer** commands are another pair of commands that can be memorized together. A fillet connects two objects with an arc that is tangent to the objects and has a special radius. Fillet can be used to round all corners on a polyline using a single command. You may access the

Fillet command button on the Modify floating toolbar (Figure 2.13).

- **The procedure of setting the fillet radius is:**

1. Click on the Fillet command button on the Modify floating toolbar.

2. ENTER R for radius.

3. Enter the fillet radius with a number.

4. Select the objects to fillet

A chamfer connects two objects with an angled line. It is usually used to represent a beveled edge on a corner. Chamfer can be used to bevel all corners of a polyline using a single command. You may access the Chamfer command button on the Modify floating toolbar (Figure 2.13).

- **The procedure of setting chamfer distance is:**

1. Click on the Chamfer command button on the Modify floating toolbar.

2. ENTER D for distance.

3. Enter the first chamfer distance with a value.

4. Enter the second chamfer distance with a value.

5. Select the lines for chamfering.

ROTATE Command

You can **rotate** objects in your drawing around a specified based point. To determine the angle of rotation, you can enter an angle value, drag using the cursor or specify a reference angle to align to an absolute angle.

- **The procedure of rotating an object is:**

1. Click on the Rotate command button on the Modify floating toolbar.

2. Select the object to rotate and press enter.

3. Specify the base point for the rotation.

4. Do one of the following:
   a. Enter the angle of rotation.
   b. Drag the object around its base point and specify a point location to which you want to rotate the object.
   c. Enter C to create a copy of the selected objects.
   d. Enter R for reference to rotate the selected objects from a specified reference angle to an absolute angle.

- **The procedure of rotating an object to an absolute angle**

1. Click on the Rotate command button on the Modify floating toolbar.

2. Select the object to rotate and press enter.

3. Specify the base point for the rotation.

4. Enter R for reference.

5. Enter a reference angle value or specify two point locations. This determines an imaginary line that will be rotated to a new angle.

6. Enter the new angle, or specify a point. The value that you enter for the new angle is an absolute angle, not a relative value. Alternatively, if you specify a point, the reference angle will be rotated to that point.

MIRROR Command

You can flip objects about a specified axis to create a symmetrical mirror image. Mirroring is useful for creating symmetrical objects because you can quickly draw half of the object and then mirror it instead of drawing the entire object. You flip objects about an axis called a mirror line to create a mirror image. To specify this temporary mirror line, you enter two points. You can choose whether to erase or retain the original objects.

- **The procedure of mirroring objects is:**

1. Click on the Mirror command button on the Modify floating toolbar.

2. Select the object to mirror.

3. Specify the first point of mirror line.

4. Specify the second point.

5. Press ENTER to retain the original objects or Enter Y to erase them.

SCALE and STRETCH Command

You can resize objects to make them longer or shorter in only one direction or to make them proportionally larger or smaller. You can also stretch certain objects by moving an endpoint, vertex or control point.

With the **Stretch** command, you relocate the endpoint of objects that lie across or within a crossing selection window. You can access Scale and Stretch command buttons in the Modify floating tool bar (Figure 2.13).

You can **scale** an object using a scale factor: A scale factor greater than 1 enlarges the object. A scale factor between 0 and 1 shrinks the object.

You also can scale an object using a Reference Distance: Using an existing distance as a basis for the new size. To scale by reference, specify the current distance and then the new desired size.

- **The procedure of scaling an object by a scale factor is:**

1. Click on the Scale command button on the Modify floating toolbar.

2. Select the object to scale and press enter.

3. Specify the base point.

4. Enter the scale factor or drag and click to specify a new scale.

- **The procedure of scaling an object by reference:**

1. Click on the Scale command button on the Modify floating toolbar.

2. Select the object to scale and press enter.

3. Specify the base point.

4. Enter R for reference.

5. Specify reference length by entering a value and pressing enter.

6. Specify new length by entering a new value.

- **The procedure of stretching an object:**

1. Click on the Stretch command button on the Modify floating toolbar.

2. Select the object using a crossing window selection. The crossing window must start from the upper right corner to lower left corner. The object will be highlighted. (If you start the crossing window from the upper left corner to the lower right corner, the object can be moved instead of stretched.)

3. Specify the base point for the stretch and then specify a second point to determine the distance and direction.

EXPLODE Command

If you need to modify one or more objects within a block separately, you can disassemble or **explode** the block reference into its component objects. When individual objects are made into a block, they become a single entity. If you need to modify the object, such as a chair that is already made to a block, you will have to explode the block into its component objects. After making the changes, you can create a new block again. You can automatically explode block references as you insert them by selecting the Explode option in the insert dialog box.

- **The procedure of Exploding a block reference is:**

1. Click on the Explode command button on the Modify floating toolbar.

2. Select the block to explode and press ENTER. The block reference is disassembled into its components. However, the block definition still exists in the drawing for insertion later.

INSERT Command

When you insert a block, you create a block reference and specify its location, scale, and rotation angle. You can specify the scale of a block reference using different X, Y, and Z values. Inserting a block creates an object called a block reference because it references a block definition stored in your current drawing. You may insert a drawing file as a block; insert Blocks from Block libraries; and insert Blocks from DesignCenter.

- **The procedure of inserting a block defined in the current drawing is:**

1. Click on the "Block" command button on the Insert menu.

2. In the Insert dialog box, in the name box, select a name from a list of block definitions (Figure 2.21).

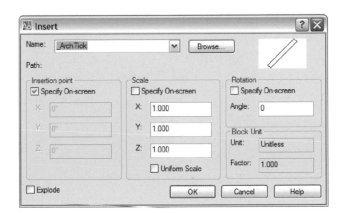

FIGURE 2.21 Insert dialog box

3. If you want to use the pointing device to specify the insertion point, scale, and rotation, check the "specify on-screen" box. Otherwise, enter value in the insertion point, scale, and rotation boxes.

4. If you want the objects in the block to be inserted as individual objects instead of as a single block, check the "explode" box.

5. Click "OK."

PURGE Command

You can remove unused named objects including block definitions, dimensions, dimension styles, layers, linetypes, and text styles with the **Purge** command.

- **The procedure of removing a block definition is:**

1. Click on the Purge command button on the File menu, Click Drawing Utilities. The Purge dialog box is displayed (Figure 2.22).

2. To purge blocks, use one of the following methods:
   a. To purge all unreferenced blocks, select Blocks. To include nested blocks, select Purge Nested Items.
   b. To purge specific blocks, double-click Blocks to expand the Block tree view. Select the blocks to be purged. If the line you want to purge is not listed, select View Items You Cannot Purge.

3. You are prompted to confirm each item on the list. If you do not want to confirm each purge, clear The Confirm Each Item To Be Purged option.

4. Click Purge. To confirm the purging of each item, respond to the prompt by choosing Yes or No, or Yes to All, if more than one item is selected.

5. Select more items to purge, or click close.

TUTORIAL PROJECTS

The following are two tutorial projects that will demonstrate the procedure of using basic 2-D AutoCAD commands.

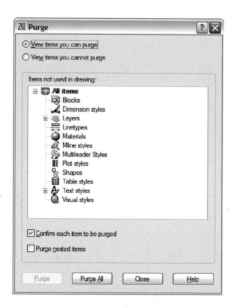

FIGURE 2.22 Purge dialog box.

Tutorial Project 2-1

ARC COMMAND, FILLET COMMAND, OFFSET COMMAND

Open up your drawing Beach-House.dwg, which was created in Chapter 1. You can create arcs in several ways. You can select a method to suit your needs. You may access ARC command under the Draw pull-down menu, shown as Figure 2.23. or you may click on the Arc command button in the floating toolbar shown as Figure 2.12. You also should use other basic 2-D commands to complete Beach-House.dwg.

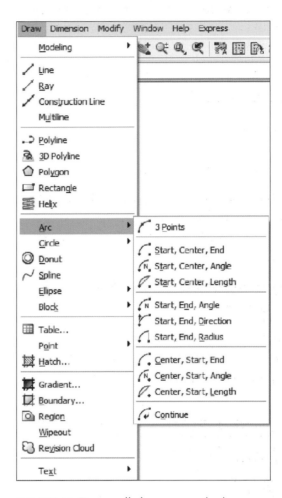

FIGURE 2.23 Draw pull-down menu (arc)

Tutorial Project 2-2

ARC COMMAND, OFFSET COMMAND, FILLET COMMAND

Open up your drawing Gallery-Lobby.dwg, which was created in Chapter 1. Use basic 2-D AutoCAD commands to complete the gallery lobby floor plan. Refer to Figure 1.7a (page 12) for dimensions. Dimensions are not required to show on the floor plan at this time.

SUMMARY

You have learned the basic 2-D AutoCAD commands in this chapter. As indicated in the beginning of the book, it is intended to give an overview of basic 2-D commands rather than give detailed procedures for each command. Readers should have had some experience using basic 2-D AutoCAD and be able to manage the basic 2-D Commands. In this chapter, 2-D command pull-down menus and floating tool bars were introduced. Some important 2-D commands, which are used extensively in drafting were reviewed. A project is provided for readers to practice in order to get familiar with basic 2-D AutoCAD commands.

KEY TERMS

Array	Modify
Basic 2-D AutoCAD	Offset
Command	PLINE
Blipmode	Pull-down menus
Dimension	Purge
Draw	Redraw / Regen
Edit	Rotate
Explode	Scale / Stretch
File	Toolbar
Fillet / Chamfer	Tools
Format	Trim / Extend
HATCH / BHATCH	View
Insert	Window
Mirror	

PROJECTS

1. Open up Beach-House.dwg drawing and create a floor plan for a beach house. The dimensions are shown in Figure 1.5a (page 9). Do not show dimensions for now.

2. Open up Gallery-Lobby.dwg and create a floor plan for a gallery lobby. The dimensions are shown in Figure 1.7a. Do not show dimensions for now.

3. Continue to work on the floor plan of the kitchen and bathroom of your houses and finish these floor plans.

Chapter Three

DesignCenter and Hatch Patterns

Objectives

A special function of AutoCAD is its capability to reuse existing or predefined data. You can avoid duplicating tasks, which saves time and increases productivity. AutoCAD contains a powerful feature called AutoCAD DesignCenter, which enables you to quickly locate, view, and import a variety of existing AutoCAD objects into the current drawing. In addition to DesignCenter, you will also explore hatch patterns. After finishing this chapter, you will be able to:

- Browse for drawing content, such as drawing or symbol libraries on your computer or a networked drive.

- Update (redefine) a block definition.

- Add content such as xrefs, blocks, and hatches to a drawing.

- Drag drawings, blocks and hatches for DesignCenter to a tool palette for convenient access.

- Define the boundaries of the area to be filled.

- Specify the pattern to be used.

- Edit a hatch pattern.

DESIGNCENTER PALETTE

You can access DesignCenter by clicking on the Tool pull-down menu and highlight Pallets and DesignCenter, shown as Figure 3.1. You will be prompted with a dialog box shown as Figure 3.2. In Figure 3.2, the DesignCenter window is divided into three views on the left side and the content area of the right side. Use the three views to browse sources of content and to display content in the content area. Below the content area, you can also display a preview or a description of a selected drawing, block, hatch pattern, or xref. A toolbar at the top of the window provides several options and operations. They are Folder, Open Drawings, History, and DC Online.

Folder Tab

The Folder Tab displays a hierarchy of navigational icons, including:

- Networks and Computers

- Web address (URLs)

- Computer Drives

- Drawings and related support files

- Xrefs, layouts, hatch styles, and named objects, including blocks, layers, linetypes, text styles, dimension styles, and plot styles within a drawing.

Open Drawings

Displays a list of the drawings that are currently open. Click a drawing file and then click one of the definition tables from the list to load the content into the content area (Figure 3.3).

History

Displays a list of files opened previously with DesignCenter. Double-click a drawing file from the list to navigate to the drawing file in the Tree view of the folder tab and to load the content into the content area.

DC Online

Provides content from the **DesignCenter Online (DC Online)** web page including blocks, symbol libraries, and manufacturer's content and online catalog.

BRINGING BLOCKS FROM DESIGNCENTER

You may bring predefined blocks from the DesignCenter to your drawing. It saves tremendous time and increases your productivity. The DesignCenter is just like a library, in which you can browse predefined blocks, such as furniture, fixture, and standard symbols and insert them

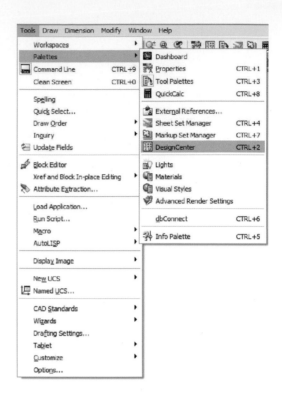

FIGURE 3.1 Tool-Palettes-DesignCenter pull-down menu

to your drawings. The procedure of browsing the predefined blocks from DesignCenter is described as the following:

1. If DesignCenter is not already open, click the Tools menu, and then highlight DesignCenter.

2. On the DesignCenter window, click on the Folders tab.

3. Under Sample, click on DesignCenter, shown as Figure 3.4.

4. Find Home-Space Planner.dwg (for example) and double click on it.

5. Click on Blocks.

6. Highlight Chair-Desk (for example) and Preview (Figure 3.5).

7. Drag it to your screen (Figure 3.6).

In this procedure, Home-Space Planner.dwg is used as an example. You may choose other drawings and browse other predefined blocks, such as tables and fixtures.

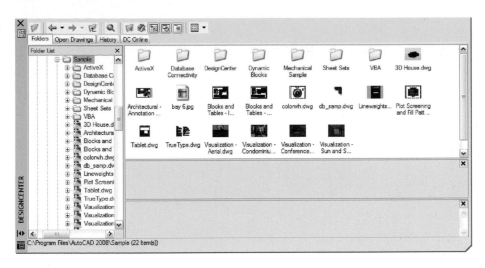

FIGURE 3.2 DesignCenter dialog box

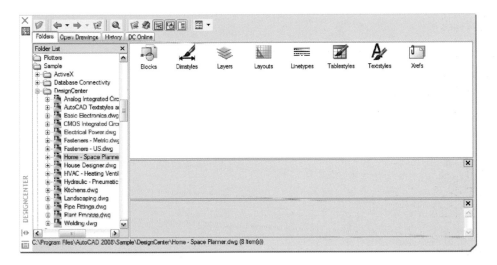

FIGURE 3.3 DesignCenter dialog box

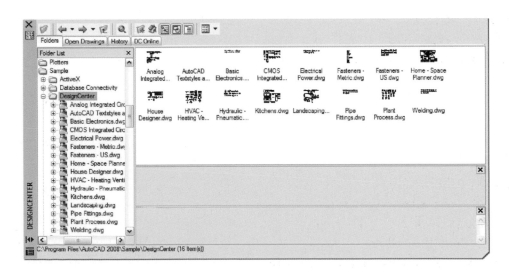

FIGURE 3.4 DesignCenter dialog box

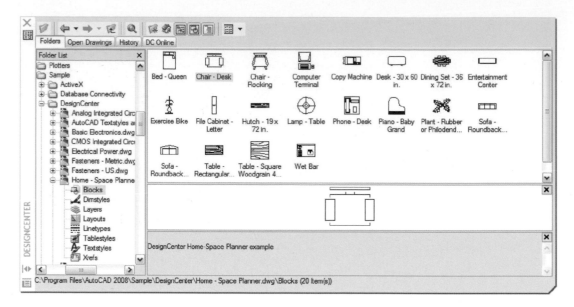

FIGURE 3.5 DesignCenter dialog box

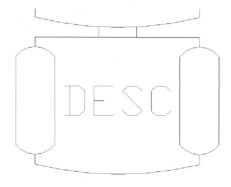

FIGURE 3.6 Chair block from DesignCenter

HATCH PATTERNS

You can hatch an area using a predefined hatch pattern, define a simple line pattern using the current linetype, or create more complex hatch patterns. One type of pattern is called solid, which fills an area with a solid color.

You can also create a gradient fill, which uses a transition between shades of one color or between two colors. Gradient fills can be used to enhance presentation drawings, giving the appearance of light reflecting on an object (CAD help menu). The critical point for creating a hatch pattern is that the boundary lines need to be closed or need to be a polyline.

Define the Boundaries of a Hatch

You can choose from several methods to specify the boundaries of a hatch:

- Specify a point in an area that is enclosed by objects.

- Select objects that enclose an area.

- Drag a hatch pattern into an enclosed area from a tool palette or DesignCenter.

Choose the Hatch Pattern

The program supplies a solid fill and more than 50 industry-standard hatch patterns that you can use to differentiate the components of objects or represent object materials. The program also comes with hatch patterns that conform to the ISO (International Standards Organization) standards. When you select an ISO pattern, you can specify a pen width, which determines the lineweight in the pattern.

You can access the Hatch Pattern command button by clicking on the floating toolbar shown as Figure 3.7, and then you will be prompted with a Hatch and Gradient dialog box shown as Figure 3.8.

FIGURE 3.7 Draw floating tool bar (Hatch)

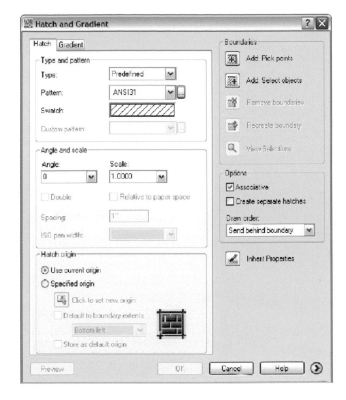

FIGURE 3.8 Hatch and Gradient dialog box

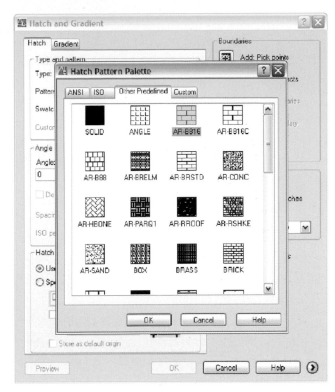

FIGURE 3.9 Hatch pattern palette

To choose the hatch pattern, click on the little square button next to Pattern in Figure 3.8, and then you will be prompted with a dialog box shown as Figure 3.9. Click on Other Predefined tab and highlight the pattern that you are going to choose and click on the OK button. It will bring you back to the Hatch and Gradient dialog box.

In the mid portion of the Hatch and Gradient dialog box, you can specify the rotation angle for the hatch pattern. You also can choose different scales to make the hatch pattern bigger or smaller. In Figure 3.10, one hatch pattern was created with a rotation angle of 45 degrees, and the other pattern was created with 0.5 scale instead of 1 scale.

Control the Hatch Origin

By default, hatch patterns always "line up" with each other. However, sometimes you might need to move the starting point, called the origin point, of the hatch. For example, if you create a brick pattern, you might want to start with a complete brick in the lower-left corner of the hatched area (Figure 3.11). In that case, use the Hatch Origin options in the Hatch and Gradient dialog box.

In the Hatch and Gradient dialog box, shown in Figure 3.8, under Hatch Origin, click on Specified Origin, and then click on Set New Origin. You will be prompted by a command line: Specify Origin Point. You just need to pick the lower left corner of the rectangle in Figure 3.11 and then pick a point inside of the rectangle. You will have a hatch pattern, shown in Figure 3.11, on the right side.

Create Associative Hatches

An associative hatch is updated when you change the boundary. Hatched areas created with Hatch are associative by default.

Under the Option section, there are two options to specify hatch patterns. One is called Associative and the other one is called Create Separate Hatches. You may click on the first one for associative hatch patterns and second one for separate hatches.

In Figure 3.12, the middle hatch pattern is the result of editing boundary with non associative hatches. The left hatch pattern is the result of editing boundary with associative hatch. It is

obvious that the associative Hatch pattern will be changed when the boundary line changes.

Create Gradient Hatches

You can also create a gradient fill, which uses a transition between shades of one color or between two colors. Gradient fills can be used to enhance presentation drawings, giving the appearance of light reflecting on an object. Figure 1.5b and Figure 1.7b are two examples of using gradient hatches in floor plans. Gradient Hatches also can be used for schematic design presentation drawings, such as floor plans and elevations.

To access the Gradient command, just simply click on the command button, shown in Figure 3.13. You will be prompted with Hatch and Gradient dialog box, shown in Figure 3.14. On top of the Hatch and Gradient dialog box, there is a section called Color. In this section, you can choose One Color or Two Color.

FIGURE 3.10 Hatch pattern palette (Brick Hatch Pattern)

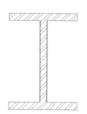  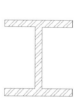

FIGURE 3.12 Associative hatch pattern sample

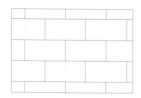 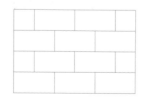

FIGURE 3.11 Control hatch origin sample

FIGURE 3.13 Draw floating tool bar (Gradient Hatch command button)

Color

- One Color—specifies a fill that uses a smooth transition between darker shades and lighter tints of one color. When One Color is selected, you also can choose your preferred color by clicking on […] button. You will be prompted with a dialog box Select Color. You may define your color choice in this dialog box.

- Two Color- specifies a fill that uses a smooth transition between two colors. When Two Color is selected, you can use browse button […] for color one and for color two. You can specify the color for the gradient fill in the dialog box Select Color shown in Figure 3.15.

Shade and Tint Slider

When One Color is selected, you also can specify the Tint (the color mixed with white) or shade (the color mixed with black) of a color to be used for a gradient fill of one color. Refer to Figure 3.14 to see Shade and Tint Slider. The "Shade and Tint Slide" is just right next to the "One Color" selection bar.

Gradient Pattern

The section Gradient Pattern in Figure 3.14 displays nine fixed patterns for gradient fills. These patterns present different color transitions.

Orientation

The section Orientation in Figure 3.14 specifies the angle of the gradient and whether it is symmetrical.

- Center—specifies a gradient configuration that is symmetrical. If this option is not selected, the gradient fill is shifted up and to the left.

- Angle—specifies the angle of the gradient fill. You may rotate the gradient fill by choosing different angles.

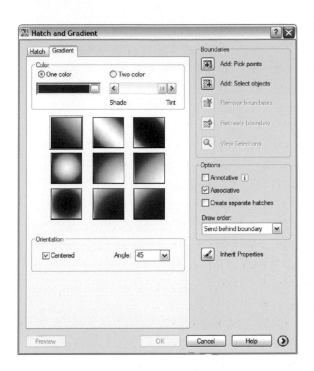

FIGURE 3.14 Hatch and Gradient dialog box

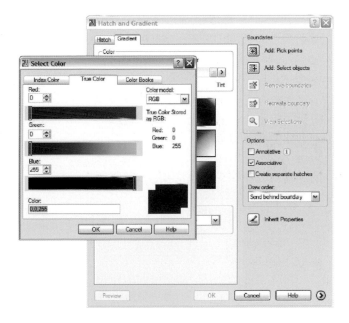

FIGURE 3.15 Select color for gradient fill

The following images are the interior elevations of a beach house with dimensions (Figure 3.16a–Figure 3.18b). You may use these images as reference for your 3-D modeling in the later chapters. Figure 3.16a–Figure 3.18b are presentation drawings with gradient hatches, as well as interior elevations with dimensions. Figure 3.19 and Figure 3.20 are interior elevations for the gallery lobby.

SUMMARY

In this chapter, you have learned how to use DesignCenter to locate source objects and bring predefined objects, such as chairs and tables, to your drawing. You may experience dragging different types of content from the palette and copying them into the current drawing. Design-Center enables you to work more productively by reusing predefined AutoCAD objects located in other drawings.

In addition to DesignCenter, you also learned how to create hatch patterns. You can choose predefined hatch patterns from the AutoCAD system. You also can rotate and scale the hatch pattern. Besides these, you also can specify hatch origin for the hatch pattern. There are two different hatch patterns. One is a non-associative hatch pattern and the other one is an associative hatch pattern. You may redefine hatch boundaries with associative hatch patterns. However, with non-associative hatch patterns, you will have to redo the hatch pattern.

The Gradient Fill Hatch command was also introduced in this chapter. It is very useful for creating presentation drawings with colored hatch patterns. You may define one or two colors for your gradient fills. You also can rotate your gradient fill patterns by specifying different angles.

KEY TERMS

DesignCenter Online
 (DC Online)
Gradient Hatch

History
Open Drawings

PROJECTS

1. Insert furniture from DesignCenter to the beach house floor plan.

2. Apply hatch patterns to the beach house floor plan and gallery lobby floor plan.

3. Create three interior elevations for the beach house. Use the beach house floor plan as reference. (The interior elevations are shown as Figure 3.16a–Figure 3.18b.)

4. Create presentation drawings for the beach house. These presentation drawings include floor plan and three interior elevations. Use Figure 3.16a–Figure 3.18b as references. You may use different colors for gradient fills. The presentation drawings should be professional.

5. Create two interior elevations for gallery lobby. Use the gallery lobby floor plan as a reference. (The interior elevations are shown as Figure 13.6a and Figure 13.7a.)

6. Create presentation drawings for the gallery lobby. These presentation drawings include floor plans and three interior elevations. Use Figure 3.19 and Figure 3.20 as references. You may use different colors for gradient fills. The presentation drawings should be professional.

7. Create presentation drawings for the kitchen and bathroom in your house. These presentation drawings must include floor plans and four interior elevations. You will have to use measuring tap to measure the dimensions in your house or apartment. You may use different color for gradient fills. The presentation drawings should be professional.

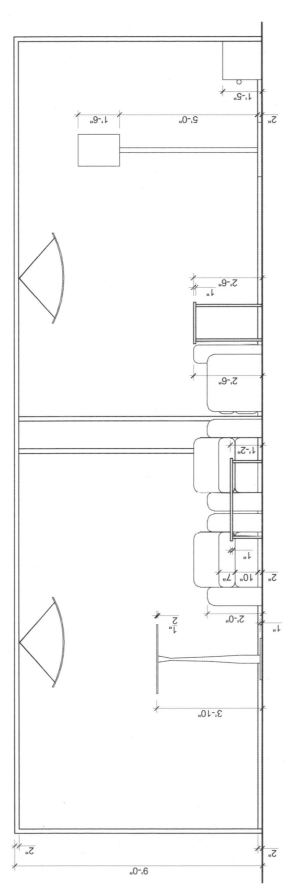

FIGURE 3.16A Interior elevation of beach house

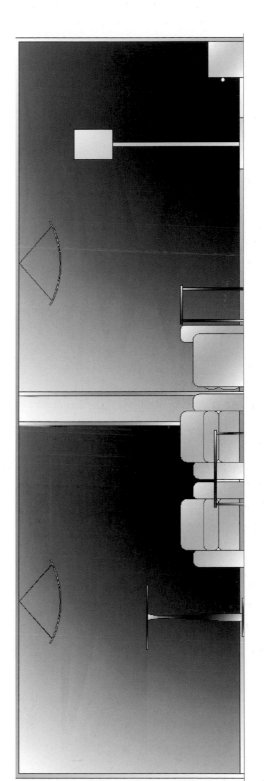

FIGURE 3.16B Interior elevation of beach house with gradient fill

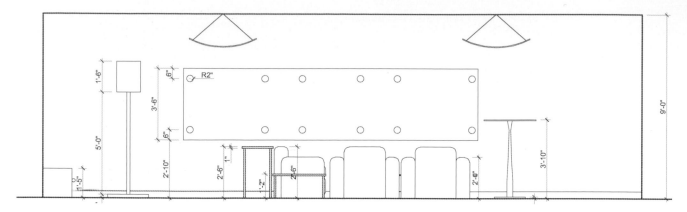

FIGURE 3.17A Interior elevation of beach house

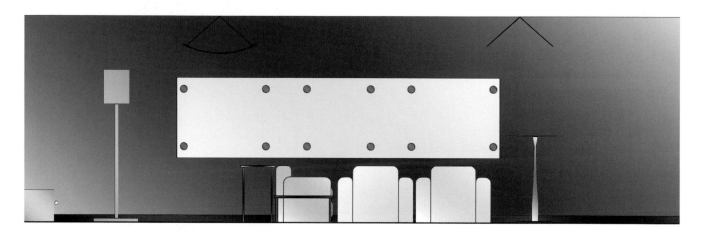

FIGURE 3.17B Interior elevation of beach house with gradient fill

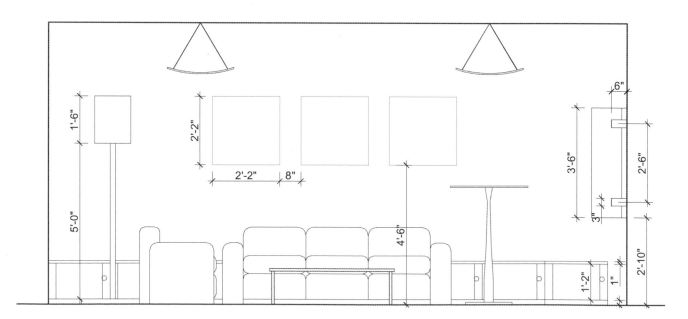

FIGURE 3.18A Interior elevation of beach house

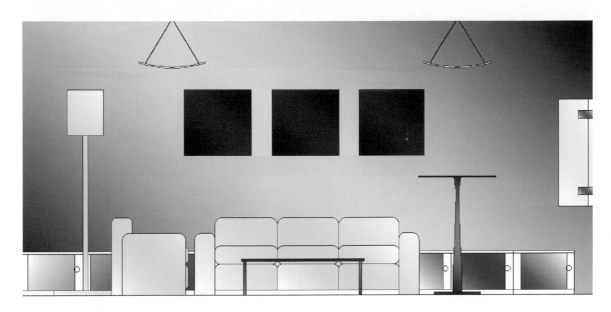

FIGURE 3.18B Interior elevation of beach house with gradient fill

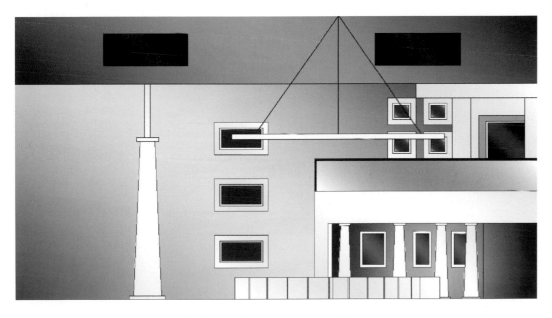

FIGURE 3.19 Interior elevation of gallery lobby with gradient fill

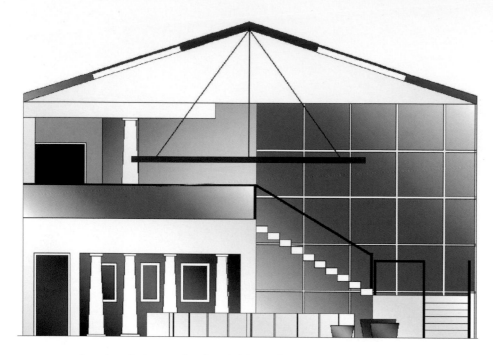

FIGURE 3.20 Interior elevation of gallery lobby with gradient fill

Chapter Four

Putting Text on a Drawing

Objectives

Text annotation is a very important component of a design document. You may need to put a single word or a short paragraph on your drawing. The ability to edit text proficiently really affects your productivity. After finishing this chapter, you will be able to:

- Determine your text height.

- Define a text style.

- Use single-line text.

- Create and modify multiline text.

- Perform text property modification and spelling check.

CHOOSING THE CORRECT TEXT HEIGHT

When you are ready to put the text in your drawing, one of the important things is to set up the correct text height. The reason for that is because you have different scales for your drawing. For example, you may have $^1/_4$" scale and $^1/_8$" scale drawings on the same sheet. You have to use the Layout tab to bring your drawings to Paper Space. Therefore, you will have to set up different text heights for each drawing in Model Space. Table 4.1 will help you to determine the correct text height. In the table, the first column shows the drawing scales. The second through the fifth columns indicate the correct text height associate with the drawing scale.

Table 4.1
TEXT HEIGHT FOR ARCHITECTURAL SCALES

Drawing Scale	Plotted Text Heights				
	$^3/_{32}$"	$^1/_8$"	$^3/_{16}$"	$^1/_4$"	$^3/_8$"
$^1/_{16}$"=1'	18"	24"	36"	48"	72"
$^3/_{32}$"=1'	12"	16"	24"	32"	48"
$^1/_8$"=1'	9"	12"	18"	24"	36"
$^3/_{16}$"=1'	6"	8"	12"	16"	24"
$^1/_4$"=1'	4.5"	6"	9"	12"	18"
$^1/_2$"=1'	2.25"	3"	4.5"	6"	9"

CHOOSING A TEXT STYLE

You can choose as many text styles as you need in a drawing. You can access the Text Style dialogue box by choosing Text Style from the Format menu (Figure 4.1). Figure 4.2 shows the Text Style dialog box. The various settings within the Text Style dialog box will be explained in more detail later in this chapter.

The following is the procedure used to creating a new text style:

1. Click on the New button in the Text Style dialog box. You will be prompted with a new dialog box, shown in Figure 4.3.

2. Type a name in the New Text Style dialog box. A duplicate style is then created from the selected style and assigned the name you provided. Click on OK. You can select a font from the font name drop down. You also can assign height for the new text style.

3. You can also rename an existing style, select the style from the list of existing styles, click the Rename button, and enter a new name.

4. You also can delete an existing style, highlight the name from the list of existing styles and click the Delete button.

5. The Standard text style cannot be deleted or renamed. The current text style cannot be deleted either.

Choosing a Font and Style

Fonts define the shapes of the text characters that make up each character. You can use True Type fonts in addition to compiled SHX fonts. True Type fonts are supplied with Windows or other Windows applications. SHX are the font files supplied with AutoCAD. A single font can be used by more than one text style. You can assign a font to a text style by selecting a font file from the list in the Text Style dialog box.

FIGURE 4.1 Format Text Style pull-down menu

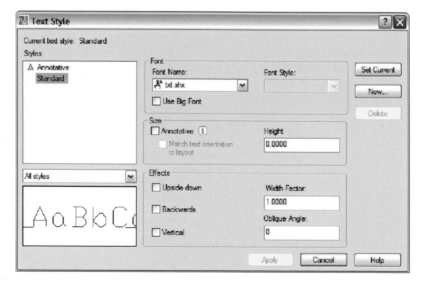

FIGURE 4.2 Text Style dialog box

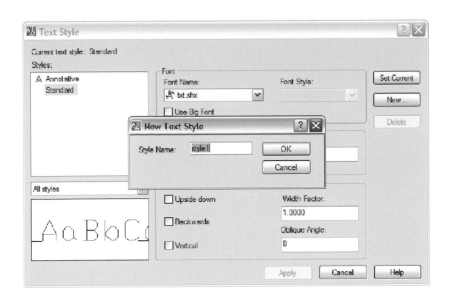

FIGURE 4.3 New Text
Style dialog box

Setting a Height

In the Text Style dialog box, you also will find the text height setting. The default height of 0 dictates that the user is allowed to set the text height at the time the text is created. Text **height** determines the size, in drawing units, of the letters in the font you are using. Except in True Type fonts, the value usually represents the size of the uppercase letters. When the height is set to 0 in the text style, you are prompted for the height each time you create single line text. Set the value to 0 if you want to specify the height as you create text.

Previewing the Text Style Settings

The Character **Preview** area enables you to view a sample of the selected style and the results of changing the various settings.

Specifying Special Effects

The **Effects** section of the Text Style dialog box contains the Upside Down, Backwards, Vertical, Width Factor, and Oblique Angle settings. Figure 4.4a shows an example of how these settings affect the appearance of the text.

Setting a Width Factor

The Width Factor determines the width of the letters. A factor of 1 results in the letters being displayed with the width as defined in the chosen font file. A factor greater than 1 results in wider letters, and a factor of less than 1 results in thinner letters. Figure 4.4b displays the effects of using different width factors. All three texts were created with the same text height.

SINGLE-LINE TEXT COMMAND

Use **single-line text** to create one or more lines of text, ending each line when you press ENTER. Each text line is an independent object that you can relocate, reformat, or otherwise modify. When you create single-line text, you assign a text style and set alignment. The text style sets the default

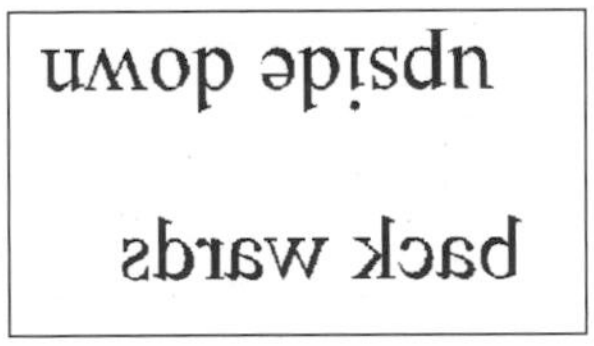

upside down

back wards

FIGURE 4.4A Upside down text

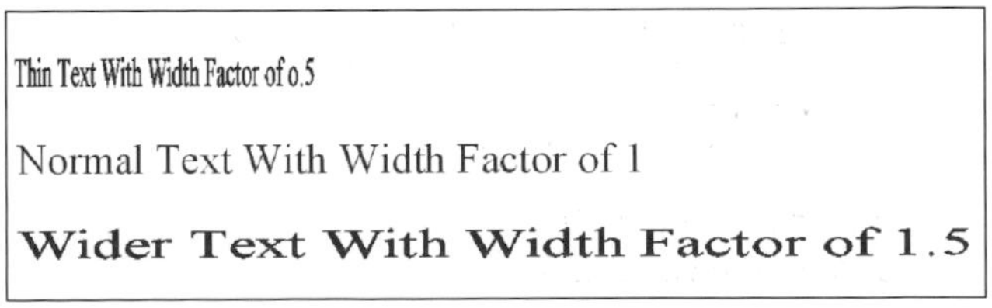

Thin Text With Width Factor of 0.5

Normal Text With Width Factor of 1

Wider Text With Width Factor of 1.5

FIGURE 4.4B Text with different width

characteristics of the text object. The alignment determines what part of the text character aligns with the insertion point. Use the Text command to enter the text in-place, or enter-text on the command line to enter the text on the command line (CAD help menu).

The text style used for single-line text is the same as those used for multi-line text. When you create text, you assign an existing style by entering its name at the style prompt. If you need to apply formatting to individual words and characters, use multi-line text instead of single-line text.

You can also compress single-line text to fit between points that you specify. This option stretches or squeezes the text to fill the designated space (CAD help menu).

You may access single line text by clicking on the Draw pull-down menu and highlighting "Text and then Single Line Text" (Figure 4.5).

When you activate the Single Line Text command, the prompt reads, Specify start point of text or [Justify/Style]. The style option allows you to select a different text style. If you type J<enter>, the prompt then becomes "Enter an option[Align/Fit/Center/Middle/Right/TL/TC/TR/ML/MC/MR/BL/BC/BR]."

Align

Align draws the text between two points that you specify by clicking. It does not condense or expand the font but, instead, adjusts the letter height so that the text fits between the two points.

Fit

Fit draws the text between two clicked points like the Align option, but instead of changing the letter height, Fit condenses or expands the font to fit between the points.

Center

Center draws the text so that the bottom of the line of the lettering is centered on the clicked point.

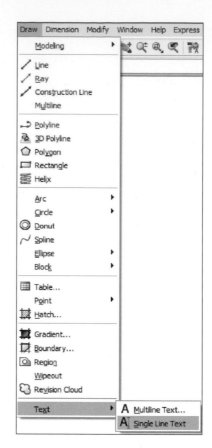

FIGURE 4.5 "Draw-text-single line text" pull-down menu

Middle

Middle draws the text so that the middle of the line of lettering is centered on a clicked point. This is very useful when a single line of text must be centered in an area such as a box.

Right

Right draws the text so that each line of text is right justified (ends at the same right margin). Right justification is not displayed until the second return is pressed.

TL/TC/TR/ML/MC/MR/BL/BC/BR

These are alignment options: Top Left, Top Center, Top Right, Middle Left, Middle Center, Middle Right, Bottom Left, Bottom Center, Bottom Right. They are used with horizontal text.

MULTILINE TEXT COMMAND

You can create one or more paragraphs of **multiline text** (MTEXT) in the In-Place Text Editor (or an alternative text editor) or use prompts on the command line. Before entering or importing text, you specify opposite corners of a text bounding box that defines the width of the paragraphs in the multiline text object. The length of the multiline text object depends on the command of text, not the length of the bounding box. You can select a defined style, change the text height and case, boldface and italicize some fonts, and make other modifications to the text (Figure 4.8).

You can access the multiline text command by clicking on the floating tool bar shown as Figure 4.6 or clicking on the pull-down menu shown as Figure 4.7. The procedure for creating multiline text is as follows:

1. Click on the Draw menu, then click on Text and then Multiline Text (Figure 4.7).

2. Specify opposite corners of a bounding box to define the width of the multiline text object.

3. To indent the first line of each paragraph, drag the first-line indent slider on the ruler. To indent the other lines of each paragraph, drag the paragraph slider.

4. To set tabs, click the ruler where you want a tab stop.

5. If you want to use a text style other than the default, click the arrow next to the Text Style control on the toolbar and then select a style.

6. Enter the text.

FIGURE 4.6 Draw floating tool bar (Multiline text)

FIGURE 4.7 Draw-text-multiline text pull-down menu

FIGURE 4.8 Text with different fonts

FIGURE 4.9 Degree symbol

```
%% C0.75
Ø0.75
```

FIGURE 4.10 Diameter symbol

```
%% P0.15
±0.15
```

FIGURE 4.11 Plus and minus symbol

```
%%UUNDERSCORE
UNDERSCORE

%%UUNDERSCORE%%U TEXT
UNDERSCORE TEXT
```

FIGURE 4.12 Underscore symbol

```
%%OOVERSCORE
OVERSCORE

%%OOVERSCORE%%O TEXT
OVERSCORE TEXT
```

FIGURE 4.13 Overscore symbol

USING STANDARD CODES TO DRAW SPECIAL CHARACTERS

You can use standard codes to obtain several commonly used symbols, such as the degree symbol, the diameter symbol, the plus-minus symbol, and underscored and overscored text. In the following figures, the top line is what you need to type; the bottom lines show the symbols you want to obtain.

Figure 4.12 and Figure 4.13 show the code for underscore and overscore: two percent symbols followed by the letter U. Notice that the first line contains only one code. The second line contains two codes: One to start the underline or overscore, and one to stop them.

SPELLING CHECK

You can check the spelling of all text in your drawing including:

- Single-line text

- Multiline text

- Text within attribution values

- Text within block references and their associated block definitions

- Text within nested blocks

Spelling is checked only in objects in the current selection set. If you enter the All option when selecting objects, spelling is checked in all objects in Model Space and in all Paper Space. Spelling is not checked in block definitions of unselected block references or in text within dimensions (CAD help menu).

You can access the spell check command by clicking on the Tool pull-down menu and highlighting Spelling, shown in Figure 4.14. When you start the command, AutoCAD prompts you to select the objects to check. If the Spelling command finds an unknown word, the Check Spelling dialog box appears, and you must choose to replace the word. If no errors are found, a message box appears, informing you that the spell check is complete.

SUMMARY

AutoCAD provides a variety of tools to edit and modify text. This chapter covered the procedures of creating single-line text and multiline text, as well as how to use standard codes to create various symbols, such as the degree symbol, diameter symbol, plus-minus symbol, and underscore/overscore symbols. This chapter also introduced detailed information on editing text and defining the text style and how to control the appearance of text.

FIGURE 4.14 Tools-Spelling pull-down menu

KEY TERMS

Effect

Height

Multiline Text

Preview

Single-line Text

Spelling Check

PROJECTS

1. Put text on the beach house floor plan with appropriate text size. You may label furniture on the floor plan.

2. Put text on the gallery lobby floor plan with appropriate text size. You may label the furniture on the floor plan.

3. Put text on the kitchen/bathroom floor plan with appropriate text size. You may label the fixtures on the floor plan.

4. Practice how to change the text font on your drawings.

Chapter Five

Dimensioning

Objectives

Dimension is a very important and critical aspect for design documents, especially for the construction documents. When working on a project in a production environment, one of the challenges is to dimension a drawing quickly and accurately. You must also be able to modify existing drawing dimensions just as quickly and accurately. When you are working on a drawing, it is recommended to create a layer called Dimension and put all the dimensions on this layer. It will allow you to turn the layer on and off as necessary.

This chapter introduces you to the settings of dimensions and various techniques necessary to dimension a drawing quickly and easily. After finishing this chapter, you will be able to:

- Set up appropriate dimension styles and settings.

- Change dimension text size and font.

- Change dimension tick size.

- Set up appropriate graphic looks for dimensions.

- Modify other dimension settings.

DEFINE DIMENSION STYLES

Before you start dimensioning a drawing, you have to set up the right settings for your dimensions. AutoCAD provides you with several tools for editing and modifying dimensions and controlling how a dimension appears in the drawing.

The following section will introduce the dimension styles, dimension options, and modifying dimensions.

A dimension style is a named collection of dimension settings that controls the appearance of dimensions, such as arrowhead, style, text location, and lateral tolerances. You create dimension styles to specify the format of dimensions quickly and to ensure that dimensions conform to industry or project standards (CAD help menu).

- When you create a dimension, it uses the settings of the current dimension style.

- If you change a setting in a dimension style, all dimensions in a drawing that use that style update automatically.

- You can create dimension substyles that deviate from the current dimension style for specified types of dimensions.

- If necessary, you can override a dimension style temporarily (CAD help menu).

Dimension Style Manager

Dimension Style Manager enables you to set the current dimension style, create a new style, modify an existing style, and override part of the current style. You can adjust the dimension variables through the Dimension Style Manager (Figure 5.1). You can access this dialog box by choosing Dimension Style from the Dimension toolbar or by choosing Style from the Dimension pull-down menu.

To modify the dimension style, simply open the Dimension Style Manager, select the style you want to edit, and click the Modify button. To create a new style, you can choose New in the Dimension Style Manager. In the dialog box (Figure 5.2), you can name a new dimension style.

Regardless of whether you choose to modify an existing dimension style or create a new one, a dialog box (Figure 5.3) appears, allowing you to modify the the individual parts of the dimension style.

Procedures of Creating a New Dimension Style

1. Start a new drawing in AutoCAD from scratch.

2. From the Dimension pull-down menu, select Dimension Style. You will get the Dimension Style Manager dialog box (Figure 5.1). You can create and edit the dimension style.

3. All drawings come with the Standard dimension style. You also can click on the New button to create a new style. This will bring you to the Create New Dimension Style dialog box (Figure 5.2).

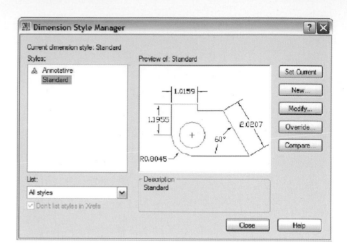

FIGURE 5.1 Dimension Style Manager dialog box

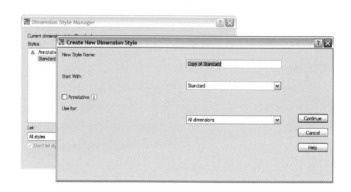

FIGURE 5.2 Create New Dimension Style dialog box

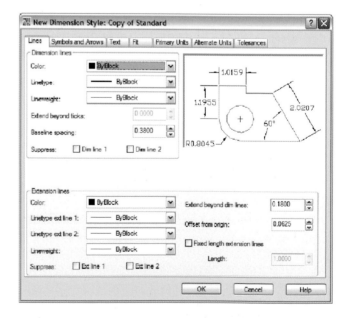

FIGURE 5.3 New Dimension Style: Copy of Standard (lines)

4. Enter a name for the new style under New Style Name.

5. Under Start With, select the dimension style you want to base the new style on. The standard style already exists in this drawing, so you can create another style based on it.

6. Click Continue and the Dimension Style Manager dialog box appears (Figure 5.1). You can make any changes to the style.

7. You can make appropriate changes in the Dimension Style Manager dialog box, such as Line and Arrow, text, and so on. The detailed information about each tab will be introduced in the following sections.

The four tabs (Primary Units Tab; Symbols and Arrows Tab; Lines Tab; and Text Tab) introduced next are the major settings you should set up when you start a new drawing for dimensions.

Primary Units Tab

The **Primary Units Tab** (Figure 5.4) is used to define the units that your dimensions will use. When you get in the Dimension Style Manager dialog box, the first tab you should click on is the Primary Units Tab. In this tab, you can change or modify the settings and appearances of the dimensions. Under Linear Dimensions, you will find Unit Format. At the drop-down of Unit Format, choose Architectural instead of Decimal. At the Precision drop-down, you can choose $1/8"$ because in architectural drawings, many dimensions are with $1/8"$ precision. For example, brick dimension is $3\frac{5}{8}" \times 7\frac{5}{8}"$. In order to show dimension as 8'-0" rather than 8', you need to uncheck the box in front of 0 inches under "Zero Suppression."

Symbols and Arrows Tab

The second tab you should click on is the **Symbols and Arrows Tab** (Figure 5.5). Under Arrowheads, you can choose Architectural tick from the

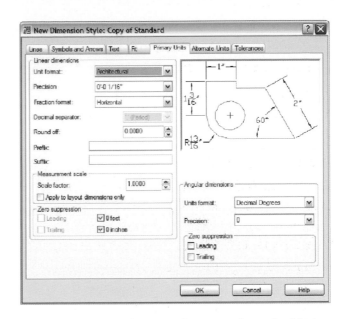

FIGURE 5.4 New Dimension Style: Copy of Standard (primary unit)

drop-down for the first and the second arrowheads. You also can change the tick size by changing the value in Arrow Size. The Arrowheads section of the Symbols and Arrows Tab provides you with control over the arrows and dimension ticks. AutoCAD provides you with standard arrowheads, including closed filled, dot, box filled, and many others. Usually the Architectural Ticks are chosen for architectural drawings.

Lines Tab

The first tab in the Dimension Manager Style dialog box is the **Lines Tab**. It enables you to control the appearance of the dimension lines (Figure 5.3). The selections found on the Lines tab enable you to control all of the dimension system variables related to dimensions. Under the Dimension Lines section, you will find Extend Beyond Ticks. By changing the value of Extend Beyond Ticks, you can make the dimension lines extended beyond ticks $3/16"$. Under the Extension Lines section, you will find Extend Beyond Dimension Lines. By changing the value of Extend Beyond Dimension Lines, you can make the dimension lines extended beyond ticks—

longer or shorter. Refer to Figure 5.6 for graphic illustrations. You also can modify the text alignment by clicking on Aligned with Dimension Lines (Figure 5.7). After you choose this option, the dimension text on the vertical dimension will be aligned with the vertical dimension line, which has been rotated 90 degrees (Figure 5.6).

Text Tab

You can control the text style and formatting used in dimension text. The appearance of dimension text is governed by the text style selected in the Dimension Style Manager's Text tab (Figure 5.7). You can choose a text style, which creates a dimension style, and specify a text color

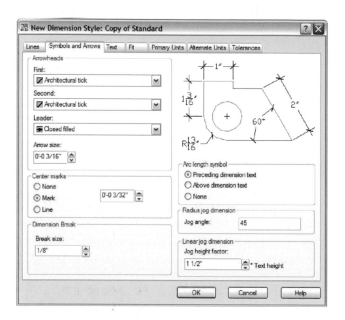

FIGURE 5.5 New Dimension Style: Copy of Standard (symbols and arrows)

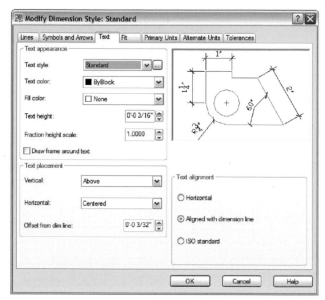

FIGURE 5.7 Modify Dimension Style: Standard (text)

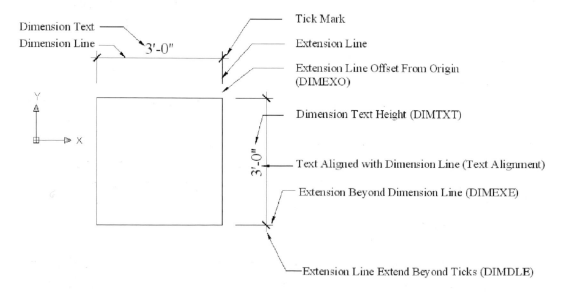

FIGURE 5.6 Dimension definitions

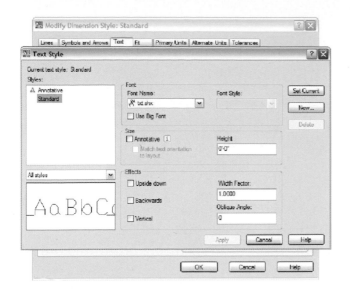

FIGURE 5.8 Text Style dialog box

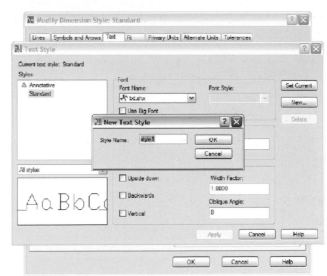

FIGURE 5.9 New Text Style dialog box

FIGURE 5.10 Dimension floating tool bar

and a height independent of the current text style's height setting. You can also specify the gap between base dimension text and the box that surrounds it. The text styles used for dimensions are the same text styles used by all text created in your drawing (CAD help menu).

To change the text style, click on the little square button next to Text Style. You will be prompted with a Text Style dialog box, shown as Figure 5.8. In the Text Style dialog box, you can specify the text font by clicking on the drop-down menu next to Font Name. You also can specify the text height by giving a value in the Height box. You also can create a new text style by clicking on the New button, and then you will be prompted by the New Text Style dialog box (Figure 5.9). You can type in the name of new text style and click on OK.

Under the Text Placement section, you will find two options for the text placement. Select Above for Vertical if you want the text to be above the dimension line. You can keep Center for Horizontal. Selecting Offset from Dim Line will allow you to specify the distance between the text and the dimension line. The Text Alignment section is for dimension text alignment. If you want your text to be aligned with your dimension line, you will need to choose this option.

DIMENSION COMMANDS

The dimension commands can be accessed from a floating toolbar (Figure 5.10) or pull-down menu shown in Figure 2.8 (page 18). Six basic types of dimensions can be automatically created using AutoCAD; they are linear, **arc length**, aligned, **ordinate**, radius, diameter, and angular.

Linear Dimensioning

Linear dimension can be horizontal, vertical, or aligned. With **aligned dimensions**, the dimension line is parallel to the line between the extension line origins; baseline (or parallel) and continued (or chain) dimensions are a series of consecutive dimensions that are based on a linear dimension. AutoCAD provides five different linear dimensions, including DIMLINEAR, DIMCONTINUE, DIMBASELINE, DIMALIGNED, and DIM-ROTATED. Each command can be accessed from the floating toolbar or command prompt.

The typical dimension command, DIMLIN-EAR, is fairly straightforward and easy to follow the command prompt.

Baseline Dimensioning

Baseline dimensions are multiple dimensions measured from the same baseline. **Continued dimensions** are multiple dimensions placed end to end. You must create a linear, aligned, or angular dimension before you create a baseline or continued dimensions. You create baseline dimensions incrementally from the most recently created dimension in the current session. Both baseline and continued dimensions are measured from the previous extension line unless you specify another point as the point of origin (CAD help menu).

To use baseline dimensioning, here is the procedure:

1. Click on the Dimension menu, and then Baseline. By default, the origin of the last linear dimension created is used as the first extension line for the new baseline dimensions. You are prompted for the second dimension line.

2. Use an object snap to select the second extension line origin or press ENTER to select any dimension as the base dimensions. The program automatically places the second dimension line at the distance specified by the Baseline Spacing option in the Dimension Style Manager, Line tab.

3. Use an object snap to specify the next extension in the line's origin.

4. Continue to select extension line origins as required.

5. Press ENTER twice to end the command (CAD help menu).

Radius and Diameter Dimensioning

You can dimension a circle with a **Radius** or **Diameter**. The command button can be accessed from the floating tool bar (Figure 5.10). The following figure shows the example (Figure 5.11).

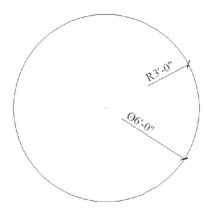

FIGURE 5.11 Example of radius dimensioning

Angular Dimensioning

You can dimension an angle with angular dimensioning. Figure 5.12 shows the example of using angular dimensioning.

Procedures for creating an angular dimension are:

1. Click Dimension Menu—Angular.

2. Use one of the following methods:
   a. To dimension a circle, select the circle at the first endpoint of the angle and then specify the second endpoint of the angle.
   b. To dimension any other object, select the first line, and then select the second line.

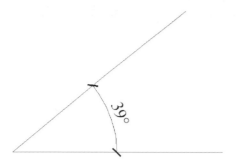

FIGURE 5.12 Example of angular dimensioning

Dimension Variables

In addition to using the four tabs mentioned above in the Dimension Style Manager dialog box to control the appearance of your dimensions, you also could use dimension variables to change the setting of your dimensions. Dimension variables are settings that determine what your dimensions look like on your drawing. For example, as shown in Figure 5.6, settings such as DIMEXO, DIMTXT, DIMEXE, and DIMDLE will determine how far the dimension line extends beyond the tick, how far the extension line extends beyond the dimension line, and so on.

When STATUS is typed in the Dim: prompt command line, a list of dimension variables and a brief description of each variable appears. Figure 5.13 shows the list of dimension variables and the default setting for each, as they appear when STATUS is typed. Some AutoCAD users prefer to use STATUS list to set dimension variables, and some other users prefer to use the Dimension Style Manager dialog box.

The following dimension variables are used often when you put dimensions on the drawing.

Dimension Variables:

DIMASZ	$^3/_{16}$"	Arrow S\size
DIMEXE	$^3/_{16}$"	Extension above dimension line
DIMEXO	$^1/_{16}$"	Extension line origin offset
DIMGAP	$^1/_{16}$"	Gap from dimension line to text
DIMTAD	0	Place text above the dimension line
DIMTSZ	0"	Tick size
DIMTXT	$^3/_{16}$"	Text height
DIMUPT	Off	User positioned text

```
AutoCAD Text Window - Drawing1.dwg

Edit

DIMSOXD      Off              Suppress outside dimension lines
DIMTAD       1                Place text above the dimension line
DIMTDEC      3                Tolerance decimal places
DIMTFAC      1.0000           Tolerance text height scaling factor
DIMTFILL     0                Text background enabled
DIMTFILLCLR  BYBLOCK          Text background color
DIMTIH       Off              Text inside extensions is horizontal
DIMTIX       Off              Place text inside extensions
DIMTM        0"               Minus tolerance
DIMTMOVE     0                Text movement
DIMTOFL      Off              Force line inside extension lines
DIMTOH       Off              Text outside horizontal
DIMTOL       Off              Tolerance dimensioning
DIMTOLJ      1                Tolerance vertical justification
DIMTP        0"               Plus tolerance
DIMTSZ       0"               Tick size
DIMTVP       0.0000           Text vertical position
DIMTXSTY     Standard         Text style
DIMTXT       3/16"            Text height
DIMTZIN      0                Tolerance zero suppression
DIMUPT       Off              User positioned text
DIMZIN       3                Zero suppression

Dim:
```

FIGURE 5.13 AutoCAD text window (dimension variables)

The Dimension Style Manager dialog box allows you to set the dimension variables by using tabs on the dialog box. If you need to use two or more different styles of dimension in the same drawing, each style and the variable settings for that style may be saved separately and recalled when needed.

SUMMARY

In this chapter, several important concepts for dimensioning a drawing were introduced:

- The Dimension Style Manager dialog box;

- Four major tabs in the Dimension Style Manager dialog box: Line tab; Symbols and Arrows tab; Text tab; and Primary Units tab;

- Dimension variables.

It is recommended to set up a specific layer for dimensions. This layer could be called DIM and all of the dimensions will be put on this layer in order to be turned on or off when necessary. It is also required to set up the right unit for dimensioning just like when you set up a new drawing. The right unit should be Architectural. This can be done by accessing the Primary Units Tab in the Dimension Style Manager dialog box. You also can change the dimension tick size from the Symbols and Arrows tab. In the Line tab, you can modify the extension of the dimension line and extension line beyond ticks. The dimension text size and font can also be changed in the Text tab.

There are two ways to change dimension settings: One is to use the Dimension Style Manager dialog box and the other is to change dimension variables. To change the dimension variables, you can type the name of dimension variables at the command prompt and follow each prompt.

You also can set more than two different dimension styles when it is necessary. To create another new style of dimension, you can access the Text tab and name the new dimension style and save it separately and recall it when it is needed.

KEY TERMS

Aligned Dimension	Lines Tab
Arc Length	Ordinate
Baseline Dimension	Primary Units Tab
Continued Dimension	Radius
Diameter	Symbols & Arrows Tab
Linear Dimension	Text Tab

PROJECTS

1. Put dimensions on the beach house floor plan and interior elevations. Use Figures 3.16a–Figure 3.18b as references.

2. Put dimensions on the gallery lobby floor plan and interior elevations. Use Figure 3.19 and Figure 3.20 as references.

3. Put dimensions on the kitchen/bathroom floor plans and interior elevations. Use the dimensions you measured with measuring tap.

Chapter Six

Productive Drafting

Objectives

This chapter presents two powerful features of AutoCAD that can greatly increase your productivity. They are WBLOCKS and external reference. After finishing this chapter, you will be able to:

- Create WBLOCKS.

- Attach and detach external reference.

- Manage external references.

- Permanently bind external references to the current drawing;

- Understand the difference between WBLOCKs and external references.

- Understand when you should use external references rather than blocks.

WBLOCKS AND EXTERNAL REFERENCE

In order to produce drawings productively and accurately, WBLOCK concept has to be used in AutoCAD. You can create drawing files for the purpose of inserting them into other drawings as blocks. Individual drawing files are easy to create and manage as the source of block definitions. Collections of symbols can be stored as individual drawing files and grouped in folders (CAD help menu). In the drawing production environment, such as architects' offices or interior design firms, WBLOCKs can be saved in a common drive that can be accessed by everyone on the project team. By using WBLOCKs, it ensures that drawing symbols are identical. It is a productive way to create drawings.

In addition to the WBLOCK concept, another important concept and productive drafting technique is External reference, also called xreference (xref). You can attach an entire drawing to the current drawing as an external reference. With xrefs, changes in the referenced drawing are reflected in the current drawing. Attached xrefs are linked to, but not actually inserted in another drawing. Therefore, with xrefs you can build drawings without significantly increasing the drawing size (CAD help menu).

By using xrefs, you can:

- Coordinate your work with the work of others by referencing other drawings in your drawing to keep up with the changes being made by others. You can also assemble a master drawing from component drawings that may undergo changes as a project develops.

- Ensure that the most recent version of the referenced drawing is displayed. When you open your drawing, each xref is automatically reloaded, so it reflects the latest state of the referenced drawing file.

- Keep the names of layers, dimensioning styles, text styles, and other named elements in your drawing separate from those in referenced drawings.

- Merge (bind) attached xrefs permanently with your drawing when the project is complete and ready to be archived (CAD help menu).

THE DIFFERENCE BETWEEN WBLOCKS AND XREFS

Both **WBLOCKs** and **xrefs** are powerful features of AutoCAD for productive drafting. You will use these two drafting techniques for your AutoCAD drawings. They are essential drafting tools in AutoCAD for producing drawings accurately and productively. The difference between WBLOCKs and XREFs are highlighted as the following:

- WBLOCK can be inserted into another drawing. However, if you need to make changes on the WBLOCK, you will have to go back to WBLOCK itself and make changes and then reinsert every single WBLOCK into your drawing.

- XREF is an individual drawing. If you make any changes in the xref, all of the changes will be reflected in the drawings, which use the modified xreferences. The changes will be made on the drawings automatically.

Therefore, XREF is very powerful in a team production environment. Only one person needs to make changes on the xreference; all the team members can use that modified xreference and make sure all the changes have been made and reflected in all drawings.

Generally speaking, when a design team is working on a big project, a base plan will be set up by the project manager. The project manager will be the person who makes all changes on the base drawing. All the drawings, such as reflected ceiling plan, floor plans, roof plan, and so on will need to xref the base plan into the drawing so that when changes are made on the base plan, the modifications will be reflected on all drawings. The drawing title block usually is an xreference because you just need to make changes on the xreference, then all of the changes will be reflected on each single drawing, such as drawing issue dates and drawing revisions.

USING XREFS VERSUS BLOCKS

External reference has some attributes that are similar to blocks. They can be attached or "xrefed" into a drawing and used to display many objects as a single object. They can be copied multiple times, and all of the insertions of that xref can be changed by editing the original reference file. The difference between these two is that blocks are inserted permanently into the current drawing as a part of the drawing; however, xrefs exist externally in independent drawing files that are only attached to the current drawing.

One situation in which you should use xrefs is when the objects in external drawings that you need to view are undergoing change. When edits are made to an externally referenced file, you can reload the xref to update it to reflect the most recent condition of the xref. Additionally, AutoCAD automatically loads the latest version of an xrefed drawing when you open your drawing. This is not true with blocks.

Another reason to use xrefs instead of blocks is when the xrefed drawing is large. Not only can you keep the current drawing's file size low by attaching large drawings as xrefs, you can also instruct AutoCAD to only load a small portion of an xref instead of the entire xrefed drawing. This reduces the number of objects in the current drawing and therefore reduces file size and regen times.

Lastly, a great benefit of xrefs is the capability to insert them into multiple drawing files. An example of this is a grid drawing for a building being attached to multiple floor plans. If the grid changes, all levels instantly reference the updated file.

FIGURE 6.1 Make a block pull-down menu

CREATING AND USING BLOCKS

To create a block, the Block Definition dialog box has to be used. You can access Make Block from the Draw pull-down menu by choosing Block, Make (Figure 6.1). Then you will be prompted by the Block Definition dialog box (Figure 6.2).

The following explanation describes the dialog box's features:

- Name: This is where you specify the name of the block. You may use the drop-down to see the list of names of all currently defined blocks. In addition to displaying block names, by selecting a name, you can also see the current settings of all blocks and redefine any of them.

- Base point: This enables you to define the X,Y,Z insertion point for the block. You can enter the coordinate values in the edit boxes, or you can click the Pick Point button and specify the insertion base point on the screen.

- Object: This area controls various options when selecting objects that define a new block, and it displays the number of objects

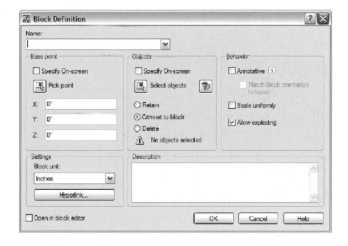

FIGURE 6.2 Block definition dialog box

selected. Click on the Select Object button; you can then choose the objects that make up the block definition on-screen.

The procedure of defining a block for the current drawing:

1. Create the objects you want to use in the block definition in a drawing.

2. On the draw menu, click Block, then Make.

3. In the Block Definition dialog box, enter a block name in the name box.

4. Under Objects, select Convert to Block.

5. Click Select Objects.

6. Use your pointing device to select the objects to be included in the block definition. Press ENTER to complete object selection.

7. In the Block Definition dialog box under Base Point, specify the block insertion point using one of these methods:
   – Click Pick Point to specify a point using the pointing device;
   – Enter the X,Y,Z coordinate value of the point.

8. In the Description box, enter a description for the block definition. This description is displayed in DesignCenter.

9. Click OK.

The block is defined in the current drawing and can be inserted at any time.

WBLOCK COMMAND

You can use WBLOCK command to make a new block. When you type WBLOCK at the command prompt, the Write Block dialog box appears (Figure 6.3). It is very easy to make a block by using the Write Block dialog box.

The Write Block dialog box displays different default settings depending on whether nothing

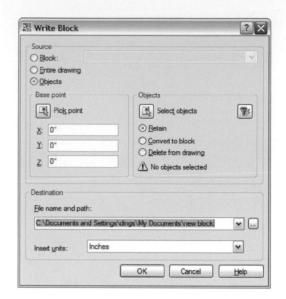

FIGURE 6.3 Write block dialog box

is selected, a single block is selected, or objects other than blocks are selected. The following is a description of each setting in the Write Block dialog box:

- Source: Specifies blocks and objects, saves them as a file, and specifies insertion points.

- Block: Specifies an existing block to save as a file. Select a name from the list.

- Entire Drawing: Selects current drawing as a block.

- Objects: Specifies a base point for the block. The default value is 0,0,0.

- Base Point: Specifies a base point for the block. The default value is 0,0,0.

- Pick Point: Temporarily closes the dialog box so that you can specify an insertion base point in the current drawing.
  X—Specifies the X coordinate value for the base point
  Y—Specifies the Y coordinate value for the base point
  Z—Specifies the Z coordinate value for the base point

- Objects: Sets the effect of block creation on objects used to create a block.

- Retain: Retains the selected objects in the current drawing after saving them as a file.

- Convert to Block: Converts the selected object or objects to a block in the current drawing after saving them as a file. The block is assigned a name in File Name.

- Delete from Drawing: Deletes the selected objects from the current drawing after saving them as a file.

- Select Object Button: Temporarily closes the dialog box so that you can select one or more objects to save to file.

- Destination: Specifies the new name and location of the file and the units of measurement to be used when the block is inserted.

- File name and Path: Specifies a file name and path where the block or objects will be saved.

- [...]: Displays a standard file selection dialog box. It allows you the specify the file destination.

- Insertion Units: Specifies the unit value to be used for automatic scaling when the new file is dragged from DesignCenter or inserted as a block in a drawing that uses different units. Select Unitless if you do not want to automatically scale the drawing when you insert it in the drop down.

The procedure of writing a block:

1. At the command prompt, enter WBLOCK.

2. In the Write Block dialog box, select Objects. (If you want the original objects used to create the new drawing to remain in your drawing, make sure the Delete From Drawing option is not selected. If this option is selected, the original objects are erased from the drawing. If necessary, you can use OOPS to restore them.)

3. Click Select Objects.

4. Use your pointing device to select the object to be included in the new drawing. Press ENTER to complete object selection.

5. In the Write Block dialog box under Base Point, specify the point to be the origin point (0,0,0) for the new drawing using one of these methods:
   a. Click specify point to specify a point using the pointing device.
   b. Enter the X,Y,Z coordinate values of the point.

6. Under Desitination, enter a file name and path for the new drawing, or click the [...] to specify the file destination.

7. [....] button to display a standard file selection dialog box. You may specify the file path and file name in the "Browse for Drawing File" dialog box.

8. Click OK (CAD help menu).

ATTACHING/DETACHING XREFS

When you attach a drawing as an xref, you link that referenced drawing to the current drawing; any changes to the referenced drawing are displayed in the current drawing when it is opened. The program treats an xref as a type of block definition with some important differences. When you insert a drawing as a block reference, it is stored in the drawing and is not updated if the original drawing changes. When you attach a drawing as an xref, you link that referenced drawing to the current drawing; any changes to the referenced drawing are displayed in the current drawing when it is opened.

A drawing can be attached as an xref to multiple drawings at the same time. Conversely, multiple drawings can be attached as external references to a single drawing.

The save path used to locate the xref can be an absolute path (fully specified), a relative (partial specified) path, or no path.

If an xref contains any variable block attributes, the program ignores them.

To attach an xref:

1. Click Insert Menu and then click on External References (Figure 6.4).

2. The External Reference dialog box will pop up (Figure 6.5).

3. Move your pointing device to the upper left corner and click on the Attach DWG button. The Select Reference File dialog box will be displayed (Figure 6.6).

4. In the Select Reference File dialog box (Figure 6.6), select the file you want to attach. Click Open. You will be prompted with the External References dialog box (Figure 6.7).

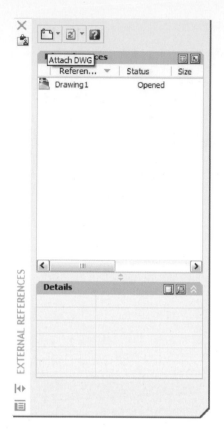

FIGURE 6.5 External References dialog box

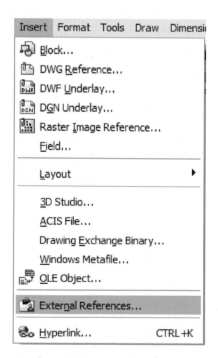

FIGURE 6.4 External References Insert pull-down menu

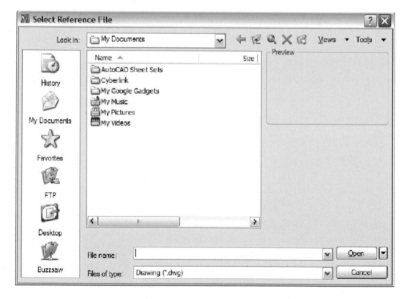

FIGURE 6.6 Select Reference File dialog box

5. In the External References dialog box, under Reference Type, select Attachment.

6. Specify the insertion point, scale, and rotation angle. Click Specify On-screen to use the pointing device in the External References dialog box (Figure 6.7).

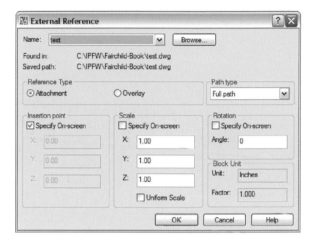

FIGURE 6.7 External Reference dialog box

You also can type XREF at the command line, and then you will be prompted with External References dialog box shown as Figure 6.5.

In the External References dialog box, click on Attach DWG; you will be prompted with the Select Reference File dialog box, shown in Figure 6.6. You can browse the Xreference file from your computer.

MANAGING XREFS

There are many advantages of using xrefs. They make the file size relatively smaller and are easily updated. However, if you are working on a big project, there will be many xrefs to be involved in the drawing. To keep track of xref drawings, you can simply type XREF at the command line, and then you will be prompted with the External References dialog box (Figure 6.5). It is very easy to identify how many xrefs are attached with the current drawing. You also will be able to find out the xref drawing name, file path, current load status, and the xref's file size and last modification date.

UNLOADING AND RELOADING YOUR XREFS

When an xref is unloaded from the current drawing, the drawing opens much faster and uses less memory. AutoCAD has the capability of enabling you to temporarily unload xrefs from a drawing so that AutoCAD does not spend time calculating the position of xref objects during regens. When you unload an xref, AutoCAD leaves its path and insertion properties. However, you can restore all the information by reloading the xref (CAD help menu).

You should unload a reference file if it is not needed in the current drawing session but may be used later for plotting. You can maintain a working list of unloaded xrefs in the drawing file that you can load, as needed (CAD help menu).

In addition to reloading xrefs that have been unloaded, you can also reload xrefs that are already loaded. When the xref has been edited and you want to refresh the drawing and see the new changes, you can reload the xrefs. All these unloading and reloading actions can be accomplished with the **Xref Manager** dialog box. To upload or unload the xref files, just right click on the xref file names; a small pull-down menu will appear, which contains Load/Unload options (Figure 6.8).

BINDING EXTERNAL REFERENCE

When you archive final drawings that contain xrefs, you have two options:

• Store the xref drawings as separate files along with the final drawing;

• Bind the xref drawings to the final drawing.

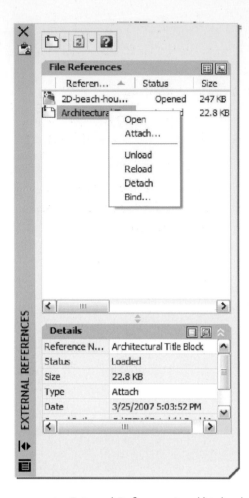

FIGURE 6.8 External Reference Load/Unload options

Storing an xref drawing along with the final drawing requires that the drawings always remain together. Any change to the referenced drawing will continue to be reflected in the final drawing.

To prevent unintentional updating of archived drawings by later changes to referenced drawings, you should **bind** the xrefs to the final drawing.

Binding an xref to a drawing makes the xref a permanent part of the drawing and no longer an external reference file. You can bind the entire database of the xref drawing, including all of its xref-dependent named objects (blocks, dimension style, layers, linetypes, and text styles) by using the XREF Bind option.

Binding xrefs to a drawing is also an easy way to send a drawing to reviewers and consultants. Rather than sending a master drawing plus each of the drawings it referenced, you can use the Bind option to merge the xrefs into master drawings. To bind xrefs, you just need to right click on the xref file name, and then you will have a small pull-down menu, which includes the Bind option (Figure 6.8) and then click OK. The xref will be binded with the drawing.

SUMMARY

In this chapter, you learned productive drafting with WBLOCKS and external reference. The difference between WBLOCKS and xrefs is that when xrefs are edited, the drawing will display the new changes automatically. However, WBLOCKS will not have such a function. When the drawing is under working process and ongoing changes will be made to the drawing, then xref needs to be used. WBLOCKS is used when there is a slight chance to make changes to the design.

In the External References dialog box, you can attach or detach xreference. You also can find out the xreference location, xref drawing file size, xref loading status, and the date that modifications are made in the External References dialog box.

Xrefs can be unloaded or reloaded. When you do not need the xreference in the current drawing, you should unload the xref because it will save the memory of the drawing. You also can reload the xrefs when new changes have been made and you want to display the changes in the current drawing.

You also should bind the xrefs when the drawing is finalized and ready to be archived. Typically, when you send the drawing to a client, you need to bind all of the external references that attach to the drawing. Otherwise, when the client opens up the drawing, all of the xrefs will be shown as Not Found.

KEY TERMS

ATTACH/DETACH   XREF

BIND   Xref Manager

WBLOCK

PROJECTS

1. Bring title block to the beach house floor plan. Create WBLOCKs for furniture and insert them into the drawing.

2. Bring title block to the gallery lobby drawing. Create WBLOCKs for furniture and insert them into the drawing.

3. Bring title block to the kitchen/bathroom drawing. Create WBLOCKs for fixtures and insert them into the drawing.

Chapter Seven

Paper Space versus Model Space

Objectives

This chapter presents two important concepts in AutoCAD, Paper Space versus Model Space. There are several benefits to switching between Model Space and Paper Space to perform certain tasks. You may use Model Space for creating and editing your objects, and use Paper Space for composing your drawings with multiple scales. After finishing this chapter, you will be able to:

- Create multiple viewports on one single sheet.

- Attach a title block to your drawing.

- Set up appropriate scales for different viewports.

- Understand the difference between Paper Space and Model Space.

- Understand the procedure of setting sheet up in Paper Space.

MODEL SPACE AND PAPER SPACE

Model Space is where you draw your objects with a 1:1 scale. That means you have to draw the object with true dimension. In Model Space, you only can print out your drawing with one scale. But in reality, you have to create a drawing sheet with multiple scales. Paper Space will enable you to have different scales in one single sheet. The method to switch from Model Space to Paper Space is using the Model tab and Layout tab at the bottom of your screen.

It is very easy to identify if you are in Paper Space or Model Space. If the UCSICON is a triangle, that means you are in Paper Space. If the UCSICON is with an X and Y axis, that means you are in Model Space.

VIEWPORTS AND MVIEW COMMAND

As mentioned before, **Viewports** are rectangles that are created by **MVIEW** command in Paper Space. Viewports can be used for setting up appropriate scale for the drawing. Each viewport presents one single drawing. You may have multiple viewports on one single sheet to present multiple different scales on one sheet.

After you create multiple viewports, one of them is the current viewport, in which you can make changes or edit your objects. When a viewport is current, the cursor is displayed as crosshairs rather than an arrow, and the viewport boundary is highlighted or bolded. You can change the current viewport at any time except when a view command is in progress (CAD help menu).

To make a viewport the current viewport, you just need to move your cursor inside the viewpoint and double-click. The viewpoint boundary will be bolded.

You can create a single layout viewport that fits the entire layout or create multiple viewports in the layout tab. Once you create the viewports, you can change their size, their properties, and also scale and move them as needed.

It is very important to create viewports on their own layer. When you are ready to plot, you can turn off the layer and plot the layout without plotting the boundaries of the viewports.

MVIEW Command

You may create viewports by using MVIEW command or going to view pull-down menu—viewports (Figure 7.1). MVIEW command creates and controls layout viewports. With the MVIEW command, you have several options for creating one or more viewports. You can also use the Copy command to create multiple viewports.

Command line: MVIEW

Specify corner of viewport or [ON/OFF/Fit/Shade plot/Lock/Object/Polygonal/Resource/2/3/4] Fit> : Enter an option or specify a point.

In a layout, you can create as many viewports as you want, but only up to 64 viewports can be active at one time.

Procedure of Creating a New Viewport

1. On the layout tab, click View menu, and highlight Viewports, and then click on 1 viewport (Figure 7.1).

2. Click to specify one corner of the new layout viewport.

3. Click to specify the opposite corner. Click on the viewport. The viewport will be highlighted with four blue dots, shown in Figure 7.2.

4. Right click on the viewport and you will be prompted with a pull-down menu. Highlight properties as shown in Figure 7.3.

5. You will be prompted with the Properties dialog box (Figure 7.4). You may stretch the viewport and make it bigger or smaller. Use the Pan command to bring your drawing into the viewport. (Figure 7.4).

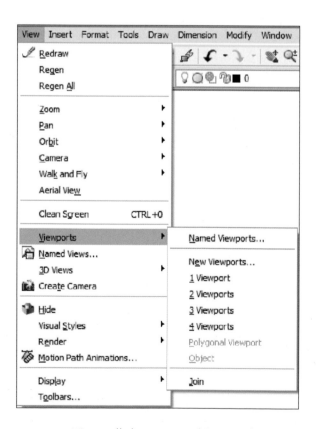

FIGURE 7.1 View pull-down menu (viewports)

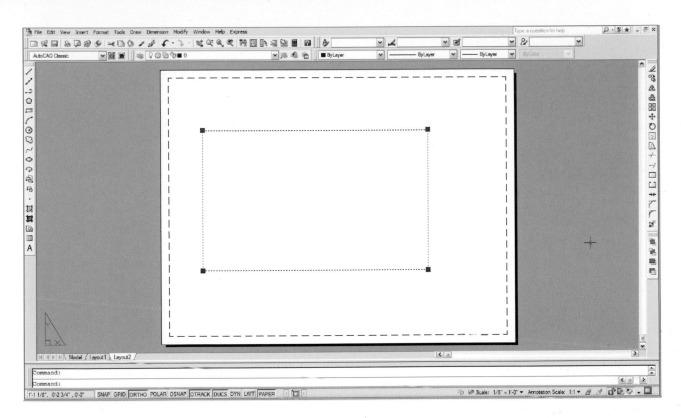

FIGURE 7.2 Paper Space screen

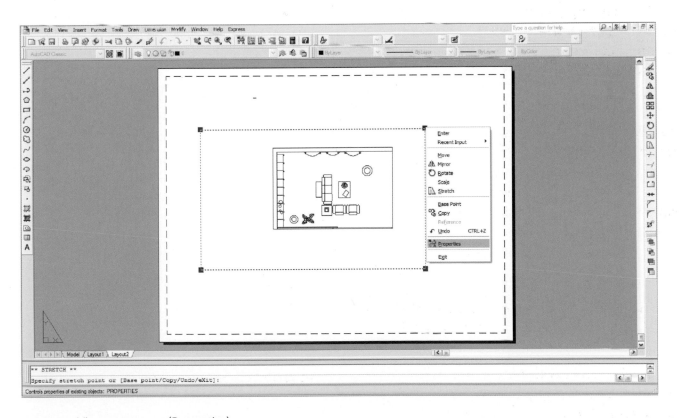

FIGURE 7.3 Viewport screen (Properties)

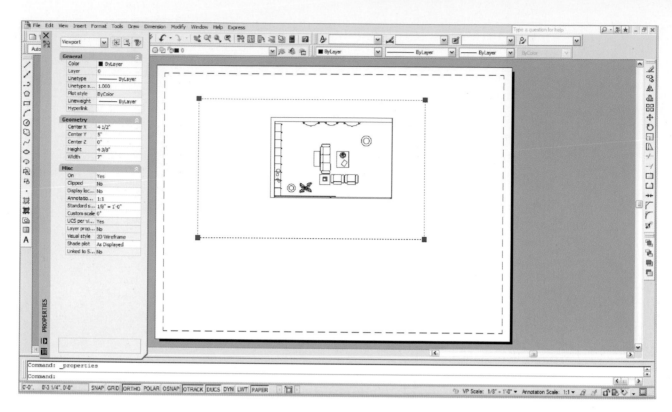

FIGURE 7.4 Viewport screen (Setting Scales)

6. You may select right scale for your viewport. In Figure 7.4, under the "Misc" section, highlight "Standard Scale" and in the drop down, select $^1/_8$" = 1'–0". The scale is $^1/_8$" =1'-0".

7. You also can lock your viewport by highlighting Display Lock. Choose Yes from the pulldown menu. (Figure 7.5). The benefit of using Display Lock is that the scale will not be changed if you accidentally zoom in or zoom out the drawing.

To adjust the view, double-click within the Layout Viewport to access Model Space. The viewport border becomes bolded and you should use the Pan command to move the object (Figure 7.6). You should click on the Model tab to switch to Model Space if you want to make any changes to your drawing.

BRINGING TITLEBLOCK IN PAPER SPACE

Titleblock is an individual drawing that can be xreferenced in Paper Space to create a frame for each individual sheet. It shows important information for the project, such as project title, project location and project team. It is recommended that titleblock should be an xref. It also should be xreferenced in Paper Space. Since you bring in the titleblock as an xreference, all the changes you made on the titleblock reference sheet will be reflected on all of the drawings. For example, you just need to make one change for the revision date on the reference sheet. All the drawings with this reference sheet will be updated automatically. Figure 7.7 shows a typical titleblock.

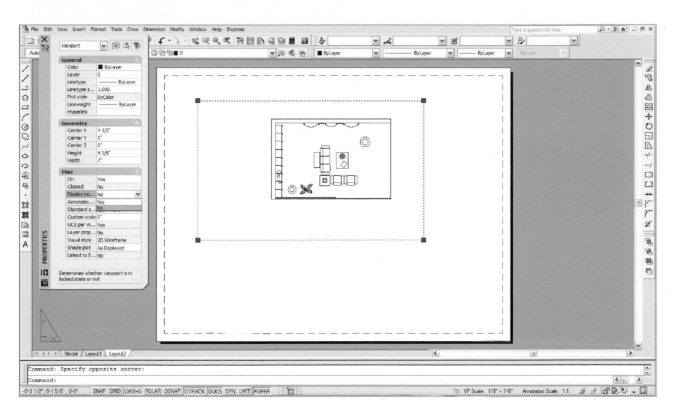

FIGURE 7.5 Viewport screen (Viewport Lock)

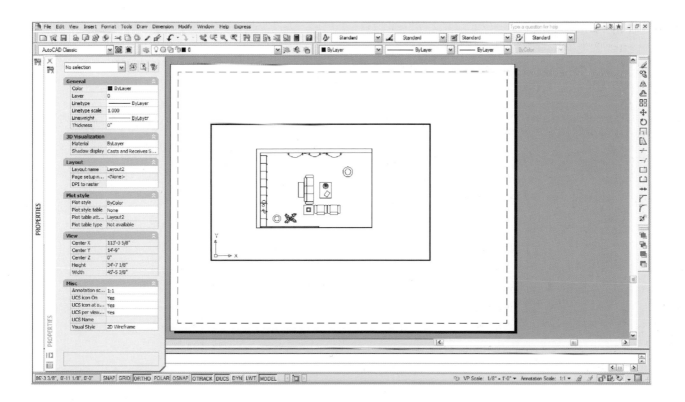

FIGURE 7.6 Viewport screen (in Model Space)

FIGURE 7.7 Titleblock

PROCEDURE OF SETTING SHEET UP

When you prepare a drawing, you typically will go through the following process:

1. Draw everything in the Model Space with accurate true dimensions, 1:1, regardless of what kind of scales you are going to print out for each individual drawing.

2. Set up right text size and dimension size for each individual drawing. Use Table 4.1 (page 41) in this book as reference for the text height.

3. Switch to Paper Space or click on Layout tab.

4. Xreference titleblock 24 × 36 to Paper Space. A generic titleblock can be found in the common drive titleblock folder. Copy the titleblock to your user drive.

5. Set up correct paper size as 24 × 36.

6. Create a new layer to be used for layout viewports–MVIEW.

7. In Paper Space, create Viewport for each individual drawing. Using command MVIEW and Cross Window.

8. Right click on the Viewport, highlight "Properties" and then a Properties dialogue box will appear.

9. In the Properties dialogue box, select the right scale for the drawing.

10. Pan your drawing and make sure it fits well.

11. Lock the viewport.

12. You may use the same procedure to create another viewport to bring another drawing from Model Space and set it to the right scale.

13. Turn off the layer containing the layout viewports—MVIEW.

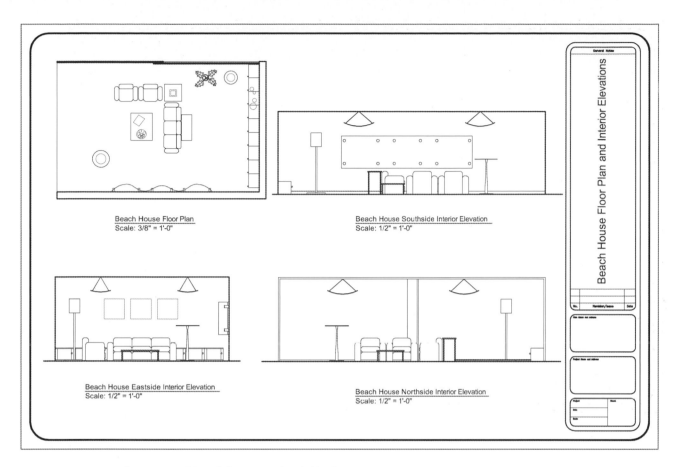

FIGURE 7.8 Interior elevations of beach house with titleblock

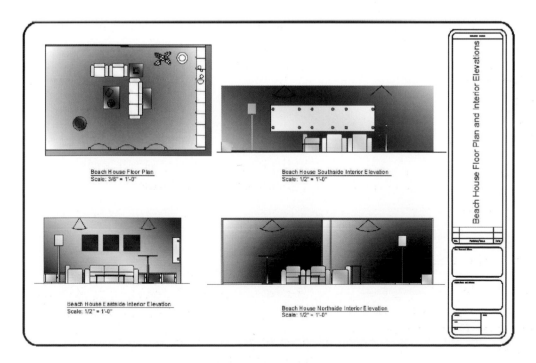

FIGURE 7.9 Interior elevations of beach house with color gradient and titleblock

14. Put project information on the titleblock.

15. Print from Paper Space. The scale should be 1:1.

Figure 7.8 and Figure 7.9 present the Paper Space with titleblocks. The scale of the interior elevations are $1/2$"=1'=0", and the floor plan scale is $3/8$" = 1'–0". Figure 7.8 is a drawing that presents the dimensions, and Figure 7.9 is a drawing that present color gradient fills. Figure 7.9 is used often for presentation drawings.

PLOTTING FROM PAPER SPACE

Plotting will be introduced in detail in Chapter 8. You may refer to Chapter 8 for more information, but when you need to plot your drawing from Paper Space, you need to set up the scale to 1":1'. (Figure 7.10).

SUMMARY

This chapter covered concepts of Model Space and Paper Space, as well as why you have to use Paper Space to set up your drawing. The reason for using Paper Space is that it allows you to set up multiple scales on a single sheet. You draw objects in Model Space with real dimension, which is a 1:1 scale.

The method to switch back and forth between Model Space and Paper Space is using the Model tab and Layout tab.

The titleblock needs to be xreferenced in Paper Space. It is an individual drawing. You only need to make changes on the titleblock drawing. All of the changes will be reflected on the xreferenced drawings.

You have to use the MVIEW command to create viewports. You can also set up the right scale for each of the viewports by right clicking on the viewport. You also can lock the viewport to avoid unexpected scale changes.

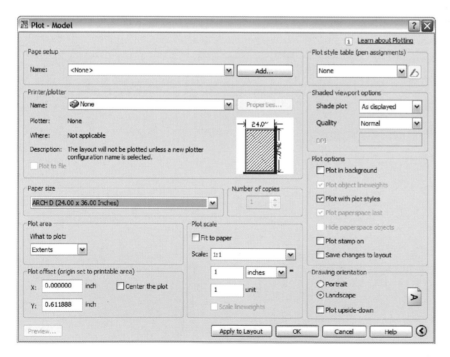

FIGURE 7.10 Plot dialog box

It is also recommended to set up an individual layer for all viewports. You can turn this layer off when you need to print your drawing.

To plot your drawing from Paper Space, you have to use a 1:1 scale no matter how many different scale viewports you have in Paper Space.

KEY TERMS

Model Space   Titleblock
MVIEW   Viewport
Paper Space

PROJECTS

1. Bring titleblock to the beach house floor plan. Create a drawing with floor plan and interior elevations.

2. Bring titlblock to the gallery lobby drawing. Create a drawing with floor plan, interior elevations, reflected ceiling plan, and section.

3. Bring titleblock to kitchen/bathroom drawing. Create a drawing with floor plan, interior elevations, reflected ceiling plan, casework details, and sections with multiple scales.

4. Visit local architectural firms to get real project drawings. You are required to produce working drawings by using Paper Space and Model Space concepts.

5. Draw the floor plan, reflected ceiling plan, interior elevation, and casework section shown in Figure 7.11, Figure 7.12, Figure 7.13, and Figure 7.14, and compose them in one single sheet by using paper space and title block. This is a house designed by Frank Lloyd Wright with typical Arts and Crafts style. The floor plan was reproduced based on the original blue prints.

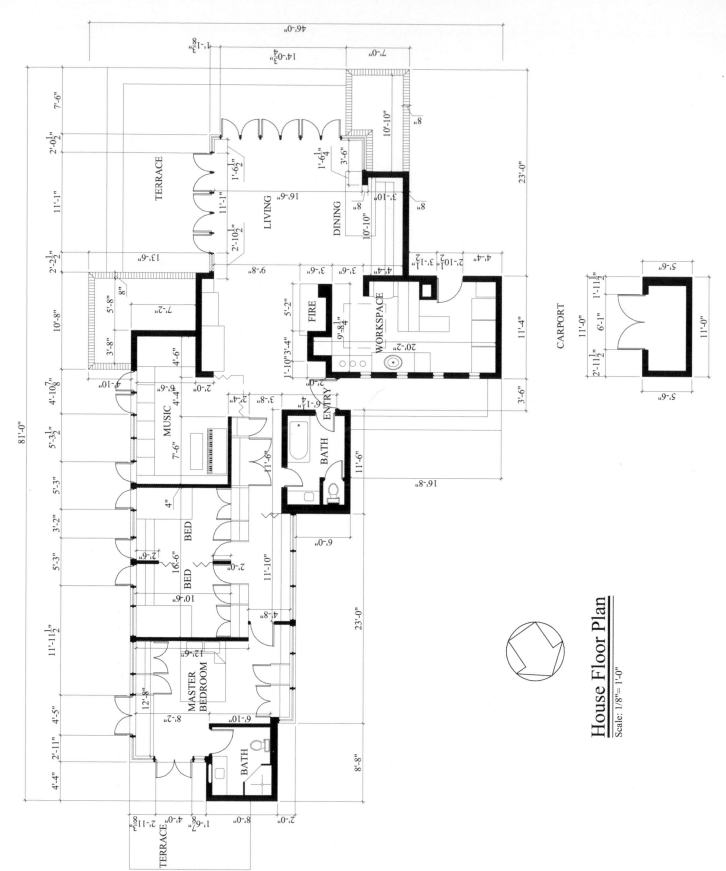

House Floor Plan
Scale: 1/8" = 1'-0"

FIGURE 7.11 Floor plan (N.T.S.)

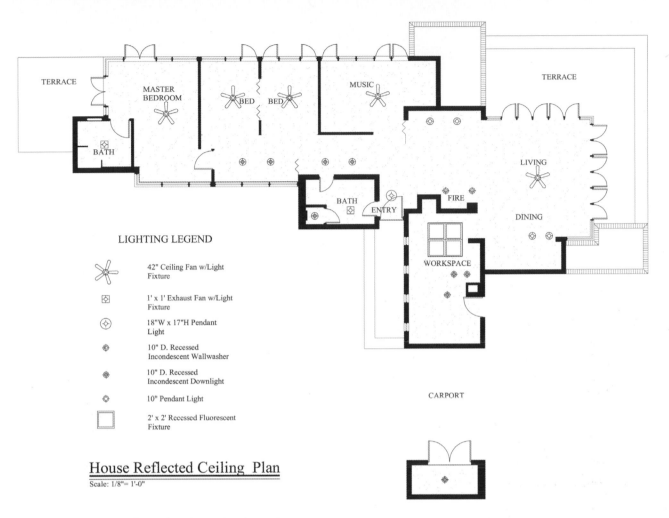

LIGHTING LEGEND

42" Ceiling Fan w/Light Fixture

1' x 1' Exhaust Fan w/Light Fixture

18"W x 17"H Pendant Light

10" D. Recessed Incondescent Wallwasher

10" D. Recessed Incondescent Downlight

10" Pendant Light

2' x 2' Recessed Fluorescent Fixture

House Reflected Ceiling Plan
Scale: 1/8"= 1'-0"

CARPORT

FIGURE 7.12 House Reflected Ceiling plan (N.T.S.)

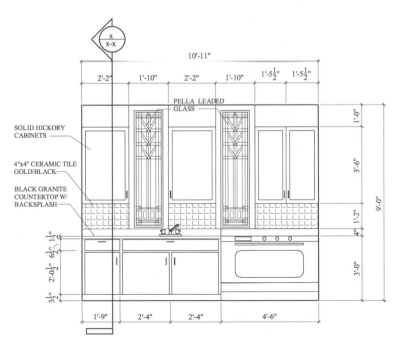

Northwest Wall Elevation in Workspace
Scale: 1/4"= 1'-0"

FIGURE 7.13 Interior Elevation

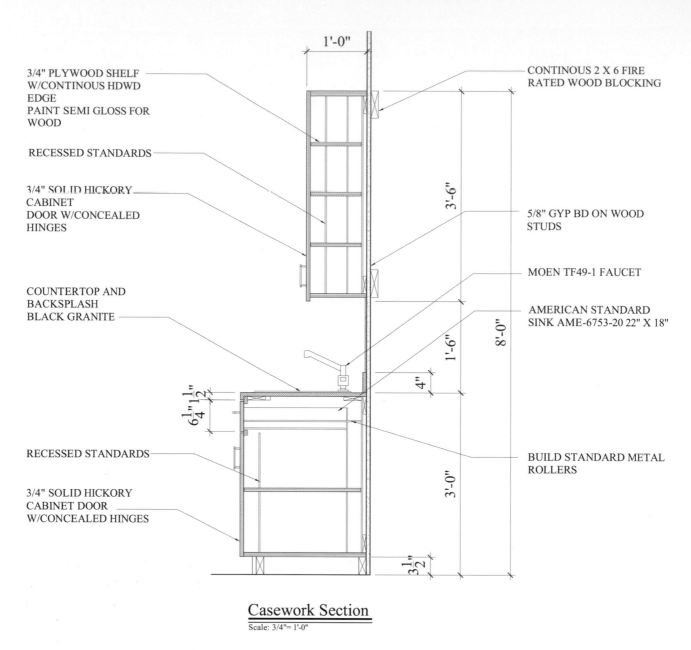

3/4" PLYWOOD SHELF
W/CONTINOUS HDWD
EDGE
PAINT SEMI GLOSS FOR
WOOD

RECESSED STANDARDS

3/4" SOLID HICKORY
CABINET
DOOR W/CONCEALED
HINGES

COUNTERTOP AND
BACKSPLASH
BLACK GRANITE

RECESSED STANDARDS

3/4" SOLID HICKORY
CABINET DOOR
W/CONCEALED HINGES

1'-0"

CONTINOUS 2 X 6 FIRE
RATED WOOD BLOCKING

5/8" GYP BD ON WOOD
STUDS

MOEN TF49-1 FAUCET

AMERICAN STANDARD
SINK AME-6753-20 22" X 18"

BUILD STANDARD METAL
ROLLERS

Casework Section
Scale: 3/4"= 1'-0"

FIGURE 7.14 Casework Section (N.T.S.)

Chapter Eight

Plotting

Objectives

This chapter walks you through the process of configuring a printer and a plotter, then defines plot styles, plot scale, and page setups. This chapter also presents how to plot from Paper Space and Model Space. After finishing this chapter, you will be able to:

- Define plot styles.
- Create page setups.
- Plot from both Paper Space and Model Space.
- Plot stamping.

PLOTTING FROM MODEL SPACE AND PAPER SPACE

Usually, you draw objects at their actual size. That is, you decide how to interpret the size of a unit and draw it on a 1:1 scale. When you plot the drawing, you either specify a precise scale or fit the image to the paper. Most final drawings are plotted at a precise scale. The method and procedure used to set the plot scale depends on whether you plot the drawing from Model Space or from Paper Space.

- On the Model tab, you can establish the scale in the Plot dialog box. This scale represents a ratio of plotted units to the world-size units you used to draw the object.

- In a Layout tab, you work with two scales. The first affects the overall layout of the drawing, which usually is scaled 1:1 based on the paper size. The second is the scale of the object itself, which is displayed in layout viewports. The scale in each of these viewports represents a ratio of the paper size to the size of the object in the viewports.

PLOT DIALOG BOX

When you finish your drafting and are ready to plot your drawing, you can click on the Plot icon on the floating tool bar (Figure 8.1) or highlight the plot command in pull-down menu (Figure 8.2). You will be prompted with the Plot dialog box (Figure 8.3), in which you need to specify several different settings or options for plotting your drawing.

Page Setup

AutoCAD provides several methods for plotting drawings, with the most traditional method being the Plot dialog box (Figure 8.3). When you execute the Plot command, AutoCAD displays the Plot dialog box. The first feature in the plot dialog box is Page Setup.

Page Setup is associated with layouts and stored in the drawing file. The settings specified in Page Setup determine the appearance and format of your final output. After you complete a drawing on the Model Space, you can begin creating a layout to plot by clicking on the Layout tab. When you click a layout tab for the first time, a single viewport is displayed on the page. A dashed line indicates the printable area of the paper for the currently configured paper size and plotter (CAD help menu).

FIGURE 8.1 Standard floating tool bar (plot)

FIGURE 8.2 File pull-down menu (plot)

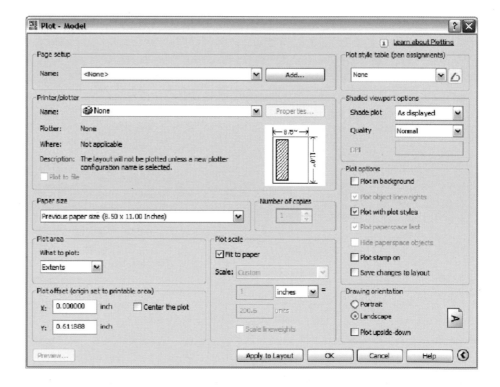

FIGURE 8.3 Plot-model dialog box

Under Page Setup section, there is a Name drop-down and an Add button.

- Name: Layout settings (the settings that control the final plot output) are referred to as page setups. This list box displays any named or saved page setups that you can select to apply to the current page setup.

- Add: When this button is clicked, the Add Page Setup dialog box is displayed. You can specify a name for the new page setup.

Page Setup Manager

1. To create a new page setup, go to File on the pull-down menu and then select Page Setup Manager. The Page Setup Manager dialog box displays, as shown in Figure 8.4. Select the New button to create a new page setup for the drawing.

2. You are prompted with the New Page Setup dialog box, shown in Figure 8.5. On the New Page Setup dialog box, type the name for the new page setup, such as "Setup1." Click on OK to continue. The OK dialog box then appears.

3. You may modify the settings in Page Setup Manager by clicking on the Modify button (Figure 8.4). After you click on Modify, it brings you the Plot dialog box, shown in Figure 8.3.

Printer/Plotter

When you create a layout, you must select a printing or plotting device in the Plot dialog box in order for the layout to be printed or plotted. Once you have selected a device, you can view the details about the name and location of the device and you can change the device's configuration. The **printer/plotter** you select in the Plot dialog box determines the printable area of the layout. This printable area is indicated by the dashed line on the layout. If you change the paper size

FIGURE 8.4 Page Setup Manager dialog box

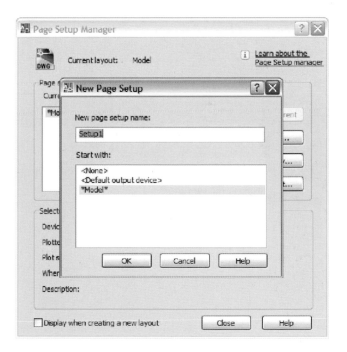

FIGURE 8.5 New Page Setup dialog box

or the printing/plotting device, it may change the printable area of your drawing (CAD Help menu). To select a printer or plotter:

1. Click File menu, and then select Plot or click on the Plot button on the floating tool bar (Figure 8.1).

2. In the Plot Dialog Box, under Printer/Plotter, select a plotter from the name list. If you have already selected a paper size and it is not supported by the plotter you have chosen, you are warned that a paper size supported by the plotter will be used. Click OK if the warning is displayed.

3. Once you have selected a plotter, you can continue to select a paper size or if the paper size is correct, click OK to plot the drawing.

Plot to File

The option Plot to File is under the section of Printer/Plotter. If you do not check the Plot to File menu, AutoCAD plots directly from your computer. If there is a cable leading from your computer to the printer or plotter, or if you are plotting from a network, do not check the Plot to File button. If you do check the Plot to File button, a file is created with the extension .plt.

Paper Size

In the Plot dialog box as shown in Figure 8.3, you have to specify the paper size when you are ready to plot. If you plot from Paper Space, you may have already specified a paper size in the Plot dialog box. However, if you plot from the Model tab, you need to specify a paper size when you plot. In the Plot dialog box, select the paper size that you want to use. This list of paper sizes depends on the printer or plotter that you have selected in the Plot or dialog box.

Plot Area

In the Plot dialog box shown as Figure 8.3, you have to specify **Plot Area**. When you prepare to plot from Model Space or Paper Space, you have to specify the plot area to determine what will be included in the plot. When you create a new layout, the default Plot Area option is Layout. Layout plots all objects within the printable area of the specified paper size. The Plot dialog box provides the following options under Plot Area:

- Layout—When you select the Layout option under What to Plot, it plots everything within the printable area of the specified paper size, with the origin calculated from 0,0 in the layout. When plotting from the Model tab, it plots the entire drawing area defined by the grid limits. If the current viewport does not display a plan view, this option has the same effect as the Extents option.

- Extents—Plots the portion of the current space of the drawing that contains objects. All geometry in the current space is plotted. The drawing might be regenerated to recalculate the extents before plotting.

- Display—Plots the view in the current viewport in the Model tab or the current Paper Space view in a Layout tab.

- Window—Plots any portion of the drawing you specify. Use a pointing device to specify opposite corners of the area to be plotted and then the Plot dialog box will appear again.

Plot Offset (Origin Set to Printable Area)

The printable area of a drawing sheet is defined by the selected output device and is represented by the dashed line in a layout. When you change to another output device, the printable area may change. The setting in the **plot offset** area of the Plot dialog box specifies an offset of the plot area relative to the lower-left corner (the origin) of the printable area or the edge of the paper. (CAD help menu).

You can offset the drawing on the paper by entering positive or negative values in the X and Y offset boxes. This may result in the plot area being clipped. If the plot area is not set to Layout (Extents, Display, View, or Window), you can also select the Center the Plot option.

Plot Scale

When you plot a final drawing, you have to specify a precise scale for it. If you just need to plot one drawing with one scale, you may plot it out from Model Space. All you need to do is to choose the right scale from the drop-down menu. If you nccd to plot multiple scales of drawings from Paper Space, you need to specify the scale as 1:1. However, when you just need a draft drawing, a precise scale is not always important. You can use the Fit to Paper option to plot the view at the largest possible size that fits the paper. The height or width of the drawing is fit to the corresponding height or width of the paper. When you plot a perspective or 3-D isometric drawing from Model Space, the view is scaled to fit the paper even when you enter a scale. This option is not available when the plot area is set to Layout.

Plot Style Table (Pen Assignment)

A plot style table (Figure 8.6) is a collection of plot styles assigned to a layout or the Model tab. A plot style is an object property, similar to linetype and color. A plot style can be assigned to an object or assigned to a layer. A plot style controls an object's plotted properties.

You can also create a new Plot style table to save in the Page Setup for the layout or edit an existing Plot style table. If you select the Display Plot option under Plot style table (pen assignment), the properties of the plot style assigned to objects are displayed in the selected layout (CAD help menu).

In Plot style table (Figure 8.6), when a plot style other than None is selected and the Edit icon (to the right of the list) is clicked, the Plot Style Table Editor (Figure 8.7) is displayed. This allows you to edit the selected Plot stylc table that

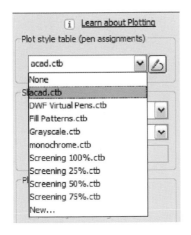

FIGURE 8.6 Plot style table

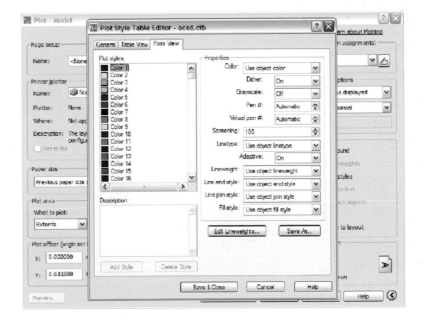

FIGURE 8.7 Plot Style Table Editor

is assigned to the plot style selected in the Name line.

Shaded Viewport Option

With the Shaded Plotting option, you can choose whether to plot a set of shaded objects using the As Displayed, Wireframe, Hidden or Rendered options. Shaded and rendered viewports are plot-previewed, plotted, plotted to file, and published with full shading and rendering. You can use realistic plots in your presentations by plotting viewports as they are displayed on the screen or otherwise.

Shaded Viewport Plotting options apply to all objects in viewports and model spaces. If you use the render option, two-dimensional wire-frame objects, such as lines, arcs, and text, are not plotted.

If you are plotting a drawing that contains 3-D solids that are shaded, you can control how the drawing is plotted. Specifically, you can choose from the following options:

- As displayed—Plots the design as it is displayed; all the shading is preserved.

- Wireframe—Displays lines and curves to represent object boundaries.

- Hidden—Suppresses the plotting of objects that are located behind other objects.

- Rendered—Renders objects before they are plotted, based on Render Options you set before you plot.

Plot Options

The following options that can be specified for layout affect how objects are plotted:

- Plot Object Lineweights—specifies that line-weights assigned to objects and Layers are plotted.

- Plot with Plot Styles—specifies that the drawing is plotted using plot styles. Selecting this option automatically plots lineweights. If you do not select this option, objects are plotted with their assigned properties and not with the plot style overrides.

- Plot Paper Space Last—specifies that objects in Model Space are plotted before those in Paper Space.

- Hide Paper Space Object—specifies whether the hide operation applies to objects in the Paper Space viewports. This option is available only from a Layout tab. The effect of this setting is reflected in the plot preview, but not in the layout.

- Plot Stamp on—turns on **plot stamping** and places a plot stamp on a specified corner of each drawing or logs it to a file. Plot Stamp settings are specified in the Plot Stamp dialog box, where you can specify the information you want applied to the plot stamp, such as drawing name, date and time, plot scale, file location, and so on. To open the Plot Stamp dialog box, select Plot Stamp in the Plot dialog box, and then click the Plot Stamp settings button.

- Save Changes to Layout—save changes you made in the Plot dialog box to the layout if you click OK.

Drawing Orientation

Drawing Orientation is a simple concept, which will not be discussed in detail here.

In either Landscape or Portrait Orientation, you can select Plot upside-down to control whether the top or bottom of the drawing is plotted first (CAD help menu).

PROCEDURE OF PRINTING/ PLOTTING

After you complete all of the drafting in Model Space, you will need to set up the sheet in Layout tab in order to have multiple scales. Or, you can just plot out the object in Model Space. When you are ready to plot, you can follow the procedure outlined below:

1. Click on the File menu and highlight Plot or click on the Plot command on the floating tool bar (Figure 8.1).

2. In the Plot dialog box, under Printer/Plotter, select a plotter from the name list.

3. Under Paper Size, select a paper size from the paper size box.

4. (Optional) Under number of copies, enter the number of copies to plot.

5. Under Plot Area, specify the portion of your drawing to plot.

6. Under Plot Scale, select a scale from the scale box when you are going to plot from Model Space. Select 1.1 from the scale box when you are going to plot from Paper Space.

7. For more options, click the More Options button on the right side.

8. (Optional) Under Plot style table (pen assignment), select a Plot style table from the Name box.

9. (Optional) Under Shaded Viewport Options and Plot options, select any appropriate settings. (Note: Plot stamping happens at plot time and is not saved with the drawing.)

10. Under Drawing Orientation, select an orientation.

11. Click OK.

SUMMARY

In this chapter you learned how to plot your drawing from Model Space and Paper Space. Several concepts were covered, such as Page Setup, Plot area, Plot offset, Plot scale, and so on. In addition, Plot Options and Shaded Plot Option were introduced. Shaded Plot Option is specifically for 3-D rendering and perspective drawings. A generic plot procedure is also presented at the end. To print your drawing from Paper Space, you need to specify your drawing scale as 1:1 even though there are multiple scales on the drawing. However, if you are going to plot your drawing from Model Space, you will have to specify different scales from the drop-down menu. No matter what, you have to create your objects in Model Space with real dimensions.

KEY TERMS

Drawing Orientation	Plot Options
Option	Plot Scale
Page Setup	Plot Stamping
Paper Size	Plot Style
Plot Area	Printer/Plotter
Plot Offset	Shaded Viewport

PROJECT

1. Plot out beach-house.dwg in Paper Space with multiple scales.

2. Plot out gallery-lobby.dwg in Paper Space with multiple scales.

3. Plot out kitchen/bathroom.dwg in Paper Space with multiple scales.

4. Plot out the real project drawing that was obtained from the local design firm in Paper Space with multiple scales.

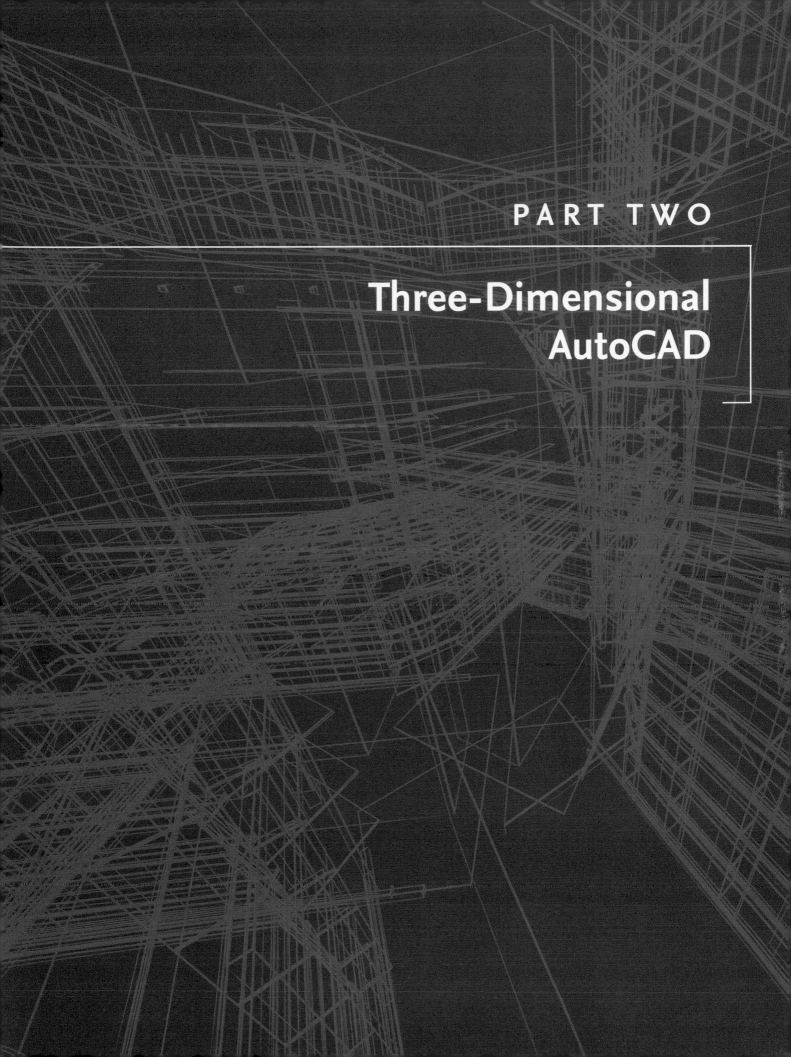

PART TWO

Three-Dimensional AutoCAD

Chapter Nine

Meshes Modeling 3-D Interior

Objectives

A step-by-step tutorial is provided to guide you through this process in this chapter. The tutorial project is to build a 3-D model for a beach house. You can start the drawing with basic commands and settings and save the drawing. When you move to the next step, you can open the drawing and keep working on it. The aim is to provide a continued tutorial process while learning how to use the commands. After completing this chapter, you will be able to:

- Switch from the AutoCAD Classic to 3-D Modeling workspace and use the Dashboard.

- Use basic 3-D Commands and settings, such as UCS, Elevation, and Thickness.

- Build 3-D models for an interior space.

- Present 3-D interiors in isometric views.

- After finishing Chapter 9 and Chapter 10, you will be able to build a 3-D interior space of a beach house, shown as Figure 9.1.

INTRODUCTION TO 3-D

AutoCAD is widely used by architects, interior designers, and engineers. Lots of design firms use AutoCAD to create construction documents during the design process. In addition to two-dimensional drawing functions, AutoCAD also provides three-dimensional drawing capabilities. 3-D AutoCAD can simulate a real scene or real world. For example, designers can create a 3-D model of an interior space and architects can create a 3-D model of architecture by using 3-D AutoCAD.

Architects and designers can also manipulate perspectives, apply materials to the building, as well as design lightings. 3-D AutoCAD also can be used to reconstruct ruins and represent the archeological sites virtually with authentic materials. The 3-D capabilities of AutoCAD are a valuable addition to your design skills.

AutoCAD provides three different modeling methods. They are: wireframe modeling, meshes modeling, and solid modeling. Each type of modeling has its own creation and editing techniques.

FIGURE 9.1 Interior perspective view of beach house

A wireframe model is a skeletal description of a 3-D object. There are no surfaces in a wireframe model. It is not in the scope of this book.

Both meshes modeling and solid modeling will be introduced with relevant tutorials. Meshes modeling defines not only the edges of a 3-D object, but also its surfaces.

Solid modeling is the easiest type of 3-D modeling to use. With the solid modeling, you can make 3-D objects by creating basic 3-D shapes: Boxes, cones, cylinders, spheres, wedges, and torus (donuts). You can then combine these shapes to create more complex solids by joining or subtracting them or finding their overlapping volume. You can also create solids by sweeping a 2-D object along a path or revolving it about an axis. Because each modeling type uses a different method for constructing and editing 3-D, you cannot convert from surface models to solid models.

One of the advantages of using meshes modeling is that it requires less computer memory than the same object if created by solid modeling. Another advantage is that meshes modeling can create some special form, which solid modeling can't, such as a curved surface in two different directions. Meshes modeling creates predefined 3-D polygon mesh objects in common geometric shapes that can be hidden, shaded or rendered. Meshes modeling includes boxes, cones, spheres, tori, and pyramids. However, solid modeling provides more flexibility to change and edit the 3-D model. The commands for making changes on 3-D objects, such as Slice and Boolean operations, have to be used on solid models. Both the Slice command and Boolean operations will be introduced in the following chapters.

In this chapter, the basic commands in meshes modeling and couple solid modeling commands will be explored in the tutorial. The basic concept of UCS (User Coordinate System), Elevation and Thickness will be introduced before the tutorial is started.

In addition to these basic concepts, you will also learn how to switch from the AutoCAD Classic user interface, which is for 2-D drafting, to a 3-D modeling working environment in order to take advantage of the 3-D modeling tools that are built in to the AutoCAD system.

3-D MODELING WORKSPACE

As mentioned earlier, there are three different workspaces predefined in the AutoCAD system. They are AutoCAD Classic, 2D Drafting & Annotation, and **3D Modeling workspaces**. Workspaces are sets of menus, toolbars, and palettes that are grouped and organized so that you can work in a task-oriented drawing environment. You can easily switch between workspaces by using the pull-down menu on the upper left corner. You just need to highlight 3D Modeling and the system will switch the workspace to 3D Modeling workspace, as shown in Figure 9.2a.

Dashboard

The **dashboard** (Figure 9.2b) is a special palette that displays buttons and controls that are associated with a task-based workspace. It is primarily for 3D modeling. When you are in 3D Modeling workspace, the dashboard displays automatically. You also can display the dashboard manually by clicking the Tools, then Palettes menu or by entering dashboard at the command prompt.

User Coordinate System

There are two coordinate systems: a fixed system called the world coordinate system (WCS) and a movable system called the user coordinate system (UCS). The User Coordinate System (UCS) is the same concept in 2-D AutoCAD. In 3-D AutoCAD, UCS allows you to change the drawing plane to any desired drawing planes, such as a horizontal drawing plane and a vertical drawing plane. By default, the UCS is set as World Coordinate System (WCS). The WCS can be thought of as being flat on the ground or floor with 0, 0 as the origin in the lower left corner. X is in the horizontal direction and Y is in the vertical direction on your screen if you are in the top view. While you are working in 3-D AutoCAD, you have to change the UCS icon and make sure it is parallel to your working surface or working plane. For example, you are going to draw an artwork on a vertical

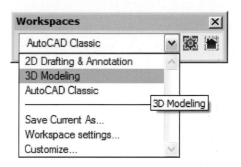

FIGURE 9.2A Workspaces switching pull-down menu

FIGURE 9.2B

wall; you have to flip the UCS icon and make X and Y to be parallel to that vertical wall. Moving the UCS can make it easier to work on particular sections of your drawing. Rotating the UCS helps you specify points in three-dimensional or rotated views. You can relocate the user coordinate system using the following methods:

- Move the UCS by defining a new origin.

- Align the UCS with an existing object or with the current viewing direction.

- Rotate the current UCS around any of its axes.

- Rotate a saved UCS (CAD help menu).

Once you have defined a UCS, you can name it and then restore it when you need to use it again. If you no longer need UCS, you can delete it.

Elevation

Elevation is a new concept in 3-D AutoCAD. In 2-D AutoCAD, you can just start drawing without worrying about the elevation. In 3-D AutoCAD, you can set the elevation or how far objects will be elevated from the ground before you make the object with **ELEV command**. The ELEV command sets the default Z value for new objects above or below the XY plane of the current UCS. This value is stored in the Elevation system variable (CAD help menu). It is critical that you set the elevation correctly. Otherwise, the object you just created will be floating in the middle of the room or buried underneath the floor.

Thickness

You can set the thickness or height of objects by using the ELEV command. **Thickness** is a property of certain objects that gives them a 3-D appearance. The 3-D thickness of an object is the distance that the object is extended, or thickened, above or below its location in space. Positive thickness extrudes upward in the positive Z direction; negative thickness extrudes downward (negative Z). Zero (0) thickness means that there is no 3-D thickening of the object. The Z direction is determined by the orientation of the UCS at the time the object was created. Objects with non-zero thickness can be shaded and can hide other objects behind them.

Tutorial Project 9-1

BEACH HOUSE INTERIOR

The following is a tutorial for creating a 3-D model for a beach house. To start the 3-D AutoCAD drawing, the basic settings will be the same as 2-D AutoCAD, such as Units, Limits, and Layers. The first step is to open up a new drawing and set up the right settings. Make sure you are in 3D Modeling workspace. You also should start your drawing in a 2-D Wireframe, which is shown in the middle of the dashboard (Figure 9.2b).

UNITS	Architectural
LIMITS	upper right corner 200', 200'

1. Save your drawing file and name it 3-D interior.dwg.

2. Make the following layers and assign colors. Make sure you create separate layers for each object that has different material because you will attach materials to each object by its layers.

LAYER NAME	COLOR
Floor	Green
Walls	Red
Sofa	White
Cabinets	White
Glass on Cabinets	Blue
Artwork	Magenta
Glass wall	Blue
Accessories	Yellow
Floor	White

Visual Styles

In AutoCAD, drawings can be displayed in different settings, which include 2-D Wireframe, 3-D Hidden, 3-D Wireframe, Conceptual, and

Realistic. Designers can choose different shading modes based on their needs. In the 3D Modeling workspace, the display mode of the model is controlled by visual styles (Figure 9.2c). You may start your model in a 2D Wireframe or 3D Wireframe mode and then you may look at your model in 3D Hidden mode, which displays the objects using 3D Wireframe representation and hides lines representing back faces. You also can use conceptual mode, which shades the objects and smoothes the edges between polygon faces. The effect is less realistic, but it can make the details of the model easier to see. Realistic mode shades the objects and smoothes the edges between polygon faces. Materials that you have attached to the objects are displayed.

3-D Box Command

The 3-D interior space you will create is a 30' (Length) × 20' (Width) × 9' (Height) beach house with two sidewalls missing. You will draw one back wall and one glass wall with furniture and art accessories. To start building the 3-D model for this beach house, you will use the **3-D Box** command first to draw the floor. Type command 3D at the command line and then respond to the prompts:

Command: **3d**

Enter an option

[Box/Cone/Dish/Dome/Mesh/Pyramid/Sphere/Tours/Wedge]: **b <enter>**

Specify corner point of box: **pick a point on screen <enter>**

Specify length of box: 30' <enter>

Specify width of box or [Cube]: **20' <enter>**

Specify height of box: **1' <enter>**

Specify rotation angle of box about the Z-axis or [Reference]: **0**

ENTER

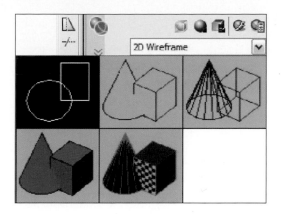

FIGURE 9.2C Visual styles selection menu

Now you should have an object resembling a box. To see this object in isometric view, you will have to use the **3D Views** command, which will be introduced in the following segment.

3D Views

When working in 3-D, you will often want to display several different views so that you can easily verify the 3-D effects of your editing. By accessing 3D Views, you can view the 3-D object in different isometric views, plan views, and side views. There are two ways to see an object in the isometric view. One is go to the floating tool bar and click on the isometric view icons shown as Figure 9.3a. The second way is to go to View pull down menu and find 3D Views and SW Isometric (Figure 9.3b). The SW Isometric view of the floor will look like Figure 9.4. You also can click on the isometric view buttons on the floating tool bar to see different isometric views, such as SE Isometric, NE Isometric, and NW Isometric.

The other options in the 3D Views can be summarized as the following:

- Viewpoint presets—Displays the Viewpoint Presets dialog box when 3D Views—Viewpoint Preset is clicked from the View menu in the menu bar

- Viewpoint—Displays the AutoCAD compass and Axis tripod

FIGURE 9.3A View floating tool bar (SW isometric)

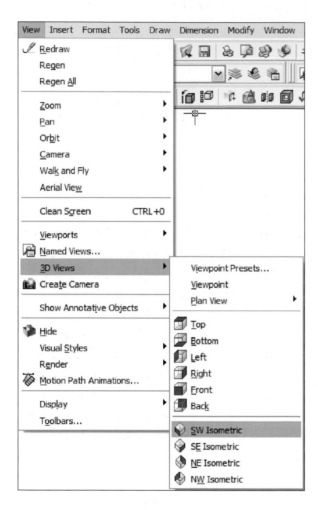

FIGURE 9.3B View-3D Views pull-down menu

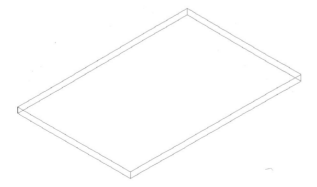

FIGURE 9.4 Isometric view of floor

- Plan view—Displays the plan view of a specified user coordinate system

- Top—Displays the top view of the 3-D model

- Bottom—Displays the bottom view of the 3-D model

- Left—Displays the left side view of the 3-D model

- Right—Displays the right side view of the 3-D model

- Front—Displays the front view of the 3-D model

- Back—Displays the back view of the 3-D model

- SW Isometric—Displays an isometric view from the front to the left and the above of the model

- SE Isometric—Displays an isometric view from the front to the right and the above of the model

- NE Isometric—Displays an isometric view from the back to the right and the above of the model

- NW Isometric—Displays an isometric view from the back to the left and the above of the model

The next step is to draw the back wall. It will be set on top of the floor. The thickness of the floor is 1'. You will have to set the elevation to 1' before you draw the back wall.

ELEV Command

The ELEV command sets the default Z value for new objects above or below the XY plane of the current UCS. This value is stored in the Elevation system variable. Once you set the elevation or thickness, all entities drawn after that point will be drawn with those settings.

Command: ELEV

Specify new default elevation <0'-0"> : **1'**

Specify new default thickness <0'-0"> :
ENTER

You do not have to set the thickness at this time. Now draw the back wall:

Type command 3D at the command line and then respond to prompts:

Command: 3d

Enter an option

[Box/Cone/Dish/Dome/Mesh/Pyramid/Sphere/ Tours/Wedge]: **b <enter>**

Specify corner point of box: pick the intersection of one corner of the floor

Specify length of box: **1' <enter>**

Specify width of box or [Cube]: **20' <enter>**

Specify height of box: **9'**

Specify rotation angle of box about the Z axis or [Reference]: **0**

ENTER

You may go to isometric view to make sure that the object you just created is at the right location. If it is not, you can use the Move command to move it to the right location.

Now you should get a box looking back wall on top of the floor. Save the changes to your drawing 3-D interior.dwg.

The next step is to build the glass wall on the side. Set the layer glass-wall to current.

Command: ELEV

Specify new default elevation: <0'-0"> : **1'**

Specify new default thickness: <0'-0"> : **ENTER**

Type command 3D at the command line and then respond to prompts:

Command: 3d

Enter an option

[Box/Cone/Dish/Dome/Mesh/Pyramid/Sphere/ Tours/Wedge]: b

Specify corner point of box: **pick the intersection of one corner of the floor**

Specify length of box: **15'2**

Specify width of box or [Cube]: **2**

Specify height of box: **9'**

Specify rotation angle of box about the Z axis or [Reference]: **0**

ENTER

To make the second glass wall, simply make a copy of the first one. You should turn on the OSNAP and pick the intersection. When you copy the first glass wall, make sure that the second one is overlapping with the first one. After you finish the back wall and the glass wall, the isometric view should look like Figure 9.5

After completing two panels of glass walls, you can add two inches of trim around the glass panels. Adding more details will make the drawing look better. To add trims, you need to move the two glass panels two inches up from the floor. Then use the BOX command to complete the trims.

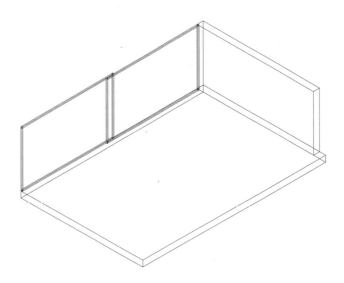

FIGURE 9.5 Isometric view of back wall and glass wall

Solid Box Command

In order to build the sofa in this beach house, you will need to use **solid box** command to build a solid model. The reason is that the corners of a sofa are round, therefore, you will need to use the FILLET command. The FILLET command can only be applied to solid 3-D models. The FILLET command will be introduced later in this chapter. The dimensions for the sofa are illustrated in Figure 9.6a and Figure 9.6b. Now, let us start building the 3-D model for the sofa. First, you need to make the furniture layer current. Then set up your drawing in SW Isometric view. The first step is to build the back of the sofa.

Command: ELEV

Specify new default elevation: <0'-0"> : **1'**

Specify new default thickness: <0'-0"> : **ENTER**

Command: BOX (or click on the Box command button on the floating tool bar (Figure 9.7) or go to the drop down menu shown as Figure 9.8 or go to the dashboard.)

Specify corner of box or [Center]: **(Click on the screen)**

Specify corner or [Cube/Length]: **L**

Specify length: **2'**

Specify width: **8**

Specify height or [2Point]: **2'6**

ENTER

The second step is to build the sofa arm on one side. You can mirror this arm to the other side.

Command: ELEV

Specify new default elevation: <<0'-0"> : **1'**

Specify new default thickness: <<0'-0"> : **ENTER**

Command: BOX (or click on Box command button in the dashboard)

Specify corner of box or [Center]: **(Click on the mid point on the side view of sofa back)**

Specify corner or [Cube/Length]: **L**

Specify length: **-8 (because it should go to the opposite direction of X axis).** You can also enter positive values for in this tutorial but you will have to move the object to the correct location after you create it.

Specify width: **-2' (because it should go to the opposite direction of Y axis)**

Specify height or [2Point]: **2'**

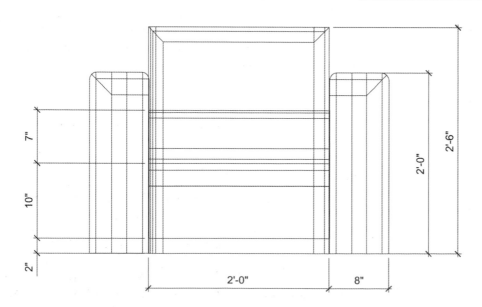

FIGURE 9.6A Elevation of sofa with dimensions

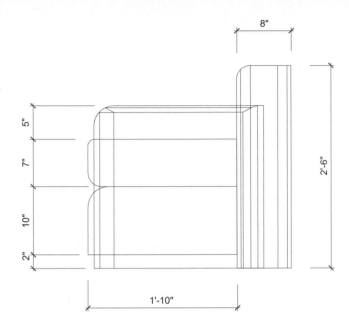

FIGURE 9.6B Side elevation of sofa with dimensions

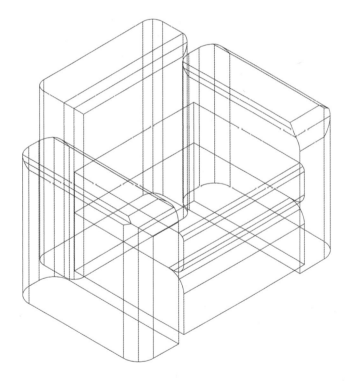

FIGURE 9.6C Isometric view of sofa

FIGURE 9.7 Modeling floating tool bar (box)

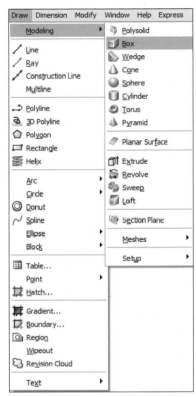

FIGURE 9.8 Draw–Modeling pull-down menu

ENTER

Click on the front view button on floating tool bar shown as Figure 9.3a and make the drawing a front view.

Command: MIRROR

Select object: **click on the left side of sofa arm and ENTER**

Specify first point of mirror line: **MID**

of Specify second point of mirror line (**turn on the ortho and click on upper screen**)

Erase source objects? [Yes/No] N> : **ENTER**

Your drawing should look like Figure 9.9 at this point. The next step is to build two cushions for sofa sitting.

One special note is that you always want to make sure that the object looks correct in all views (top view, side views, and isometric view). Sometimes the object looks correct from the isometric view but not from the top and side views.

Command: ELEV

Specify new default elevation: <<0'-0"> : **1'2 (because the lower cushion is 2" away from the floor and 1' floor thickness plus 2" equals 1'-2")**

Specify new default thickness: <<0'-0"> : **ENTER**

Command: BOX (or click on Box command button on the floating tool bar or click on the Box command button in the dashboard.)

Specify corner of box or [Center]: **(Click on a point on the back of sofa)**

Specify corner or [Cube/Length]: **L**

Specify length: **2'**

Specify width: **-1'10 (because it should go in the opposite direction of the Y axis)**

Specify height: **10**

After you build the lower cushion for the sofa, the drawing should look like Figure 9.10. You can use the Front view to adjust the lower cushion location, which is 2" away from the floor. The following step is to build the upper cushion for the sofa.

Command: ELEV

Specify new default elevation: <<0'-0"> : **2' (because the upper cushion is on top of lower cushion, which has 10" thickness. Plus 2' away from the floor and 1' thickness for the floor)**

Specify new default thickness: <<0'-0"> : **ENTER**

Command: BOX (or click on the Box command button on the floating tool bar or go to the drop down menu shown as Figure 9.8 or simply click on the Box command button in the dashboard.)

Specify corner of box or [CEnter]: **(Click on the left side intersection of the lower cushion)**

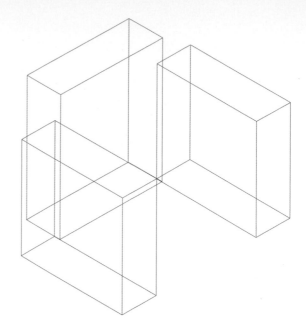

FIGURE 9.9 Isometric view of sofa

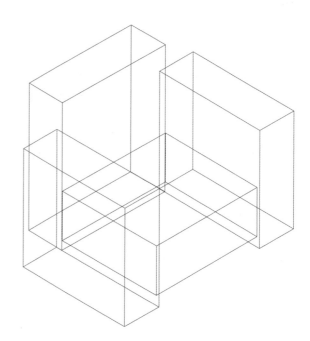

FIGURE 9.10 Isometric view of sofa

Specify corner or [Cube/Length]: **L**

Specify length: **2'**

Specify width: **1'10**

Specify height: **7**

After you complete all these steps, your drawing should look like Figure 9.11.

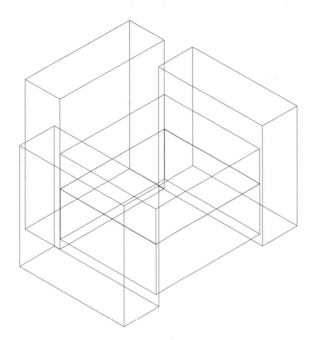

FIGURE 9.11 Isometric view of sofa

FILLET Command

Now it is the time to demonstrate how to use the FILLET command. It is similar to the command in 2-D AutoCAD. However, it is important to remember that FILLET command only can be used on solid 3-D models. The corners on the sofa are round and the FILLET command can accomplish this task. You can add rounds and fillets to selected edges of 3-D solids. The default method is specifying the fillet radius and then selecting the edges to fillet (CAD help menu). You can still work in SW Isometric view. Click on the command button on floating tool bar shown as Figure 9.12.

FIGURE 9.12 Modify floating tool bar (Fillet)

Command: _fillet

Current Settings: Mode = Trim, Radius = 0'- 1"

Select first object or [Undo/Polyline/Radius/Trim/Multiple]: **R**

Specify fillet radius (0'-0"): **4**

Select first object or [Undo/Polyline/Radious/Trim/Multiple]: **Click on one of the vertical lines on sofa arm**

Enter fillet radius 0'-4"> : **ENTER**

Select an edge or [Chain /Radius]: **ENTER**

Repeat same procedure four times to make four corners on vertical sides rounded.

Command: _fillet

Current Settings: Mode = Trim, Radius = 0'- 4"

Select first object or [Undo/Polyline/Radious/Trim/Multiple]: **R**

Specify fillet radius (0'-4"): **2**

Select first object or [Undo/Polyline/Radius/Trim/Multiple]: **Click on one side of the top of the sofa arm**

Enter fillet radius 0'-2"> : **ENTER**

Select an edge or [Chain /Radius]: **ENTER**

Repeat same procedure four times to make four corners on top of the arm rounded.

Do the exact same thing on the other side of sofa arm. You can use the FILLET command with 2" radius to make round corners for the back and two cushions.

The completed drawing should look like Figure 9.13.

After you complete one sofa, you may use the Copy command to generate two sofas side by side. The three seat couch can be created by the Copy command as well. Just remove one arm and copy the sofa twice and use the Mirror command to add the other side of arm. The completed drawing should look like Figure 9.14. Tip: Always remember to save the changes periodically.

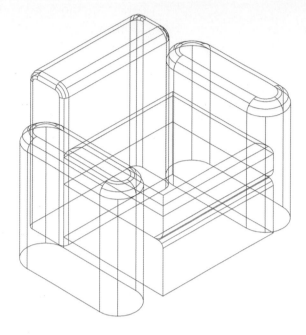

FIGURE 9.13 Isometric view of sofa after fillet command

Building Tables and Other Furniture

The next step is to use the Box command (Surface modeling) to build 3-D models for a coffee table, end table and console table. Open 3-D interior.dwg drawing. The first step is to build the table leg.

Command: ELEV

Specify new default elevation: <0'-0"> : **1'**

Specify new default thickness: <0'-0"> : **ENTER**

Command: 3d

Enter an option

[Box/Cone/Dish/Dome/Mesh/Pyramid/Sphere/Tours/Wedge]: **b**

Specify corner point of box: **pick a point on the screen**

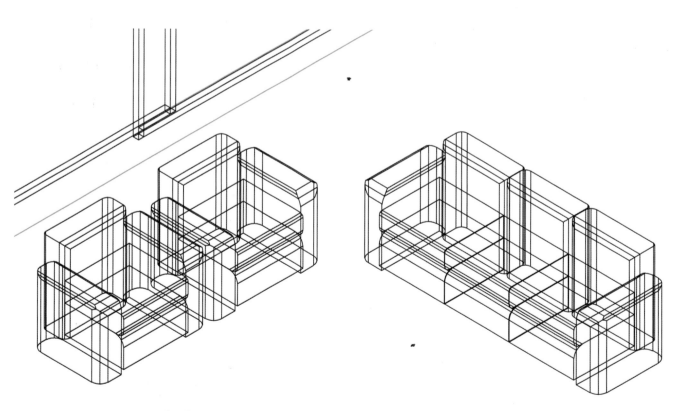

FIGURE 9.14 Isometric view of sofa

Specify length of box: **1**

Specify width of box or [Cube]: **1**

Specify height of box: **1'2**

Specify rotation angle of box about the Z axis or [Reference]: **0**

ENTER

You can use the Copy command to make the other three table legs. Place them in the location shown as Figure 9.15

Now you can use the same method to build the tabletop. But you have to set ELEV as 2'-2" because the floor thickness is 1' and the table leg height is 1'-2". Therefore, the ELEVATION is 2'-2".

Command: ELEV

Specify new default elevation: <0'-0"> : **2'2**

Specify new default thickness: <0'-0"> : **ENTER**

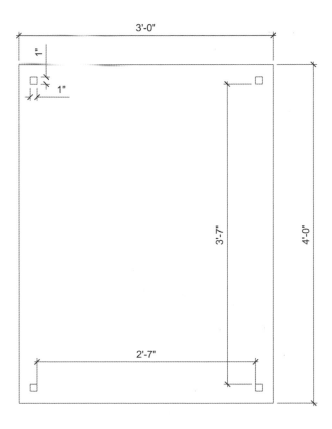

FIGURE 9.15 Dimensions for the coffee table (top view)

Command: 3d

Enter an option

[Box/Cone/Dish/Dome/Mesh/Pyramid/Sphere/Tours/Wedge]: **b**

Specify corner point of box: **pick a point on the screen**

Specify length of box: **3'**

Specify width of box or [Cube]: **4'**

Specify height of box: **1**

Specify rotation angle of box about the Z axis or [Reference]: **0**

You can use the same command and procedure to build the end table and console table. The dimensions for the end table are 2'-4" (L) × 2'-4" (W) × 1'-2" (H). The dimensions for the console table are 3'-9" (L) × 1'-6" (W) × 2'-6" (H).

The following tutorial shows you how to build the 3-D model for the cabinets. The cabinets' dimensions are shown as Figure 9.16a, Figure 9.16b, and Figure 9.16c.

First, build the bottom board of the cabinet:

Command: ELEV

Specify new default elevation: <0'-0"> : **1'**

Specify new default thickness: <0'-0"> : **ENTER**

Command: 3d

Enter an option

[Box/Cone/Dish/Dome/Mesh/Pyramid/Sphere/Tours/Wedge]: **b**

Specify corner point of box: **pick a point on the screen**

Specify length of box: **1'6**

Specify width of box or [Cube]: **2'**

Specify height of box: **2**

Specify rotation angle of box about the Z-axis or [Reference]: **0**

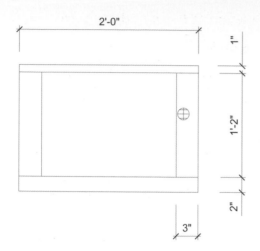

FIGURE 9.16A Elevation of cabinet with dimensions

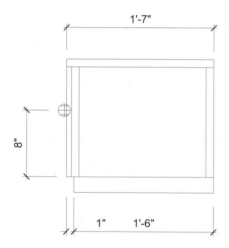

FIGURE 9.16B Side view of cabinet with dimensions

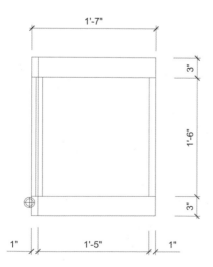

FIGURE 9.16C Top view of cabinet with dimensions

Second, build the sideboard of the cabinet:

Command: ELEV	
Specify new default elevation: <<0'-0">> : **1'2**	
Specify new default thickness: <<0'-0">> : **ENTER**	
Command: 3d	
Enter an option	
[Box/Cone/Dish/Dome/Mesh/Pyramid/Sphere/ Tours/Wedge]: **b**	
Specify corner point of box: **pick the intersection of the cabinet base**	
Specify length of box: **1'7**	
Specify width of box or [Cube]: **3**	
Specify height of box: **1'2**	
Specify rotation angle of the box about the Z axis or [Reference]: **0**	

1. Adjust the location of the sideboard as necessary.

2. Use the Copy command to place the sideboard on the other side.

3. The drawing should look like Figure 9.17a.

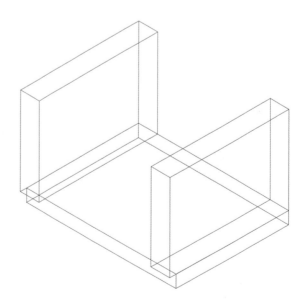

FIGURE 9.17A Isometric view of cabinet

Third, build the backboard of the cabinet:

Command: ELEV

Specify new default elevation: <<0'-0">> : **1'2**

Specify new default thickness: <<0'-0">> : **ENTER**

Command: 3d

Enter an option

[Box/Cone/Dish/Dome/Mesh/Pyramid/Sphere/
Tours/Wedge]: **b**

Specify corner point of box: **pick the intersection
of the cabinet base**

Specify length of box: **1**

Specify width of box or [Cube]: **1'6**

Specify height of box : **1'2**

Specify rotation angle of box about the Z axis or
[Reference]: **0**

1. Adjust the backboard location as necessary.

2. Copy the backboard and place it at the location shown in Figure 9.17b.

3. The drawing should look like Figure 9.17b .

Fourth, build the top board of the cabinet:

Command: ELEV

Specify new default elevation: <0'-0"> : **2'4**

Specify new default thickness: <0'-0"> : **ENTER**

Command: 3d

Enter an option

[Box/Cone/Dish/Dome/Mesh/Pyramid/Sphere/
Tours/Wedge]: **b**

Specify corner point of box: **pick the intersection
of the cabinet sideboard**

Specify length of box: **1'7**

Specify width of box or [Cube]: **2'**

Specify height of box: **1**

Specify rotation angle of box about the Z axis or
[Reference]: **0**

1. Adjust the location of the top of cabinet

2. Use Sphere Command to create the handle on the cabinet door

3. Then the drawing should look like Figure 9.17c

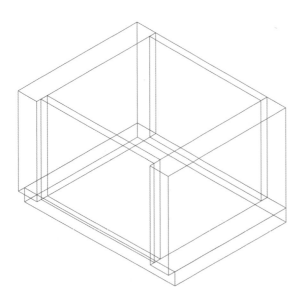

FIGURE 9.17B Isometric view of cabinet

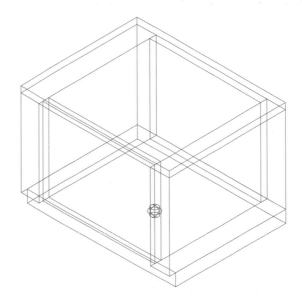

FIGURE 9.17C Isometric view of cabinet

Lastly, build the ball handle on the cabinet:

Command: ELEV

Specify new default elevation: <<0'-0"> : **1'8**

Specify new default thickness: <<0'-0"> : **ENTER**

Command: 3d

Enter an option

[Box/Cone/Dish/Dome/Mesh/Pyramid/Sphere/
Tours/Wedge]: **s**

Specify center of sphere: **(click on the sideboard)**

Specify radius of sphere or [Diameter]: **1 (ENTER)**

Enter number of longitudinal segments for surface of sphere <16> : **ENTER**

Enter number of latitudinal segment for surface
of sphere <16> : **ENTER**

After completing one cabinet, you can copy it
and make the layout look like Figure 9.18. Figure
9.19 shows the layout after applying materials and
using the Render command.

Basic Materials Application

In Chapter 12 and Chapter 15, lighting design
and materials applications will be introduced in
detail. In this tutorial, only basic materials and
lighting applications are introduced. Rather than
create a material from scratch, you can use or
modify a predefined material imported from a
library of materials supplied with thc AutoCAD
program. The materials in the materials library
need to be imported from the library to your
drawing first before you can apply them to your
model. The following procedures show the basic
material applications.

1. Click on the Materials tool icon in the dashboard as shown in Figure 9.20a and a dialogue
   box, like Figure 9.20b, will appear on your
   screen.

2. Click the Materials tool icon as shown in Figure 9.21a. A Material Editor palette will show
   up on your screen (Figure 9.21b).

3. Click the Flooring tab on the Materials palette
   (Figure 9.20b). Drag Finishes. Flooring. Wood.

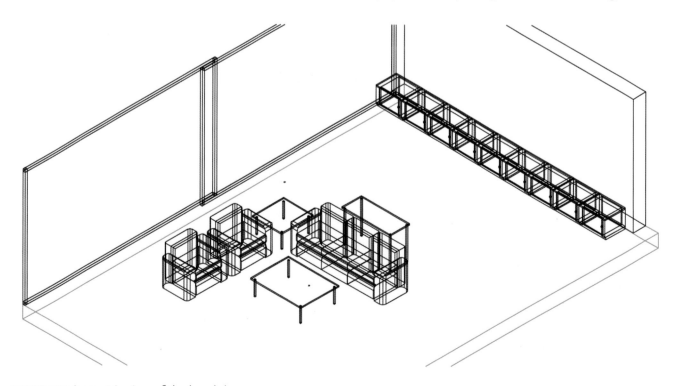

FIGURE 9.18 Isometric view of the beach house

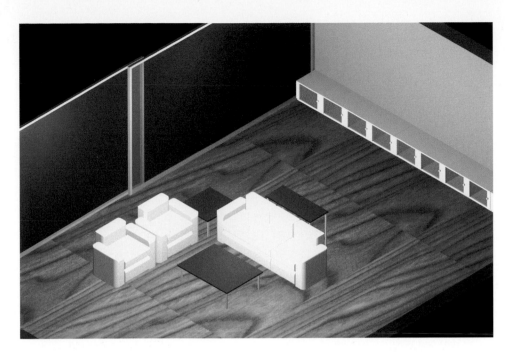

FIGURE 9.19 Rendered Isometric view of beach house

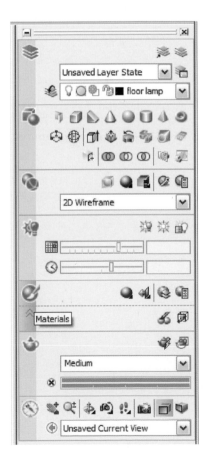

FIGURE 9.20A Dashboard (materials)

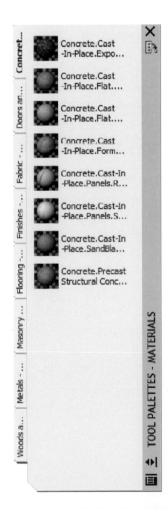

FIGURE 9.20B Tool palettes (Materials)

FIGURE 9.21A Dashboard (Materials)

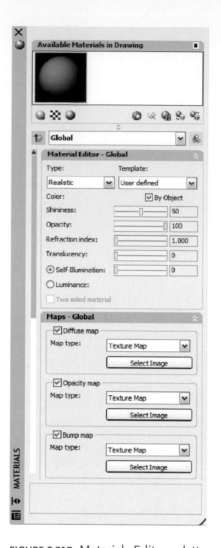

FIGURE 9.21B Materials Editor palette

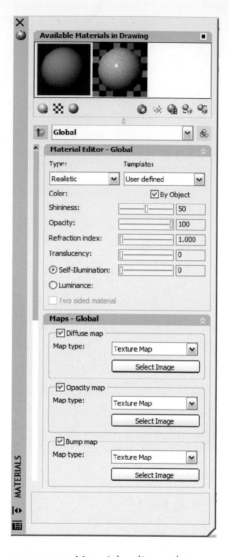

FIGURE 9.22 Materials editor palette

Plank. Beech and drop into the top window of the Materials palette, as shown in Figure 9.22.

4. Repeat step 3 to import the following materials:
   - Doors and Windows—Materials Samples (tab)
     § Doors—Windows. Glazing. Glass. Frosted.
   - Finishes—Material Samples (tab)
     § Finishes. Gypsum Board. Painted. White.
   - Woods and Plastics—Material Samples (tab)
     § Woods. Plastics. Finish. Carpentry. Plastic Laminates. Navy.

   - Fabric—Material Samples (tab)
     § Furnishings. Fabrics. Canvas. White.
   - Woods—Material Samples (tab)
     § Woods. Plastics. PVC. White.

5. Attach materials to the objects in your drawing:
   a. Double click on Finishes. Flooring. Wood. Plank. Beech material swatch in the Material Editor to make it active.
   b. Follow the prompt as the following:
      Prompt:
      Select objects: With the Paintbrush, click on the floor.
      Select objects or [Undo]: ENTER

You may use beige color or white color for the back wall; frosted glass for the glass sliding doors and low cabinet doors; wood plank for the floor; and navy plastics for table surface. You may choose different materials and colors for this tutorial. Figure 9.23 shows the materials that have been imported into your drawing from the materials library.

Basic Lighting Application

Lights are the first step in adding realism to a rendering. The way light strikes each surface in a model is affected by angle, distance, color, and the reflective qualities of the surface material. You can add distant light, point lights and spot lights, and set the color, location, and direction for each. When there are no lights in a scene, the scene is shaded or rendered with default lighting. More detailed information about lighting design will

be described in Chapter 12. The following is the procedure of adding lighting to this beach house:

1. Click on the Lighting icon (New Point light), shown as Figure 9.24, or click on the lighting icon in the middle of dashboard.

FIGURE 9.24 Lights Floating Tool Bar

2. The Viewport Lighting Mode dialog box pops up.

3. Click |Yes| and follow the command line.
   Specify source location 0,0,0> : .XY
   Of (point near the front of the room)
   (need Z): 8'
   Enter an option to change [Name/Intensity/ Status/Shadow/Attenuation/Color/ eXit] <eXit> : N
   Enter light name Pointlight1> : Point-1
   Enter an option to change [Name/Intensity/ Status/Shadow/Attenuation/Color/ eXit] <eXit> : ENTER

4. You may adjust the lighting intensity by doing the following:
   Click on the just-created light, right-click, and choose Properties (Figure 9.25). The Properties palette pops up (Figure 9.26).

5. Change the value of the intensity of the point light you just created in the Properties palette.

You may add another light in the drawing. You should name it differently, such as point-2. In the mean time, you may change the location of the light by clicking on a different point and different Z value.

Another type of AutoCAD light is the distant light. You might use this to simulate the sun

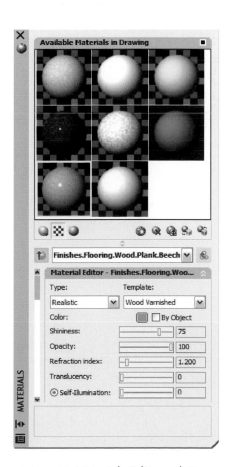

FIGURE 9.23 Materials Editor palette

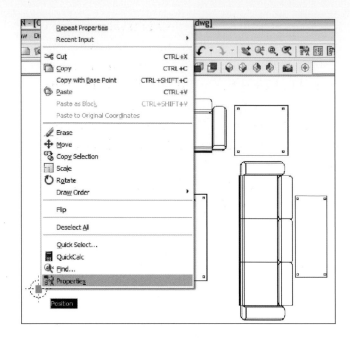

FIGURE 9.25 Lights Properties pull-down menu

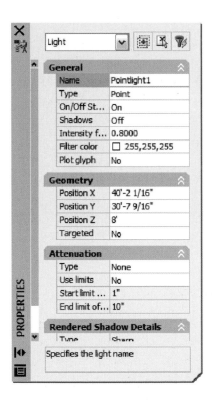

FIGURE 9.26 Properties dialog box

coming through a window. Sunlight simulation will be introduced in detail in Chapter 15.

1. Click on the Distant Light icon in the floating tool bar, as shown in Figure 9.24 or click on the Distant Light icon on the dashboard.

2. The Photometric Distant Light dialog box pops up.

3. Click [OK] and follow the command line.

   Command: _ distantlight

   Specify light direction FROM 0,0,0> or [vector]: **.XY**

   Of (point near the front of the room) (need Z): **12'**

   Specify light direction To <1,1,1> : point to the back corner of the room

   Enter an option to change [Name/Intensity/Status/Shadow/Attenuation/Color/eXit] <eXit> : **N**

   Enter light name <Pointlight1> : Distant-1

   Enter an option to change [Name/Intensity/Status/Shadow/Attenuation/Color/eXit] <eXit> : **ENTER**

4. You may add another distant light by changing the name and location.

There are two different distant lights and one point light in the drawing shown as Figure 9.1. More detailed information about lighting applications will be introduced in Chapter 12. You may adjust lighting intensity by accessing the Lighting List on the dashboard (Figure 9.27a). Click on the lighting list icon; a dialog box pops up as shown in Figure 9.27b. Highlight the lighting name and right click, and then you will have the lighting properties dialog box, like in Figure 9.26.

Render Command

The **Render** command produces images that have shading, shadows, and assigned materials. There-

FIGURE 9.27A Dashboard (light list)

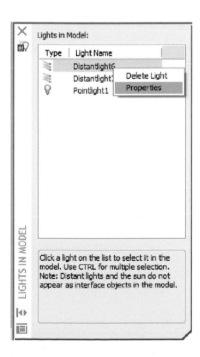

FIGURE 9.27B Lights in Model dialog box

fore, the Render command can make a realistically shaded image of your 3-D models.

Command: RENDER or click on the command button (little green pot) shown as Figure 9.28. In a few seconds, a rendering of the SW Isometric view of this 3-D interior with materials associated with each object will be shown on your screen like Figure 9.19.

More details about the Render command will be introduced in Chapter 11.

FIGURE 9.28 Render dialog box

SUMMARY

Several new concepts were introduced and demonstrated with the tutorial in this chapter. When you start creating a 3-D model, it is recommended to follow this procedure:

- Switch to 3D Modeling workspace;

- Set up right Unit, which is architectural;

- Set up appropriate Limits;

- Set up appropriate Layers with different colors;

- Set up right Elevation.

You can use the Meshes Modeling method to create a 3-D model, which will save lots of memories of your drawing. However, some of the commands only can be used on solid objects, such as Fillet and Chamfer. You will have to use solid modeling commands to create solid objects. You can see your model in an isometric view with 3D Views options. You can also apply materials to the surface of the object from the pre-defined materials library. You also can apply lightings to the 3-D model. The Render command enables you to see a photo-like, realistic three-dimensional object.

This tutorial will be continued through Chapter 10. You will explore more surface modeling commands in the following tutorial.

KEY TERMS

3-D MODELING	ELEV
WORKSPACE	MATERIALS
3-D BOX	RENDER
3D VIEWS	Solid box
DASHBOARD	THICKNESS

PROJECTS

1. Create a 3-D model of a chair / sofa of your choice. Apply materials to it from the materials library. Add lighting to your rendering.

2. Create a 3-D model of a bookshelf of your choice and add some details such as books, photos, and accessories. Apply materials to it from the materials library. Add lighting to your rendering.

3. Create a 3-D model of your choice. Apply materials and lightings to your rendering.

Chapter Ten

3-D Furniture and Interior Accessories

Objectives

The tutorial in this chapter is a continuation of previous tutorial. You will continue to explore Meshes modeling method and commands. You will also explore how to create 3-D furniture and interior accessories. A project of creating 3-D models of table lamps is also demonstrated with the Meshes modeling technique in this chapter.

After completing this chapter, you will be able to:

- Change UCS settings and work on vertical surfaces.

- Build 3-D models for furniture and interior accessories, such as table lamps, shown in Figure 10.1.

- Continue the drawing you have been working on in Chapter 9.

- Build a 3-D interior space of a beach house as shown in Figure 9.1 (page 90).

Tutorial Project 10-1

BEACH HOUSE INTERIOR, CONTINUED

You have been working on drawing 3-D-interior. dwg in Chapter 9. In this chapter, you will learn several new commands as indicated in the list of Key Terms. The first new command that will be introduced is the Plan Command. A plan view is a view aimed toward the origin (0,0,0) from a point on the positive Z-axis. This results in a view of the XY plane. You can restore the view and coordinate system that is the default for most drawings by setting the UCS orientation to World and then setting the 3D view to Plan View (CAD help menu). Sometimes, you will need to set your drawing in a plan view, such as when you create the perspective.

Plan Command

The **Plan** Command generates a view parallel to the UCS. Since the current UCS is WCS, it will generate a floor plan view.

Command: PLAN

Enter an option [Current ucs/Ucs/World]
Current> : **(press ENTER)**

Your drawing should look like Figure 10.2 after you use the Render command.

Viewports

Another important feature to help you with your work in 3-D is AutoCAD's ability to simultaneously display more than one Model Space viewport. Setting up a different coordinate system in individual viewports is useful if you typically work on 3-D models. Multiple viewports are especially useful when you are working in 3-D because you can set up a top (or plan) view in one viewport, set up a front (or elevation) view in another viewport, and have a third and fourth viewport show an isometric view of your model (Figure 10.5). You can see the effects of changes in one view reflected in the other views.

The Viewports setting allows you to generate multiple views. With Model Space viewports, you can do the following:

- Pan, Zoom; Set Snap; and UCS icons and restore named views.

- Save user coordinate system orientations with individual viewports.

- Draw from one viewport to another when executing a command.

To access the Viewport command, click on View on top of your screen and highlight the drop down menu Viewports—4 Viewports shown as Figure 10.3. Then you will get a screen, like Figure 10.4. To make the viewport active, just double click on the viewport and you will see the border of the viewport becomes bolded.

1. Double click on the upper left corner and make this viewport active. Then click on Plan view, and then you will get a top view of the drawing, like in Figure 10.5.

2. Double click on the lower left corner and make this viewport active. Then click on Front view and you will get a front elevation of the drawing, like Figure 10.5.

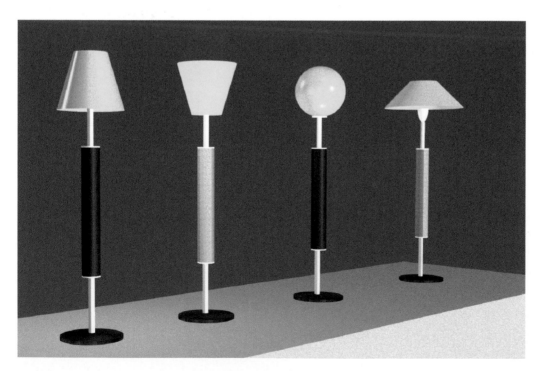

FIGURE 10.1 3-D models of table lamps

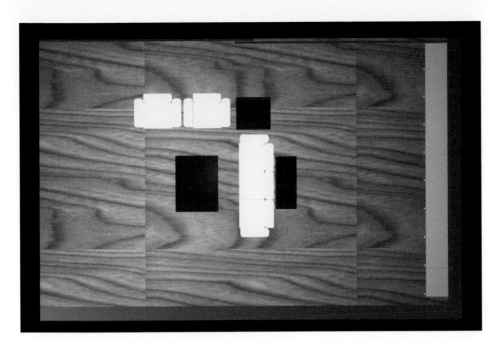

FIGURE 10.2 Rendered beach house floor plan

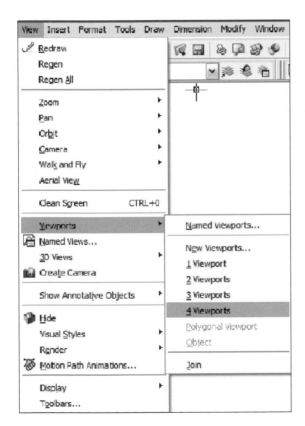

FIGURE 10.3 View pull-down menu (viewports)

3. Double click on upper right corner and make this viewport active. Then click on SE Isometric view and click on "Realistic" in the middle of Dashboard. You will get an SE Isometric view rendering, shown as Figure 10.5.

4. Double click on the lower right corner and make this viewport active. Then click on "Realistic" in the middle of Dashboard; you will get an SW Isometric view rendering, shown as Figure 10.5. (Your screen may look different than figure 10.5 due to different materials.)

There is another useful concept that needs to be mentioned. It is UCSVP. The UCS in each viewport is controlled by the UCSVP system variable. When UCSVP is set to 1 in a viewport, the UCS last used in the viewport is saved with the viewport and is restored when the viewport is made current again. When UCSVP is set to 0 in a viewport, its UCS is always the same as the UCS in the current viewport (CAD help menu).

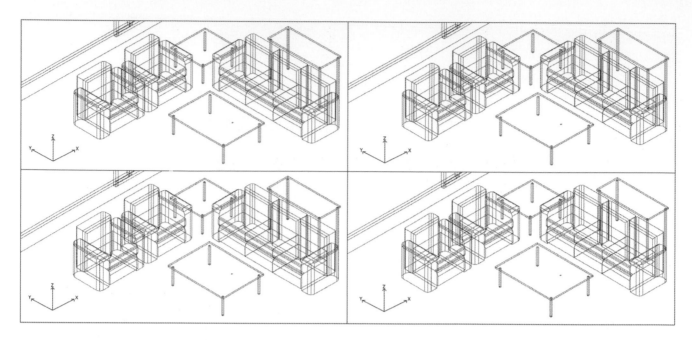

FIGURE 10.4 Viewports on screen

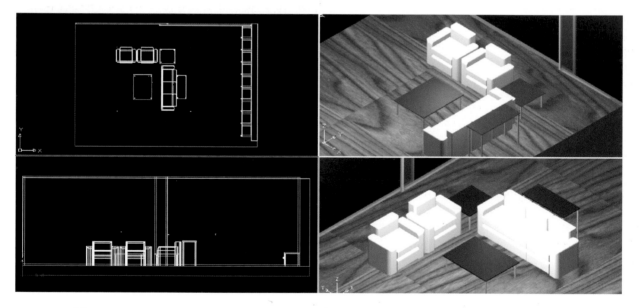

FIGURE 10.5 Viewports on screen

ORBIT Command

The Viewports setting allows you to have static views of a 3-D model. But the Orbit command enables you to view 3-D models interactively. When the Orbit command is active, you manipulate the view with the screen-pointing device (the mouse) and you can view the model from any point in 3-D space. The 3-D Orbit view displays an arcball, which is a circle, divided into four quadrants by small circles. When Orbit is active, the target of the view stays stationary and the camera location, or point of view, moves around target. The center of the arcball is the target point (CAD help menu). The icon is found on the floating tool bar and drop down menu under View, as shown in Figure 10.6 and Figure 10.7.

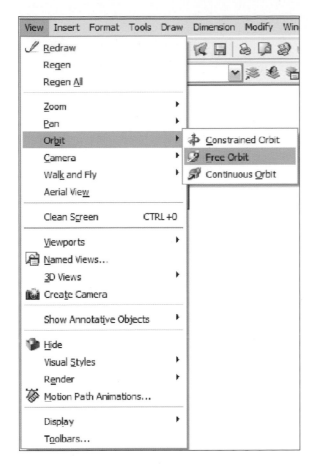

FIGURE 10.6 View pull-down menu (orbit)

FIGURE 10.7 Orbit floating tool bar

Command: ORBIT

1. Double click on the right viewport shown as Figure 10.8

2. Click on one of the small circles on the large circle and drag to rotate the room.

3. Right click to see a shortcut menu and click on EXIT to exit this command.

Using Continuous Orbit

While Orbit is active, you can click and drag in the Orbit view to start a continuous motion. When you release the pick button on your pointing device, the orbit continues in the direction that you were dragging it (CAD help menu). Such continuous motion studies can help to reveal information about the structure and geometric relationships in a 3-D model that are less apparent in static views. The command can be found in the floating tool bar shown as Figure 10.9.

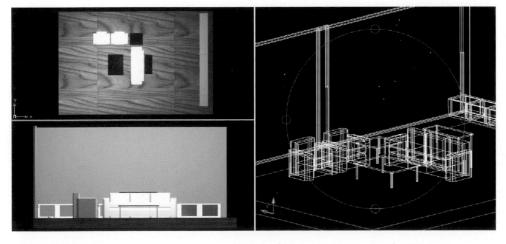

FIGURE 10.8 Viewports on screen

FIGURE 10.9 Orbit floating tool bar

Hide Command

When you use viewports to see a 3-D model, a wireframe is displayed in the current viewport. All lines are presented, including those hidden by other objects. The **Hide** command eliminates the hidden lines from the screen. The Hide command regenerates a three-dimensional wireframe model with hidden lines suppressed. When the drawing is regenerated, all lines of the model become visible again. To use:

1. Select the right viewport to make it active.

2. Use the HIDE command to hide lines that are behind other surfaces (Figure 10.10).

> Command: **HIDE (or TYPE: HI <enter>)**

You also can display your model with 3D Hidden mode from Visual Styles, as shown in Figure 9.2c.

Working on the Vertical Surfaces

Next, you will make 3-D art work on the back wall. It is the rule of thumb that you have to align the UCS to the vertical surfaces that you are working on before you start building any 3-D model. First, you will need to rotate the UCS around the X-axis and then attach the UCS origin to the lower left corner of the back wall. It is very easy to rotate or flip your UCS if the model is created with solid modeling command. You may just simply follow the following generic procedure:

> Command: **UCS**
>
> ---
>
> Specify origin of UCS or [Face/Named/Object/Previous/View/Word/X/Y/Z/ZAxis] World> : **F and ENTER**
>
> ---
>
> Select face of solid object: **Click on the surface that you want your** XY UCS
>
> ---
>
> Enter an option [Next/Xflip/Yflip] accept> : **ENTER**

You will use this procedure in the following chapters when you work on the solid modeling.

However, if the model is created with Meshes modeling like in this tutorial, you will have to set the thickness back to 0 and set the elevation to 1' and follow the following procedure:

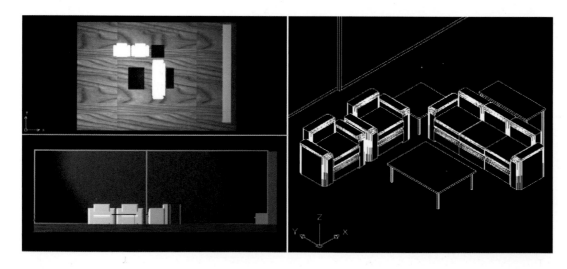

FIGURE 10.10 Viewports on screen

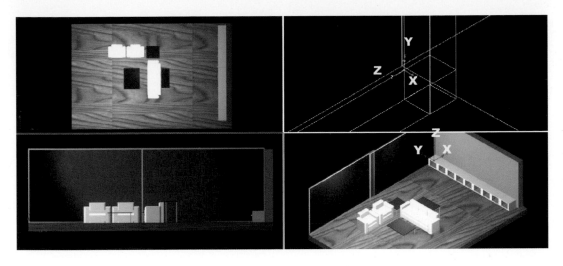

FIGURE 10.11
Viewports on
screen

Command: ELEV

Specify new default elevation <<0'-0"> : **1'**

Specify new default thickness <0'-0"> : **0**

In the upper right viewport, use the ZOOM command for a closer view (Figure 10.11)

Command: UCS

Current UCS name: "NO NAME"

Specify origin of new UCS or [Face/Named/Object/Previous/View/World/X/Y/Z/ZAxis]: World> : **Y**

Specify rotation angle about Yaxis <90> : **-90**

Command: UCS

Current UCS name: "NO NAME"

Specify origin of new UCS or [Face/Named/Object/Previous/View/World/X/Y/Z/ZAxis]: World> : **ZA**

Specify new origin point or [Object]0,0,0,> : **INT (pick the intersection at the corner as shown in Figure 10.13) then press ENTER**

Specify point on positive portion of Z-axis65'-5$^1/_2$", -21'-3 $^1/_4$", <0'-1"> : **ENTER**

The UCS icon should appear like in Figure 10.13. Of one special note for the UCS command, you only can use Face and Object options when you click on the solid objects. For Meshes modeling objects, you will have to use X, Y or Z options in the command line. The next step is to build the 3-D model for the artwork hung on the wall. You may use the Box command. The dimensions for the artwork are: 2'-2" (Width) × 2'-2" (High) × 1" (Thickness). The mounting height is 4'-6" away from finished floor.

Command: ELEV

Specify new default elevation <0'-0"> : **7'8 (because floor thickness 1' plus mounting height 4'-6" plus art work height 2'-2")**

Specify new default thickness <0'-0"> : **1'**

Command: 3d

Enter an option

[Box/Cone/Dish/Dome/Mesh/Pyramid/Sphere/Tours/Wedge]: **b**

Specify corner point of box: **click on the back wall**

Specify length of box: **2'2**

Specify width of box or [Cube]: **2'2**

Specify height of box: **1**

Specify rotation angle of box about the Z axis or [Reference]: **0**

ENTER

You also can attach a material from the Material Library to the artwork. Your drawing should look like Figure 10.12.

Building Floor Lamp and Accessories

To build a 3-D model for the floor lamp, make the Floor lamp layer current and assign white color to it. The dimensions for the floor lamp are shown as Figure 10.14. You will need to specify the thickness for the circle in order to create a cylinder-looking object for the lamp shade. The first step is to build the lamp base. It can be built by 1' radius and 2" high solid cylinder.

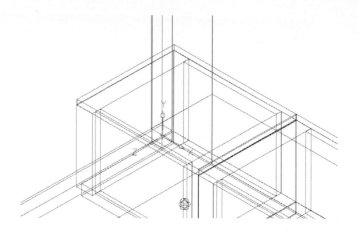

FIGURE 10.13 Isometric view of cabinets with UCS icon

Command: **ELEV**

Specify new default elevation <0'-0"> : **1'**

Specify new default of thickness <0'-0"> : **ENTER**

Command: **_cylinder (or you can access this command from Dashboard Figure 10.41)**

Specify center point of base or [3P/2P/Ttr Elliptical]: **Click on the screen**

Specify base radius or [Diameter]: **1'**

Specify height or [2Point/Axis endpoint]: **2**

ENTER

The next step is to build the lamp support stick, which is 5' tall with 1" radius:

Command: **ELEV**

Specify new default elevation <0'-0"> : **1'2**

Specify new default of thickness <0'-0"> : **5'**

Command: **c**

Circle Specify center point for circle or [3P/2P/Ttr (tan tan radius)]: **pick the center point of the lamp base**

Specify radius of circle or [Diameter]: **1**

The last step is to build the lamp shade, which is 7" radius and 1'-6" thickness

Command: **ELEV**

Specify new default elevation <0'-0"> : **5'11**

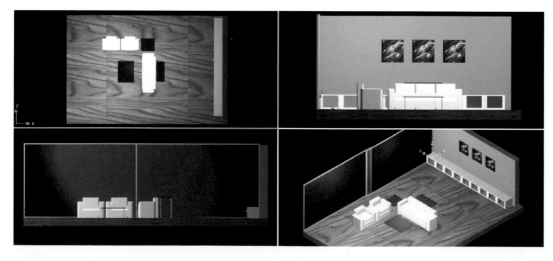

FIGURE 10.12 Viewports on screen

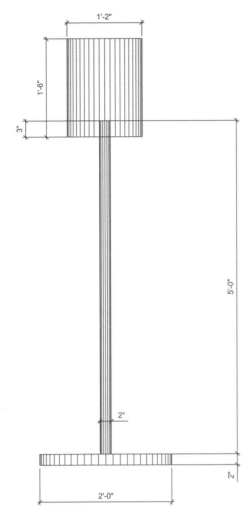

FIGURE 10.14 Accessory elevations with dimensions (floor lamp)

Specify new default of thickness <0'-0"> : **1'6**

Command: c

Circle Specify center point for circle or [3P/2P/Ttr (tan tan radius)]: **pick the center point of the lamp base**

Specify radius of circle or [Diameter]: **7**

Command: Render

The accessories on low cabinets, such as vases and dishes, can be built by the same procedure as demonstrated above. The dishes can be built by using the Dish command. All accessories dimensions are shown as Figure 10.15.

Command: ELEV

Specify new default elevation <0'-0"> : **2'5** (floor thickness plus cabinet height)

Specify new default of thickness <0'-0"> : **0**

Command: 3d

Enter an option

[Box/Cone/Dish/Dome/Mesh/Pyramid/Sphere/Tours/Wedge]: **di**

Specify center point of dish: **click on the top of low cabinet**

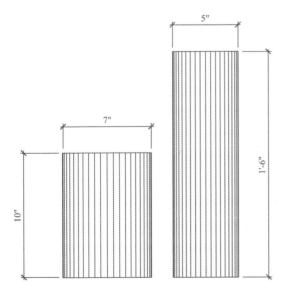
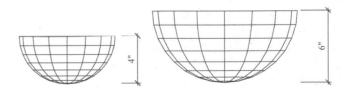

FIGURE 10.15 Accessory elevation with dimensions

Specify radius of dish or [Diameter]: **4**

Enter number of longitudinal segments for surface of dish <16> : **ENTER**

Enter number of latitudinal segments for surface of dish <8> : **ENTER**

The rest of the accessories, such as cubes, books, and balls in the dish can be built by using the Box, Dish, and Sphere commands. The dimensions are shown as Figure 10.16, Figure 10.17a, and Figure 10.17b.

The following demonstrates the process of building the model of using Sphere to create models of balls and using the Box command to build a model of a book.

Command: ELEV

Specify new default elevation <0'-0"> : **2'7**

Specify new default of thickness <0'-0"> : **0**

Command: 3d

Enter an option

[Box/Cone/Dish/Dome/Mesh/Pyramid/Sphere/Tours/Wedge]: s

Specify center of sphere: **click a point inside of the dish**

Specify radius of sphere or [Diameter]: **2.5 and press ENTER**

You will get a ball inside of the dish. You can copy it several times and fill in all balls in the dish shown in Figure 10.17a and Figure 10.17b.

The following is the procedure of creating a 3-D model for a book. There are three steps in the process. The first is to build a back cover for the book using the Box command. The second step is to create the book pages, using the same command. The third step is to copy the back cover and make it a front cover of the book. Then, apply materials to both the front and back covers

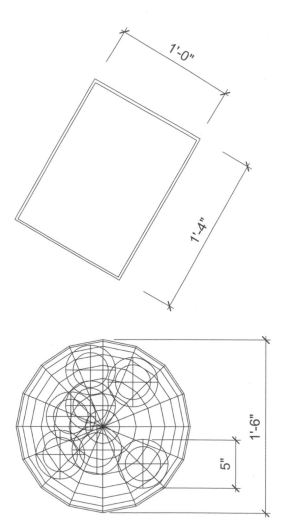

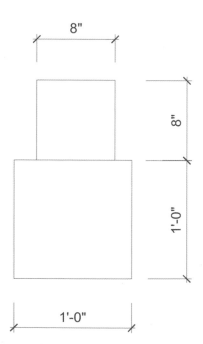

FIGURE 10.16 Accessory elevation with dimensions

FIGURE 10.17A Top view of accessory with dimensions

from the Materials Library. Remember to change the elevation before you start the next step. Go to the top view.

> Command: **ELEV**
>
> Specify new default elevation <0'-0"> : **2'3**
>
> Specify new default of thickness <0'-0"> : **0**
>
> Enter an option
>
> Command: **3d**
>
> [Box/Cone/Dish/Dome/Mesh/Pyramid/Sphere/Tours/Wedge]: **b**

> Specify corner point of box: **click on a point on top of the table**
>
> Specify length of box: **1'1**
>
> Specify width of box or [Cube]: **1'5**
>
> Specify height of box: **¹/₄**
>
> Specify rotation angle of box about the Z axis or [Reference]: **135**
>
> **ENTER**

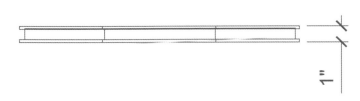

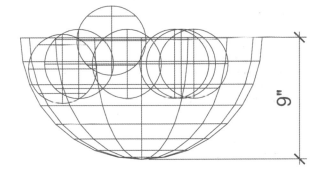

9"

1"

FIGURE 10.17B Side view of accessory with dimensions

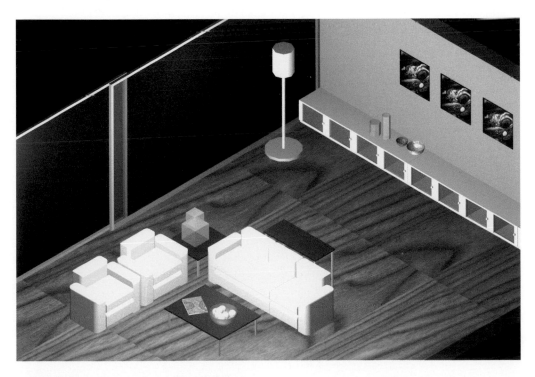

FIGURE 10.18 Isometric view of beach house

Remember to change the elevation to 2'-3¹/₄" before the second step. The dimension of the box is a little smaller than the first one. It is 1'-0" (Length) × 1'-4" (Width) × 1" (Height).

Now you have finished this 3-D interior with artwork and accessories. The drawing should look like Figure 10.18.

Basic Landscaping

In an older version of AutoCAD, such as AutoCAD 2006, there is a landscaping library, which allows you to import basic landscaping into your rendering. This book is to be used by people using different versions of AutoCAD. Therefore, basic landscaping will be introduced.

Now you are working on the last step on this 3-D interior, which is bringing landscaping into the interior. You may refer to Chapter 11 for more detailed information. Landscape Library provides predefined realistic landscape items, such as trees and bushes. You can add these items to your drawing. A landscape object is an extended-editing object with a bitmap image mapped onto it. You can manipulate the object directly in the drawing as well as in the Landscape New dialog box. The geometry of the object depends on whether you choose one or two faces for it and whether it is viewed aligned (CAD help menu).

You may use the same method like the method of building the lamp shade to build the planter. The dimension for the planter is 2'-0" high and 2'-0" diameter.

To bring the landscaping to the drawing, you can use the following procedure:

1. Click on the Landscaping New button on the floating tool bar, as shown in Figure 10.19a.

2. Then you will have a dialog box as shown in Figure 10.19b. Highlight the landscaping name from the library and click on Preview.

3. Change the height value from 20 to 60 or depending on your drawing needs.

FIGURE 10.19A Render Floating toolbar (Landscape New . . .)

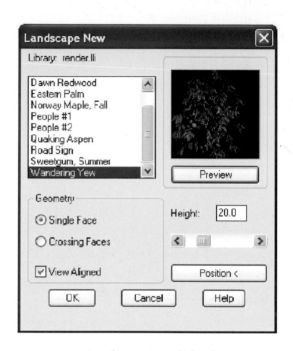

FIGURE 10.19B Landscape new dialog box

4. Click on Position.

5. Click on the location where you want your plants to be.

6. Render the drawing and make an SW Isometric view. Your drawing should look like Figure 9.20.

In the new version of AutoCAD (2008), you may go to the Internet and download free 3-D models of landscaping and insert them into your drawing.

Basic Perspective

You can define perspective views of a model to create realistic effects. The difference between defining perspective views and defining parallel projections is that perspective views require a

FIGURE 10.20 Isometric view of beach house

FIGURE 10.21 Perspective view of beach house

distance between a theoretical camera and target point. Small distances produce severe perspective effects; large distance produce mild effects (CAD help menu). You may create a perspective for this interior space. The command you will be using is DVIEW. Here, the basic perspective concept is introduced and you will make a perspective view for this room as in Figure 10.21. Refer to Chapter 11 for more information. When making a perspective view, you will need to change the view to top view or plan view as shown in Figure 10.22a. Bringing an image into the drawing as background will be introduced in Chapter 11.

You first enter the target point, which is where you are looking at and then the camera location, which is where you are viewing from. You need to use .xy in order to be prompted for a height for these points. Finally, you will enter a distance, which is how far you are away from the object.

When you set up perspective views, you need to:

- Click the Visual Styles list to select 2D Wireframe;

- Switch to Top View through the view list on the Dashboard;

- Zoom at the floor plan and turn off the OSNAP.

Command: DVIEW

Select objects or use DVIEWBLOCK> : **ALL**

Select objects or use DVIEWBLOCK> : **ENTER**

Enter option

[Camera/Target/Distance/Points/Pan/Zoom/ Twist/Clip/Hide/Off/Undo]: **PO**

Specify target point 49'-7^7/$_{16}$", 31'-5^3/$_4$", 5'—0^3/$_8$" > : **.xy**

Of **(point A)**

(need Z): **3'**

Specify camera point 49'-10^5/$_{16}$", 31'-1^5/$_8$", 5'-5^7/$_8$"> : **.xy**

of **(point B)**

(need Z): **5'**

Enter option

[Camera/Target/Distance/Points/Pan/Zoom/ Twist/Clip/Hide/Off/Undo]: **D**

Specify new camera-target distance 7'-3^9/$_{16}$"> : **28'**

Enter option

[Camera/Target/Distance/Points/Pan/Zoom/ Twist/Clip/Hide/Off/Undo]: **PA**

Specify displacement base point: **VIEW**

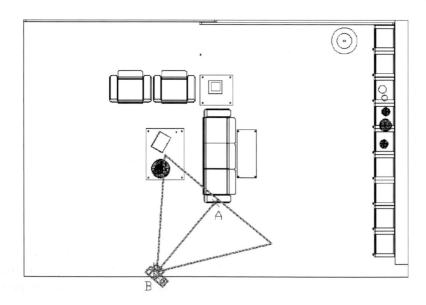

FIGURE 10.22A Floor plan of beach house with camera point

Specify second point: (**move to get whole view in viewport**)

Enter option

[Camera/Target/Distance/Points/Pan/Zoom/Twist/Clip/Hide/Off/Undo]: **ENTER**

Many operations are not available in perspective view, including panning and zooming and operations that require using object snap or input from the pointing device. The DVIEW command can be used in both older versions and the newer version of AutoCAD. The following is the new feature in new versions of AutoCAD.

Command: _camera (or click on the Create Camera tool icon in the Dashboard, Figure 10.22b)

Specify camera location: pick point B

Specify target location: **.xy**

Of **pick point A** (need Z): **5'5**

Enter an option [?/Name/Location/Height/Target/Lens/Clipping/View/eXit]<eXit> : **H**

Specify camera height <5'> : **5'5**

Enter an option [?/Name/Location/Height/Target/Lens/Clipping/View/eXit]<eXit> : **LE**

FIGURE 10.22B Dashboard (create camera)

Specify lens length in mm <50.0000> : **24**

Enter an option [?/Name/Location/Height/Target/Lens/Clipping/View/eXit]<eXit> : **N**

Enter name for new camera <Camera1> : **ENTER**

Enter an option [?/Name/Location/Height/Target/Lens/Clipping/View/eXit]<eXit> : **V**

Switch to camera view? [Yes/No] No> : **Y**

Now your rendering should look like Figure 10.22c.

FIGURE 10.22C
Perspective view of beach house

CREATE MESHES

The Meshes modeling method creates faceted surfaces using a polygonal mesh. Because the faces of the mesh are planar, the mesh can only be approximate curved surfaces. You can create meshes if you need hiding, shading, and rendering capabilities that wireframe models cannot provide, but do not need the physical properties that solid models provide. Meshes are useful if you want to create geometry with unusual mesh patterns, such as a 3-D topographical model of mountainous terrain (CAD help menu). Meshes are displayed as wireframe representations until you use the Hide or Render commands.

The following are several different meshes commands, which will be demonstrated in the tutorial:

- Tabulated Mesh (**TABSURF**)—creates a polygon mesh representing a general tabulated surface defined by the extrusion of a line or curve (called a path curve) in a specified direction and distance (called a direction vector, CAD help menu).

- Edge-defined Mesh (**EDGESURF**)—creates a mesh surface from four edges with two different directions of curve.

- Revolves Mesh (**REVSURF**)—creates a polygon mesh approximating a surface of revolution by rotating a path curve or profile (lines, circles, arcs, ellipses, etc.) about a specified axis (CAD help menu).

- Ruled Mesh (**RULESURF**)—creates a polygon mesh representing the ruled surface between two lines or curves (CAD help menu).

TABSURF Command

The TABSURF command creates a tabulated surface, or a surface that is extruded along a linear path. You can access the TABSURF com-

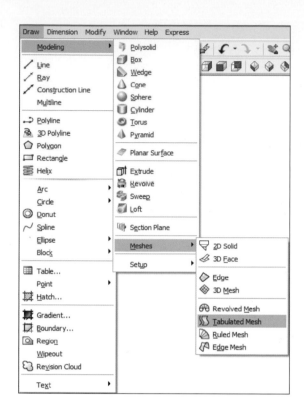

FIGURE 10.23 Pull-down menu (tabulated meshes)

mand by choosing the Draw pull-down menu, Modeling, Meshes, Tabulated Mesh, shown as Figure 10.23.

To create a surface with the TABSURF command, you need to have two elements, such as an outline or a curve to be extruded and a direction vector indicating the direction and distance the curve is to be extended. In Figure 10.24, the curved artwork on the east sidewall is created by the TABSURF command.

The dimension of the artwork are shown in Figure 10.25. The material for the art is white glass and the material for the bolt is grey metal from the Material Library. The height of the artwork is 3'-6". You will have to use the PEDIT command to create a curved polyline before you use the TABSURF command.

Go to top view of the beach house.

Command: ELEV

Specify new default elevation <0'-0"> : **2'10**

FIGURE 10.24

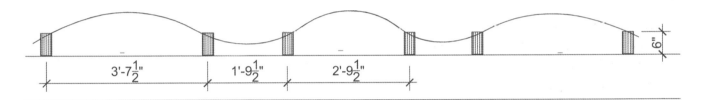

FIGURE 10.25 Dimensions of artwork

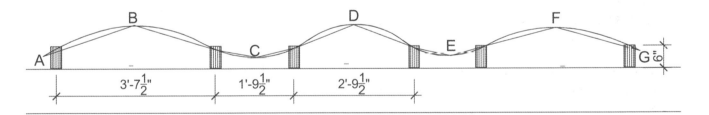

FIGURE 10.26 Dimensions of artwork

Specify new default of thickness <0'-0"> : **ENTER**

Command: **PL (or click on floating tool bar)**

Specify start point: **click on a point A on screen (Figure 10.26)**

Current line-width is 0'-0"

Specify next point or [Arc/Halfwidth/Length/Undo/Width]: **click on point B**

Specify next point or [Arc/Close/Halfwidth/Length/Undo/Width]: **click on point C (Figure 10.26)**

Specify next point or [Arc/Close/Halfwidth/Length/Undo/Width]: **click on point D (Figure 10.26)**

Specify next point or [Arc/Close/Halfwidth/Length/Undo/Width]: **click on point E (Figure 10.26)**

Specify next point or [Arc/Close/Halfwidth/Length/Undo/Width]: **click on point F (Figure 10.26)**

Specify next point or [Arc/Close/Halfwidth/Length/
Undo/Width]: **click on point G and ENTER**

Command: PEDIT

Select polyline or [Multiple]: **M**

Select objects: **Click on the pline 1 found**

Select objects: **ENTER**

Enter an Option [Close/Open/Join/Width/Fit/
Spline/Decurve/Ltype gen/Undo]: **F**

Enter an Option [Close/Open/Join/Width/Fit/
Spline/Decurve/Ltype gen/Undo]: **ENTER**

Then you should have a curved line, just like Figure 10.25. Go to isometric view.

Draw a vertical line which is 3'-6" from the end point of the curved line, as in Figure 10.27.

Before you start the TABSURF command, check your SURFTAB value. The resolution of the 3-D surface generated by the TABSURF command or any other surfacing commands is con-

trolled by two system variables: SURFTAB1 and SURFTAB2. The default value of both SURFTAB1 and SURFTAB2 is 6. By increasing these values, you can get more accurate surfaces because more individual faces are generated between the bounding edges. Figure 10.38b and Figure 10.39b (page 136) show the difference between surfaces with both variables set to 6 and the same surface with both variables set to 30.

Command: SURFTAB1

Enter new value for SURFTAB1 6> : **60**

Command: SURFTAB2

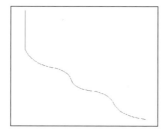

FIGURE 10.27 Reference lines for TABSURF command

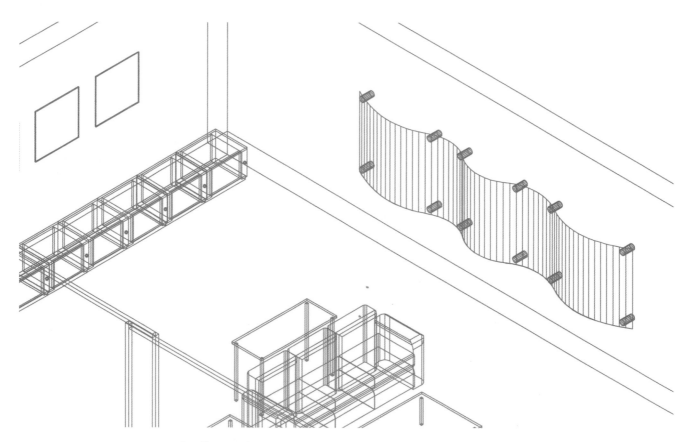

FIGURE 10.28A Isometric view of wall artwork

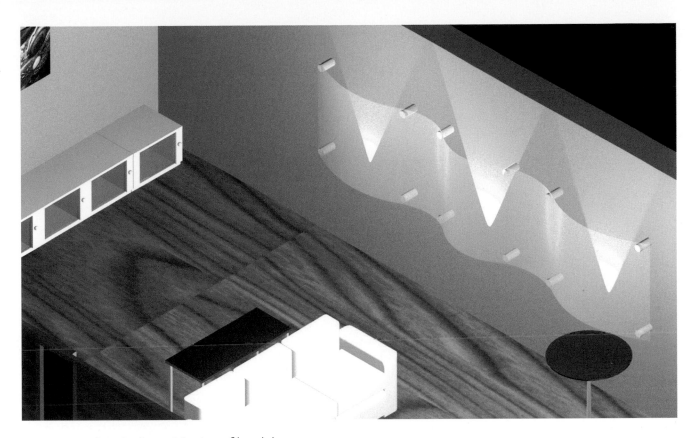

FIGURE 10.28B Interior isometric view of beach house

FIGURE 10.28C Interior perspective of beach house

Enter new value for SURFTAB2 6> : **60**

Command: _ **tabsurf (or click on the command button. Figure 10.23b)**

Current wire frame density: SURFTAB1 = 60

Select object for path curve: **click on curve line (Figure 10.27)**

Select object for direction vector: **click on vertical line (Figure 10.27)**

You may need to adjust the location of this curved art work.

You can set up the thickness as 6" and use the CIRCLE command to build the metal bolts for the artwork on the wall. Be sure that you have made the UCS to be parallel to the eastside wall.

Then you should have the artwork shown as Figure 10.28a, Figure 10.28b, and Figure 10.28c. The lightings used are spotlights. Refer to Chapter 12 for a detailed introduction of lighting.

EDGESURF Command

The EDGESURF command is used to create a 3-D surface between four connected lines or polylines. The EDGESURF command can be found under the Draw pull-down menu, Modeling, Meshes, Edge Mesh (Figure 10.29). The lighting fixtures on the ceiling in Figure 10.24 are created by using the EDGESURF command. Before you start to build the light fixture on the ceiling, it is a good idea to build the ceiling first. You can use the Box command and set the elevation to 10'. Create a layer called Ceiling because you might want to turn off the ceiling layer later.

Command: **ELEV**

Specify new default elevation <0'-0"> : **10'**

Specify new default thickness <0'-0"> : **Enter**

Command: **3d**

Enter an option

[Box/Cone/Dish/Dome/Mesh/Pyramid/Sphere/Tours/Wedge]: **b**

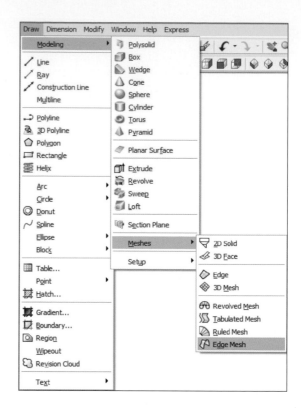

FIGURE 10.29 Draw pull-down menu (edge meshes)

Specify corner point of box: **click on a point on top of the wall**

Specify length of box: **30'**

Specify width of box or [Cube]: **20'**

Specify height of box: **4**

Specify rotation angle of box about the Z axis or [Reference]: **0**

You just finished the ceiling. To build a model for the lighting fixture, use the dimensions shown in Figure 10.30. First you need to use the ARC command to create four arcs. You will have to create two arcs in the Front view and create another two arcs in the Left side view. Make sure all of the end points are connected.

Command: _ **edgesurf (or click on the pull-down menu Figure 10.29)**

Current wire frame density: SURFTAB1 = 20, SURFTAB2 = 20

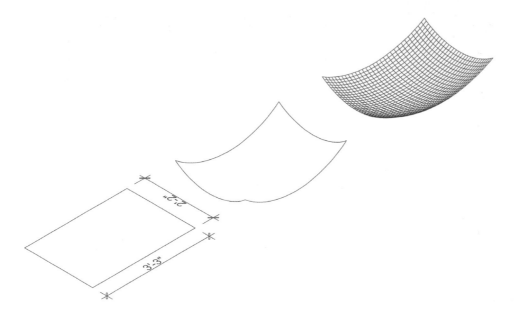

FIGURE 10.30 Illustrations for ceiling fixture

Select object 1 for surface edge: **click on first arc line**

Select object 1 for surface edge: **click on second arc line**

Select object 1 for surface edge: **click on third arc line**

Select object 1 for surface edge: **click on fourth arc line**

At this point, you will have an object just like in Figure 10.30. You can set up the elevation to 8'6" and thickness to 1'10" and use the Circle command to build the lighting fixture hanger and then adjust the location by rotating and copying the hangers for each lighting fixture. The diameter for the lighting fixture hanger is ½". You can copy the lighting fixture you just completed for the rest of the three fixtures. The ball shape fixture can be built by using the Sphere command. The perspective view of the lighting fixtures is shown in Figure 10.31a and Figure 10.31b.

REVSURF Command

The REVSURF command is perhaps the most useful of the 3-D Meshes modeling commands. **REV-SURF** generates a 3-D mesh object in the form of a surface of revolution by taking an outline (straight line or curved line) and revolving it about an axis. The REVSURF command can be found under the Draw pull-down menu, Modeling, Meshes, Revolved Mesh shown as Figure 10.32.

The path curve is the outline that will be revolved. It must be a single entity, such as a line, arc, circle, ellipse, polyline, spline, and so on. The axis of revolution is the axis about which the path curve is revolved. The axis can be a line or a polyline.

The Table shown in Figure 10.24 is built by using the REVSURF command. The detail dimensions of the table are indicated in Figure 10.33. The table base and tabletop can be built by using the Circle command with thickness as 1" and ½". Now let's build the model for the table support. Use PLINE to draw the profile of the table support and draw a vertical line from the center point of table base to center point of tabletop.

Command: _ revsurf (or click on the pull- down menu Figure 10.32)

Current wire frame density: SURFTAB1 = 20, SURFTAB2 = 20

FIGURE 10.31A Interior perspective of beach house

FIGURE 10.31B Interior perspective of beach house

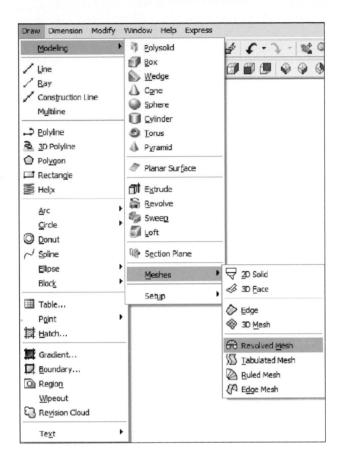

FIGURE 10.32 Draw pull-down menu (revolved meshes)

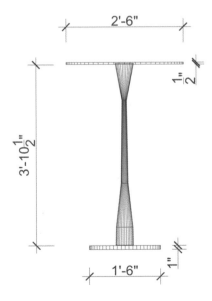

FIGURE 10.33 Table elevation

Select object to revolve: **click on the pline (Figure 10.34a)**

Select object that defines the axis of revolution: **click on the vertical line (Figure 10.34a)**

Specify start angle 0> : **ENTER**

Specify included angle (+=ccw, -=cw) 360> : **ENTER**

Now your drawing should look like Figure 10.34b. A note regarding the polyline: Do not try to use the PEDIT fit option to modify the polyline. Otherwise, it will generate something else.

Tutorial Project 10-2

TABLE LAMPS

For the following table lamps, two circles are two entities. You may use the RULESURF command to create the lamp shades. The dimensions for all table lamps are shown as Figure 10.36.

RULESURF Command

The RULESURF command will apply a surface connecting any two known entities, such as two arcs of different shapes, two lines, a point and a circle (which creates a cone), a point and a line, a triangle and a point (to make a pyramid), and so on.

Command: **RULESURF (click on the pull-down menu shown as Figure 10.37)**

Current wire frame density: **SURFTAB 1=6**

Select first defining curve: **(point to lower circle)**

Select second defining curve: **(point to upper circle)**

Apply yellow plastic to the lamp shad surface and RENDER the drawing. The cone shape is not very smooth (Figure 10.38a and Figure 10.38b).

ERASE the Rulesurf by clicking on the ruled surface. To fix this problem, it is important to set SURFTAB1, a system variable to a higher value

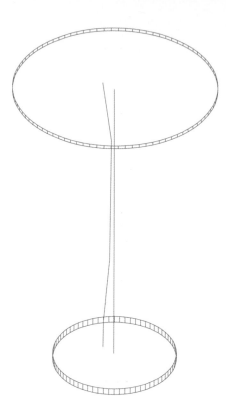

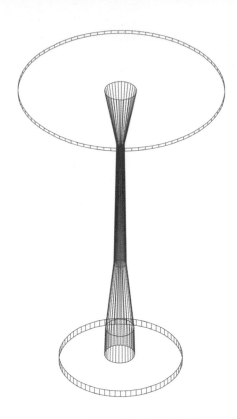

FIGURE 10.34A Isometric view of table

FIGURE 10.34B Isometric view of table

FIGURE 10.35 Interior perspective of beach house

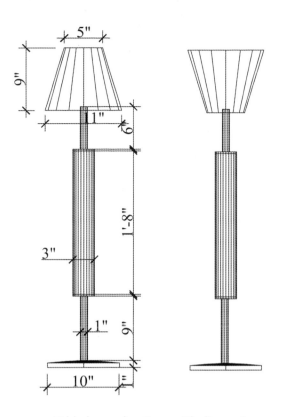
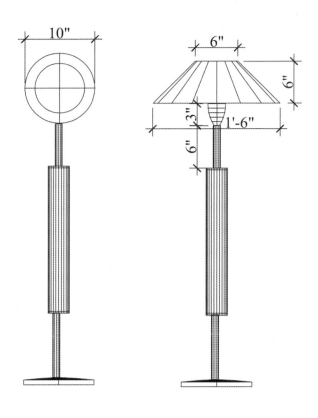

FIGURE 10.36 Table lamp elevations with dimensions

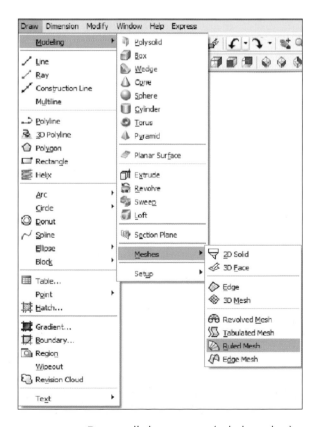

FIGURE 10.37 Draw pull-down menu (ruled meshes)

because it controls the vertical mesh. The procedure is:

Command: SURFTAB1

Enter new value for SURFTAB1 6> : **60**

- Redo the RULESURF on the two circles;
- Apply yellow plastic to the lamp shad surface and RENDER the drawing.

A smoother cone by setting the mesh variable to a higher value will be shown as Figure 10.39a and Figure 10.39b.

To build the table lamps shown in Figure 10.1, you should start a new drawing and name it table-lamp.dwg. Set up the units as architecture and appropriate limits, as well as appropriate layers. You may build a table base first. The dimension for the table base is 12' (Length) × 4' (Width) × 3' (Height). You can use the Box command to build the table base. Then, you may set up the Elevation at 3' and build the lamp base and the

FIGURE 10.38A Lamp shade isometric view

FIGURE 10.38B Rendered lamp shade

FIGURE 10.39A Lamp shade isometric view

FIGURE 10.39B Rendered lamp shade

lamp sticks by setting up different elevations. You can use the Cylinder command to complete this assignment. In this project, the only commands you will be using are RULESURF and CYLINDER commands (with the thickness). The lamp bases are identical for four lamps. You only need to use the RULESURF command to build the lamp-shade according to the dimensions shown in Figure 10.36. After you get four lamps completed, you make a different perspective view for this

art project. See Figure 10.40. Assuming you have completed the table base, which is created by the Box command.

Command: ELEV

Specify new default elevation <0'-0"> : **3'**

Specify new default of thickness <0'-0"> : **0**

Command: _cylinder (or you can access this command from Dashboard Figure 10.41)

Specify center point of base or [3P/2P/Ttr Elliptical]: **Click on a point on top of the table**

Specify base radius or [Diameter]: **5**

Specify height or [2Point/Axis endpoint]: **1**

ENTER

To build the lamp stick, you can do the following steps:

Command: ELEV

Specify new default elevation <0'-0"> : **3'1**

Specify new default of thickness <0'-0"> : **0**

Command: _cylinder (or you can access this command from Dashboard Figure 10.41)

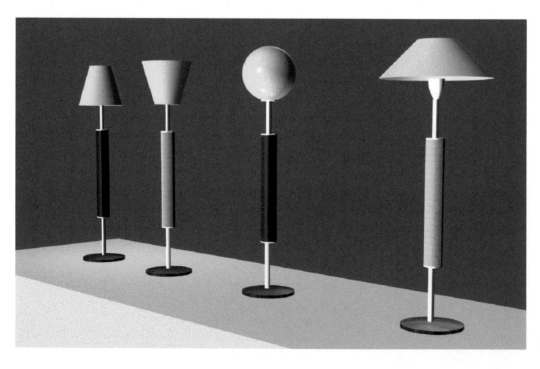

FIGURE 10.40 Perspective view of table lamps

FIGURE 10.41

Specify center point of base or [3P/2P/Ttr Elliptical]: **Click on the center point of the lamp base**

Specify base radius or [Diameter]: **$^1/_2$**

Specify height or [2Point/Axis endpoint]: **9**

ENTER

You can use the same procedure to finish up the rest of table lamp.

Other Meshes Commands

The predefined 3-D surface (3-D)—Create three-dimensional polygon mesh objects in common geometric shapes, including boxes, cones, spheres, tori, wedge, and pyramids are demonstrated above. In addition to these, here are couple more options:

- 3-D face (3DFACE)—Creates a planar surface with either three or four sides.

- General surface meshes (3DMESH)—Creates three-dimensional polygon meshes objects in any shape.

SUMMARY

The tutorial in this chapter is the continuation of the tutorial in Chapter 9, which is to create a 3-D model for a beach house. You have explored Meshes modeling techniques through this tutorial. Furniture and interior accessories can be created by BOX, SPHERE, DISH, and other predefined 3-D commands. Your final rendering should look similar to Figure 9.1 (page 90) and Figure 10.24 (page 127).

In this chapter, the UCS concept was reinforced with the explanation of rotating UCS in order to work on the vertical surface. Orbit and Continuous Orbit allow you to view the 3-D model from different angles, especially Continuous Orbit, which provides continuous motion rather than a static view. The Viewports command allows you to divide the screen in more than one portion, and you can view the changes in other viewports when you are working on a 3-D object. You can set up different views, such as elevation or isometric views, in each viewport. UCSVP is the system variable that controls UCS in each viewport.

Basic landscape and perspective concepts were introduced. You can refer to Chapter 11 for more information. To create a curved meshes object, you can use meshes modeling commands. RULESURF, TABSURF, REVSURF, and EDGESURF were demonstrated in the tutorial.

In addition to the Beach House tutorial, another tutorial of creating table lamps was demonstrated. It demonstrated the RULESURF command and reinforced using CYLINDER commands to create cylinder-looking objects. You have practiced creating perspective views and adding lightings to your rendering through this tutorial.

KEY TERMS

3-D Orbit

CONTINUOUS ORBIT

EDGESURF

HIDE

PLAN

REVSURF

RULESURF

TABSURF

UCSVP

PROJECTS

1. Create a 3-D model of a lighting fixture with any type of curved shade and render it in a perspective view.

2. Create a 3-D model of abstract artwork with curved surfaces. Render it in a perspective view.

Chapter Eleven

Perspectives and Rendering Interiors

Objectives

This chapter provides more detailed information about creating and rendering perspectives. It not only reinforces the following concepts, but also provides new information on rendering background in the drawing. After completing this chapter, you will be able to:

- Make different perspective views for interior space.

- Render the perspective view with different background.

For older version AutoCAD users:

- Insert landscape from the Landscape Library.

- Insert figures of people from the Landscape Library.

PERSPECTIVES

The following drawings are perspective views of the beach house you have created. The goal of this chapter is to provide in-depth information about perspective and rendering. Your ability to create perspectives will be reinforced. For older version of AutoCAD users, you will also be able to insert landscape and figures of people in your rendering. Figure 11.1a and Figure 11.1b are perspectives that have been rendered with materials and lightings. It also includes two elevations by using 3-D viewports. Figure 11.1c and Figure 11.1d show different perspective views of the

interior space without render command. Figure 11.d and Figure 11.1e are created by using the Hide command.

As a designer, sometimes you will just need a line drawing perspective and then use markers or colored pencils to render the drawing. The line drawing perspective can be created by using the Hide command.

Creating Perspectives

Perspectives are very important for a rendering. No matter how much effort you dedicated to design, selecting materials, and designing

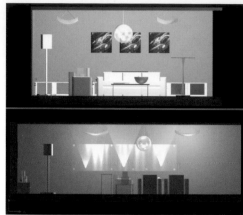

FIGURE 11.1A Interior elevations and perspective of beach house

FIGURE 11.1B Perspective of beach house

lightings, if the perspective is created from an uninteresting point of view, it will make your effort seem unprofessional. In other words, it could make a drawing look more attractive if you choose an interesting angle for the rendering. Although you can use 3-D views, such as different isometric views and ORBIT to view a 3-D model from different angles, these commands are used during the model-creating process to give you a sense of the model's spatial relationship. For a final rendering, however, it is usually required to have a perspective view of the 3-D model.

DVIEW command provides flexibility and control of perspective view of a 3-D model. It defines parallel projection or perspective views by using a camera and target. DVIEW enables you to view the model from a perspective just like we view objects in the real world.

Before the DVIEW command is introduced, you will have to know two other concepts:

- **Camera location**—The point in the model from which you are viewing objects.

- **Target location**—The point in the model that you are viewing.

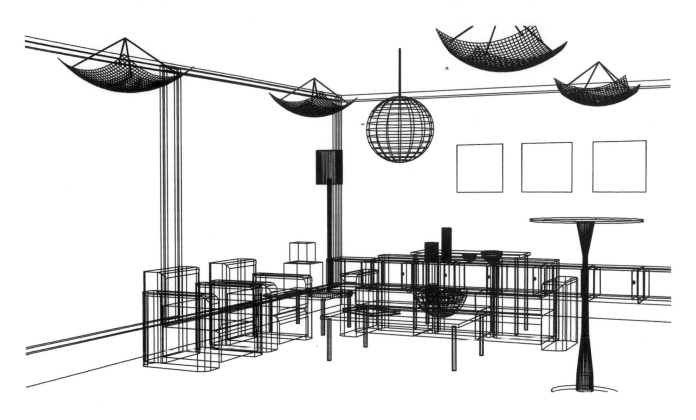

FIGURE 11.1C Perspective of beach house without rendering

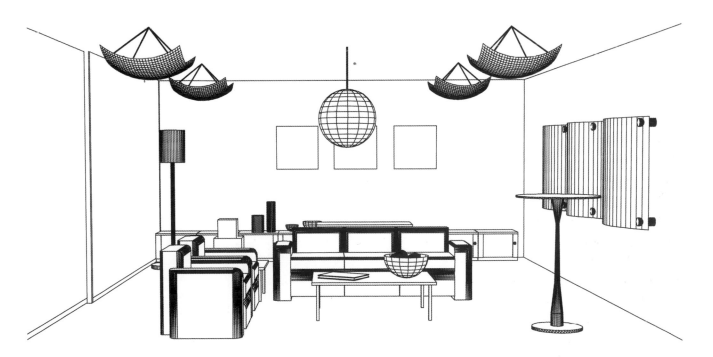

FIGURE 11.1D Perspective of beach house with Hide command

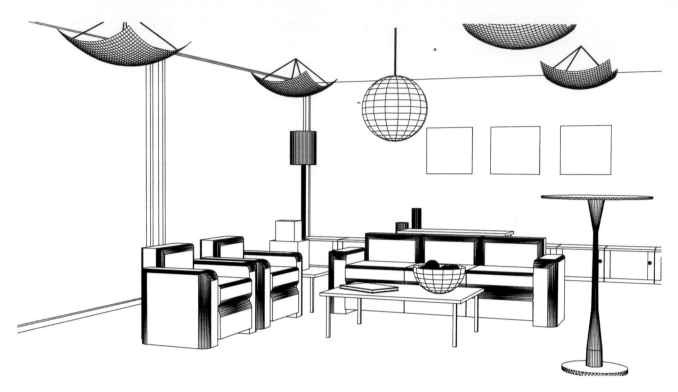

FIGURE 11.1E Perspective of beach house with Hide command

Perspective in Figure 10.21 (page 123) was created with camera location at B point (Figure 10.22a), and target location at A point (Figure 10.22a, page 124).

As soon as you establish these points, you can adjust the perspective until you are happy with it. After you set up a perspective view, use NAMED VIEWS to save the view so that you do not have to re-create a perspective view later. The following is a typical procedure to create a perspective view:

1. Open up drawing 3-D-interiors.dwg.

2. From the View pull-down menu, select 3-D views, then top view to make your drawing a plan view (Figure 10.22a).

3. To start the DVIEW command, at the command line, type DVIEW and press ENTER. When you are prompted to select objects, type ALL for select all objects and then type ENTER.

4. When prompted for "Enter Option", type PO and press ENTER to select the Points option of the DVIEW command.

5. When prompted for the **target point**, type .xy and press ENTER to indicate that you will specify the A point as the target point.

6. When prompted for the Z value, type 3' or a different value. This establishes the target position for the view.

7. When prompted for the **camera point**, type .xy and press ENTER to indicate that you will specify the B point as the camera point.

8. When prompted for the Z value, type 5' or a different value. This establishes the camera position for the view.

9. Type D and press ENTER to choose the Distance option of the DVIEW command. At this moment, you will get a slide tool bar on top of your screen. You may slide the tool bar to specify the distance from your screen and ENTER.

10. Type PA to pan the object. This provides the opportunity for you to adjust the location of

the object on the screen. After you have made your decision, click on the screen and press ENTER.

11. You need to save your perspective views although you have saved your drawing. To save your perspective views, from the View pull down menu, select Named Views. A dialogue box will be prompted (Figure 11.2).

12. Click on the New button; you will be prompted by a dialog box for the name of perspective view (Figure 11.3).

13. Type the name of the perspective view and click on OK. Your perspective view has been saved.

The following is a generic DVIEW command prompt line:

Command: dview

Select object or <use DVIEWBLOCK>

Enter option

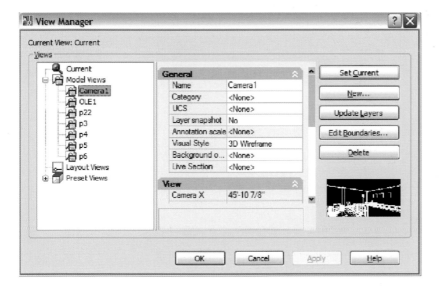

FIGURE 11.2 View manager dialog box

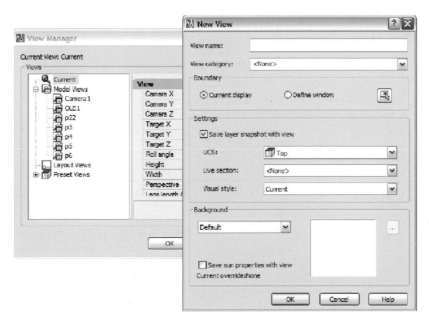

FIGURE 11.3 New view dialog box

[Camera/Target/Distance/Points/Pan/Zoom/
Twist/Clip/Hide/Off/Undo]:

Specify a point with your pointing device, or
enter an option

As mentioned earlier, DVIEW can be used in both older versions and new versions of AutoCAD. The Camera command is another way to set up perspectives in the newer version of AutoCAD. The following is a generic procedure of making perspectives by using the Create Camera tool icon.

1. Open up drawing 3-D-interiors.dwg.

2. Click on the Visual Style list to select 2D Wireframe (Figure 9.2c).

3. Switch to Top View through the view list on the Dashboard.

4. Click the Create Camera tool icon (Figure 10.22b).

5. You will be prompted with the command line:

    Command: _camera

    Current camera settings: Height = 0" Lens
    Length = 50.0000mm

6. You also will be prompted to specify camera location. Just pick point B.

7. You will be prompted to specify target location. Type .xy and pick point A and press ENTER.

8. Specify Z value for target location as 5'5 or a different value.

9. Enter an option to specify camera height. The height could be 5'5 or a different value

10. Enter an option to specify Lens in mm. The value could be 24 or a different value.

11. Enter an option to name the new camera.

12. Enter an option to view the perspective.

13. You will be prompted with a choice of switching to camera view.

FIGURE 11.4 Beach house background

Restore a Saved View and Plot a Hideline Perspective View

You may bring a saved perspective view back at any time. The following is the procedure to restore a saved view:

1. Enter command VIEW.

2. You will be prompted with the View Manager dialog box (Figure 11.2).

3. Highlight Camera1.

4. Click Set Current.

5. Click OK.

6. The saved perspective "Camera1" is shown.

You may plot out a perspective view with hidelines and you may render it by hand, like perspectives in Figure 11.1c, Figure 11.1d, and Figure 11.1e. The following is the procedure to plot a perspective with hidden lines:

1. Set Visual Style as 3D Hidden through the Visual Style Control Panel.

2. Start the Plot command.

3. Set the Shade Plot option under Shade Viewport options to As Displayed.

4. Preview the plot and click OK to plot.

Changing Background

From the previous tutorial, you have been using a solid background, which is black. AutoCAD also provides options to change the background. Figure 11.1b shows the perspective view of the beach house with image background. Importing a digital image to AutoCAD drawing creates a special background. The image shown in Figure 11.4 is a photo, which looks like a beach scene in a real setting.

The Background command defines the type, color, effects, and position of the background for your drawing. There are three different options you can have in AutoCAD when you create a rendering. They are Solid, Gradient, Image, and Merge. The first three options are used more often.

- **Solid**—Selects a one-color background. You can use color controls to specify the color.

- **Gradient**—Specifies a two or three-color gradient background. Use the color controls and Horizon, Height, and Rotation to define the gradient. A three-color gradient is the default. To create a two-color gradient, set Height to 0, so that Render uses only the Top and Bottom colors (CAD help menu).

- **Image**—Uses a bitmap file for the background.

The following is a typical procedure to change the background with a bitmap file:

1. Start the View command. You will be prompted with the View Manager dialog box, like in Figure 11.5.

2. In the View Manager dialog box, highlight Camera1 and click <None> to the right of Background and highlight Image from the drop-down menu.

3. You will be prompted with a dialog box, like in Figure 11.6.

4. Click on Browse.

5. Find the file and browse the image from your computer.

6. Double click the file name to open it.

7. Click OK.

8. Click on Set Current in the View Manager dialog box, Figure 11.5.

9. Click OK again.

10. Render the perspective. Your drawing should look like Figure 11.1.

You may open up the drawing lamp.dwg, which was created in the previous tutorial. Set the drawing in a perspective view. The typical procedure

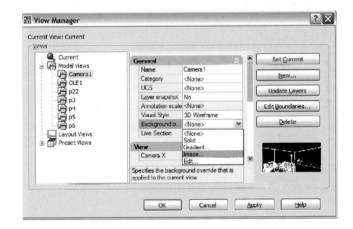

FIGURE 11.5 View manager dialog box

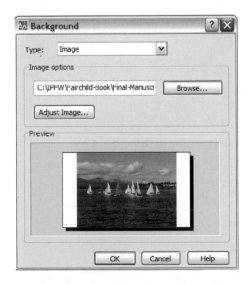

FIGURE 11.6 Background dialog box

of making a gradient background is shown as the following:

1. Start the View command. You will be prompted with the View Manager dialog box, like in Figure 11.5.

2. In the View Manager dialog box, highlight Camera1 and click <None> to the right of Background and highlight Gradient from the drop-down menu.

3. You will be prompted with a dialog box like Figure 11.8.

4. Adjust the value in the Rotation box to 45 degrees, like in Figure 11.8.

5. Click on the color bars (Top, Middle, and Bottom) in the Background dialog box and you will be prompted with the Select Color dialog box, like Figure 11.9a.

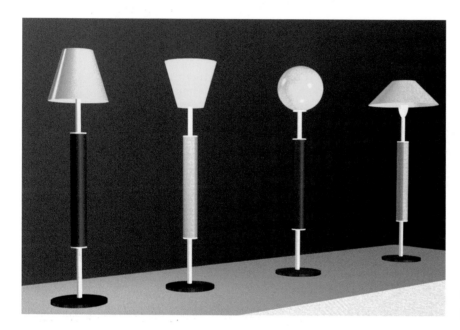

FIGURE 11.7 is the lamp drawing with gradient background.

FIGURE 11.8 Background dialog box

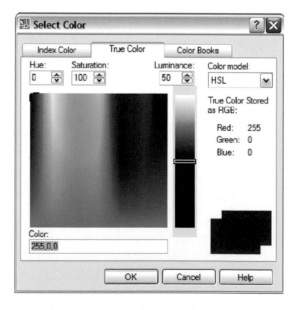

FIGURE 11.9A Select color dialog box

6. Choose colors from the True Color tab, shown in Figure 11.7.

7. Click on OK.

8. Click on Set Current in the View Manager dialog box, like Figure 11.5.

9. Click on OK again.

10. Render your drawing. You will get a rendering that looks like Figure 11.7.

Rendering

You can view your model in several different ways, such as 3-D Hidden, Conceptual, and Realistic. Figure 11.9b presents the interior space in a conceptual mode and Figure 11.9c displays the interior space in Realistic visual style. These different modes can be controlled through Visual Styles (Figure 9.2c, page 93).

When you render a model, you may set the output image quality. The preset quality-control settings in AutoCAD are ranked as follows:

- Draft
- Low
- Medium
- High
- Presentation

The default setting is Medium. When you are ready for the final high quality rendering, you may choose the High or Presentation setting. But it will take a longer time to render the image. Figure 11.9d presents the different settings in the Dashboard.

When you need to show a high quality and larger size rendering, you need to save rendering to the file. The following is the procedure to save rendering to a file:

1. You can access the save rendering to a File tool icon on the Dashboard (Figure 11.9e).

2. Click the Browse button […]. The Render Output File dialog box pops up.

3. Specify the location where you want to save the rendered image file.

4. Click the file type list and select TIF (*.tif).

5. Enter a name for the file.

6. Click Save and the TIFF Image Option dialog box pops up (Figure 11.9f).

7. Click OK to take the default setting.

8. Click on the Output Size drop-down and specify output size. The Output Size dialog box pops up (Figure 11.9g).

9. Click the lock icon to lock the Image Aspect to 4.25.

10. Change the Width to 2040.

11. Click OK.

Figure 11.10a is a rendering created with high image quality with shadow off. Figure 11.10B is a rendering created with high image quality with shadow on. With shadow on, it takes a longer time to finish the rendering.

In addition to presetting quality control settings in the Dashboard, two more new concepts are very useful for the quality of your rendering. You can adjust the values for these two settings so that you can get better quality images. You can control the display accuracy of curved objects by using **VIEWRES** command and **FACETRES** system variable.

- **Viewres**—Viewres controls the appearance of circles, arcs, and ellipses using short vectors. The greater the number of vectors, the smoother the appearance of the circle or arc. Increasing zoom percentage in Viewres may increase the time it takes to regenerate the drawing. The following is the procedure of changing the value of VIEWRES (CAD help menu).

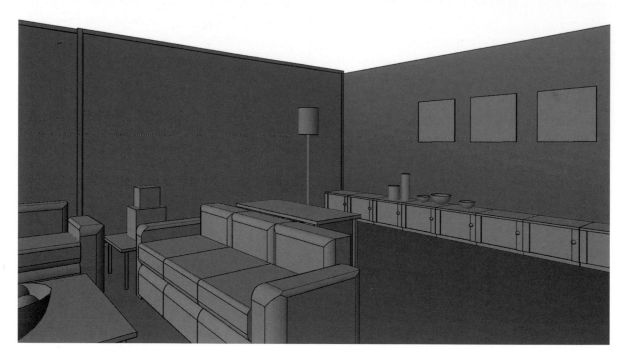

FIGURE 11.9B Perspective of beach house (conceptual)

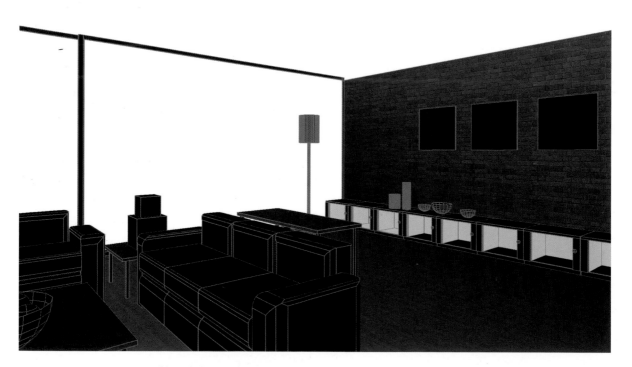

FIGURE 11.9C Perspective of beach house (realistic)

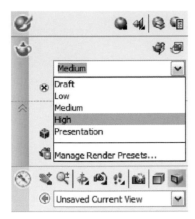

FIGURE 11.9D Dashboard (rendering quality selection)

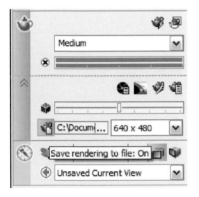

FIGURE 11.9E Dashboard (rendering file destination selection)

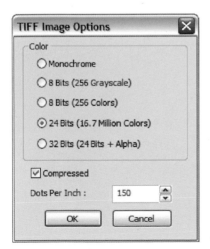

FIGURE 11.9F TIFF image options

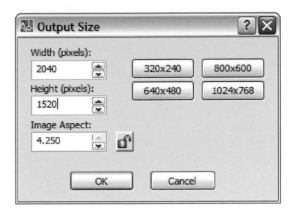

FIGURE 11.9G Output size dialog box

Command line: **viewres**

Do you want fast zooms [Yes/No] Y> : **ENTER**

Enter circle zoom percent (1-2000) <Current> :

Enter integer from 1-20,000 or press **ENTER**

- **Facetres**—Facetres controls the smoothness of shaded and rendered curved solids. It is linked to the value set by VIEWRES. The default value of FACETRES is 0.5. The range of possible value is 0.01 to 10. (CAD help menu).

Command line: **facetres**

Enter new value for FACETRES <0.5000> :

Enter integer from 1-10 or press **ENTER**

You also can use the Advanced Render Setting dialog box, as shown in Figure 11.11 by clicking on the Dashboard render section. You can change many settings for your rendering from there, such as shadows on or off, rendering's quality, rendering output size and destination and so on. The High option gives you higher quality for your rendering.

LANDSCAPING AND PEOPLE FIGURES

The following paragraph is written for an older version of AutoCAD (such as 2006). For the newer

FIGURE 11.10A Perspective of beach house

FIGURE 11.10B Perspective of beach house (with shadow)

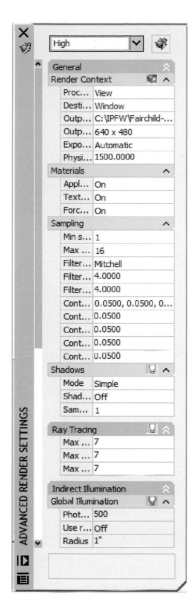

FIGURE 11.11 Render setting selection box

version of AutoCAD, you can browse pre-made 3D models from the Internet, like furniture, people, and landscaping. The landscaping and People Figure section is for users who have older versions of AutoCAD. You have used the Basic Landscape command in Chapter 10. You can manipulate the object directly in the drawing or in the Landscape New dialog box. The geometry of the object depends on whether you choose one or two faces for it or whether it is viewed aligned. You make these choices according to your rendering requirement (AutoCAD help menu). The following are the basic settings in a landscape dialog box:

- **Single face / Crossing faces:** Specifies a single-face object or a crossing-face object depending on your rendering requirement. A single-face object is faster to render but not quite as realistic as a cross-face object, especially for animation and raytraced shadows (CAD help menu).

- **View Aligned:** View aligned makes the object always face the camera. This is generally a good choice for trees and other non-planar objects.

- **Height:** Specifies the height of the landscape object in the current drawing units. The default is 20, and the height is always in the position Z direction of the current user coordinate system (UCS). Use the scroll bar or enter a value (CAD help menu).

- **Position:** Uses the pointing device to specify a location in the drawing. The default position is at the origin of the UCS.

Figure 11.12 shows a rendering with people figures in the drawing. It adds more interest to an interior space. The procedure of bringing people figures from the Landscape Library is the same as the procedure of bringing trees from the Landscape Library.

SUMMARY

This chapter covered topics of perspective and rendering as well as inserting people figures from the Landscape Library into the drawing. Key concepts for making a perspective are camera location and target location. Camera location is the point in the model from which you are viewing the object, and target location is the point in the model from which you are viewing. By using the DVIEW command and following .xy prompt, you can specify camera and target locations, as well

FIGURE 11.12 Interior perspective of beach house with people figure and landscape

as Z values. You also can use the Named Views option to save your perspective views. You may use Create Camera in the Dashboard to set up perspectives too.

AutoCAD also provides several different options for your rendering background. They are solid/color, gradient, and image. You can simply choose a color and make a solid background. You also can browse a bitmap file and use this image as rendering background. For gradient background, you can specify a different value in the Rotation box to achieve different color combinations.

As far as rendering, there are several different options for your image quality. High and Presentation options take a longer time to generate the rendering. Medium is the default setting for your rendering. If you need to generate high quality and a larger size image, you will have to use Render to File. It can be accessed through Dashboard.

VIEWRES controls the appearance of circles, arcs, and ellipses using short vectors. The greater the number of vectors, the smoother the appearance of the circle or arc. FACETRES controls the smoothness of shaded and rendered curved solids. The default value of FACETRES is 0.5. The range of possible values is 0.01 to 10.

Basic settings in a Landscape dialog box are Single face/Crossing faces; View Aligned; Height and Position. View Aligned makes the object always face the camera. This is generally a good choice for trees and other non-planar objects.

KEY TERMS

camera point	single face
crossing face	target point
DVIEW	view aligned
FACETRES	VIEWRES
perspective	

PROJECTS

1. Practice the DVIEW command by creating different perspective views for the beach house.

2. Change the background for table-lamp.dwg. Create different perspective views.

3. Create different perspective views for your other renderings, such as chairs, table lamps, bookshelves, accessories, and so on.

4. Change the background for your renderings.

Chapter Twelve

Lighting Design

Objectives

You will explore different type of lighting commands as well as some important concepts, such as intensity and color in lighting design. The way light affects each surface in a model is by its angle, distance, color, and by the reflective qualities of the surface material. After completing this chapter, you will be able to:

- Use light command.

- Create different lighting effects in a setting.

- Manipulate the lighting commands and settings to generate images as shown in Figure 12.1, Figure 12.2 and Figure 12.3.

LIGHTING A SPACE

Lighting design is an important component in interior design. It can change people's psychological perception of a space. A good lighting design definitely will enhance the quality of built environment. After you generate a 3-D model of an interior and apply the materials to the surfaces of the furniture and space, the next logical step is to add lighting to the interior or to the architectural model. Otherwise, the model looks like a two-dimensional form without volume. In this chapter, the AutoCAD light command will be introduced.

You can add distance light, point light, and sport light, as well as set lighting color, location, and direction for your drawing. These are the key

concepts indicated in the summary, which will be explained in the following. Adding lighting to your drawing is the simplest way to improve the appearance of your models. You can use lights to illuminate a whole model or to highlight selected objects and parts of objects in your drawing. In the previous chapters, some of lighting applications are for the entire model and some of the lighting applications are just for selected parts of the model.

Light Command

You can access the Light command by clicking on the LIGHT icon (Figure 9.24, page 107) on the floating tool bar or by typing LIGHT at the command prompt or click on the lighting command

FIGURE 12.1 Vase with spot light in perspective

FIGURE 12.2 Vase with point light in perspective

FIGURE 12.3 Vase with point light (a different color) in perspective

in the Dashboard. Then you should follow the prompts at the command line. After you create a light in your model, right click on the light you just created and highlight the properties (Figure 9.25, page 108), and then you will be prompted with the Properties dialog box like Figure 9.26. You may change the color and intensity of lightings or turn on or off the shadow cast for your 3-D model from there.

Types of Lights

AutoCAD provides three types of lights, point light, spot light, and distance light. AutoCAD also provides a default light, which is built in with the program and gives an overall appearance of lighting. But with these three different types of lightings, you can create a more realistic interior space and architectural model.

1. **Point Light**—This type of light is more like a single light bulb. It radiates light in all directions from its point location. Generally, Point Light is used to simulate a can light or to give general illumination with low intensity. You can combine point lights with spotlights for a special lighting effect. Point lights are an alternative to default light for providing fill in of a localized area.

2. **Spotlight**—This type of light is more like track lighting. Light from a spotlight is cast in a cone shape. You can define the angle of the cone to make it become smaller or bigger. Spotlight is used when you want to have a focal point or want to increase the contrast in the interior space. Typically, you will use spotlight to create the down light on the ceiling or soffit. Hotspot and Falloff angles are two settings of spotlight that together specify how light diminishes along the edge of the cone.

3. **Distance Light**—This type of light is more like sunlight. Distance light emits parallel light beams in one direction. Distance light source cannot cast shadows on the object. Typically, you will use distance light to simulate sunlight or to increase the level of luminance without shadows. Because a distant light is so frequently used to simulate the sun in this way, especially in architectural render-

ing, AutoCAD provides a special sun angle calculator that calculates the sun's position based on both the hour of the day and geographic location. To position a distant light to simulate the sun light, you can use the Sun Properties dialog box to control the effect of sunlight. The sunlight simulation will be introduced in detail in Tutorial Project 12-3 in this chapter.

4. **Default Light**—When there are no lights in a scene, the scene is shaded or rendered with default lighting. Default lighting is derived from two distant sources that follow the viewport as you move around the model. You can control brightness and contrast, but you do not need to create or place lights yourself. When inserting custom lights or enabling the sun, you will be given the option of disabling default lighting (CAD help menu).

Lighting Design Settings

Lighting Design Settings can be controlled in the Properties dialog box. You may specify whether you want to have shadow cast on or off, as shown in Figure 12.4a. You also can choose Select Color in the Filter Color drop-down to specify lighting colors (Figure 12.4b). The Properties dialog box is the place whereyou may change lighting attributes.

You will have to give a name to each light when you create it. You cannot use the Copy command to create the second light. You will have to create them separately and name them as Spot-1 and Spot-2. In the Properties dialog box (Figure 12.4a), you can see several attributes, which you can modify.

- **Intensity**—Intensity controls the brightness or darkness of the light. When you set it to zero, the light is turned off.

- **Color**—You can assign a different color to each light in the scene. Settings in Figure 12.2 and Figure 12.3 are exactly the same except for the color of light, back wall color and

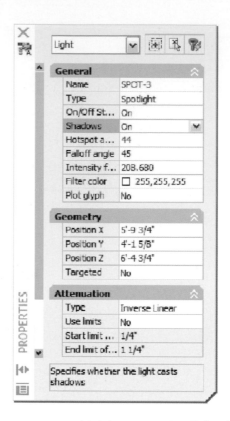

FIGURE 12.4A Lighting properties dialog box

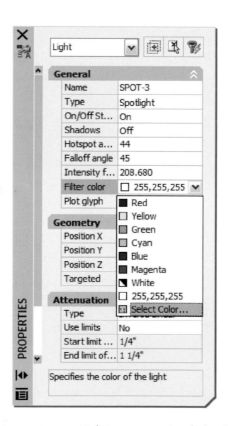

FIGURE 12.4B Lighting properties dialog box

countertop color. You can see the huge difference in these two settings. You can modify the lighting color by clicking on File Color in the drop-down and selecting Select color (Figure 12.4b). You can select from the 255 colors in the AutoCAD Color Index (ACI) (Figure 12.5), or true colors (Figure 12.6) and color book (Figure 12.7) colors to define the color of light. Usually, you can set up the color as slight blue when you want a fluorescent lighting setting and make the color as slight yellow when you want an incandescent lighting. For a special setting like sunrise or sunset, you may want to give a distant light a slightly red color.

- **Shadows**—In Figure 12.4a, you can see Shadow On in the check box. Shadow On makes the spotlight cast shadows. The shadow type can be controlled by Rendered Shadow Details drop-down menu in the Properties dialog box.

- **Hotspot and Falloff**—In Figure 12.4a, you also see Hotspot and Falloff drop-down menus. You can adjust the angle of the cone and its

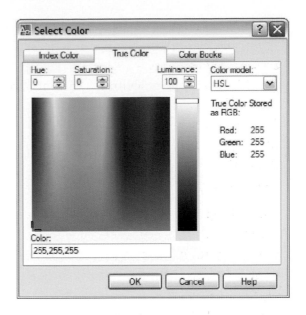

FIGURE 12.6 Select Color dialog box (true color)

FIGURE 12.7 Select Color dialog box (color book)

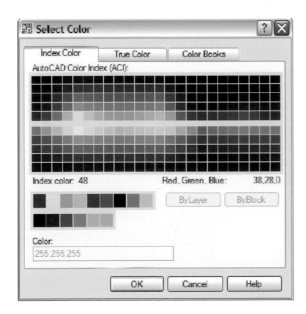

FIGURE 12.5 Select Color dialog box (index color)

falloff for a spotlight. The value of Hotspot should be smaller or equal to the value of Falloff. The greater the difference between the Hotspot and Falloff angles, the softer the edge of the light beams. If the Hotspot and Falloff angles are equal, the edge of the light beam is sharp. Both values can range from 0 to 160 degrees.

– **Hotspot cone angle:** Defines the brightest part of a light beam. This is also known as the beam angle.

– **Falloff cone angle:** Defines the full cone of light. This is also known as the field angle.

You can delete a light or modify its position, color, and intensity. The only change you cannot make is the type of light. For example, you cannot change a point light to a Spotlight. Instead, you must delete the point light and insert a new spotlight (CAD help menu). You can add as many lights as you want to your drawing. You can set the color, location, and direction of each light you create. Don't worry about creating too many lights; you can always delete them, exclude them from the current scene, or turn them off by setting their intensity to zero.

Tutorial Project 12-1

CREATING SPOTLIGHT

You can follow this tutorial to explore how to add spotlights to a design setting as shown in Figure 12.1. Before you start this tutorial, it is recommended that you consult Chapter 15 and follow the tutorial in order to create the 3-D model of vases. Now open up drawing vase.dwg and save it as vase-lighting1.dwg.

1. Make the drawing in a Plan View setting. Click the Visual Style list to select 2-D Wireframe. Switch to Top View by clicking on the floating tool bar shown as Figure 9.3a (page 94)

2. Click on the New Spotlight command button shown as Figure 9.24, and then follow the prompt at the command line.

   Command: _spotlight

   Specify source location 0,0,0> : **.xy and ENTER**

   of **(Pick point near back wall in the plan view shown as Figure 12.8)**

of (needZ): **5'10**

Specify target location 0,0,0> : **.xy and ENTER**

of **(pick almost the same point near back wall in the plan view shown as Figure 12.8)**

(need Z): **4'**

Enter an option to change [Name/Intensity/Status/Hotspot/Falloff/ShadoW/Attenuation/Color/eXit] <eXit> : **N**

Enter light name Spotlight1> : **ENTER**

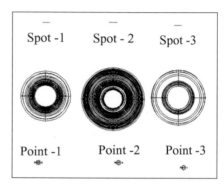

FIGURE 12.8 Lighting locations for vase rendering

Enter an option to change [Name/Intensity/Status/Hotspot/Falloff/ShadoW/Attenation/filterColor/eXit] <eXit> : **ENTER**

3. Right click on the light you just created and highlight Properties. You will be prompted with the Properties dialog box.

4. Adjust all lighting design settings in the Properties dialog box as shown in Figure 12.9. Hotspot Angle 35, Falloff Angle 35, and Intensity 150.

5. You also can go to front view to check the spotlight location shown as Figure 12.10.

6. In the Select Color dialog box, set the RGB value shown in Figure 12.11 for the color of light.

7. Add two more spotlights in the setting. The locations are shown in Figure 12.8 and Figure 12.10.

8. Add three point lights in the setting. The locations are shown in Figure 12.9 and Figure 12.10. (Refer to the next tutorial for more information of point light design.)

9. You can check the Shadows On box in the Properties dialog box.

10. Render the perspective view. You should get an image that looks like Figure 12.1.

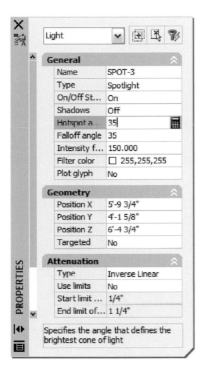

FIGURE 12.9 Lighting Properties dialog box

FIGURE 12.10 Vase elevations with lighting location

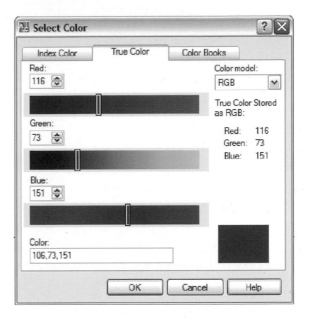

FIGURE 12.11 Select Color dialog box (true color)

Tutorial Project 12-2

CREATING POINT LIGHT

You can follow this tutorial to explore how to add point light to a design setting as shown in Figure 12.2 and Figure 12.3. You can save the previous drawing as vase-lighting2.dwg.

1. Make the drawing in a plan view setting. Click the Visual Style list to select 2D Wireframe. Switch to Top View by select clicking on floating tool bar shown as Figure 9.3a.

2. Click on the New Point light command button shown as Figure 9.24, and then follow the prompt at the command line.

Command: _pointlight

Specify source location 0,0,0> : **.xy and ENTER**

of **(Pick point near back wall in the plan view shown as Figure 12.13)**

(needZ): **6'4**

Enter an option to change [Name/Intensityfactor/Status/Photometry/ShadoW/Attenuation/filterColor/eXit] <eXit> : **N**

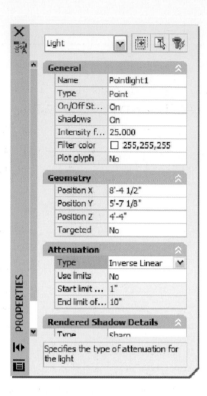

FIGURE 12.12 Lighting Properties dialog box

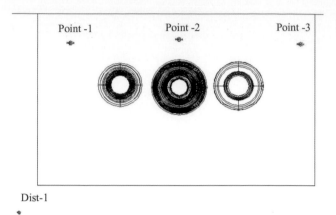

FIGURE 12.13 Lighting locations for vase rendering

Enter light name Pointlight1> : **ENTER**

Enter an option to change [Name/Intensityfactor/ Status/Photometry/ShadoW/Attenation/ filterColor/eXit] <eXit> : **ENTER**

3. Right click on the light you just created and highlight Properties. You will be prompted with the Properties dialog box (Figure 12.12).

4. Adjust all lighting design settings in the Properties dialog box.

5. You also can go to front view to check the spotlight location shown in Figure 12.14.

6. In the Select Color dialog box, set the RGB value shown in Figure 12.11 for the color of light.

7. Add two more point lights in the setting. The locations are shown in Figure 12.13 and Figure 12.14.

8. You can check the Shadows On box in Properties dialog box.

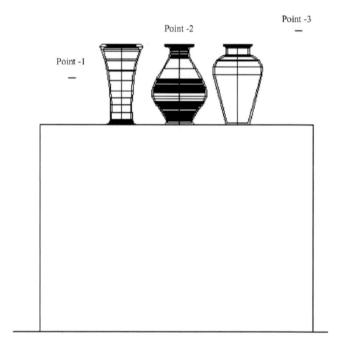

FIGURE 12.14 Vase elevations with lighting locations

FIGURE 12.15 Dashboard (changing default lighting brightness)

9. Render the perspective view. You should get an image that looks like Figure 12.2.

10. By changing the light color, back wall color and counter top color you can generate an image like Figure 12.3.

You may change the brightness and contrast of the default lighting from the Dashboard (Figure 12.15). Adjust the sliders to make the lights brighter or darker.

Tutorial Project 12-3

CREATING SUNLIGHT

You can use distant light to create sunlight for an architectural model. The 3-D model of Falling Water House was completed by adding sunlight. (Figure 12.16a and Figure 12.16b). Figure 12.25 is a 3-D model of the Sears Tower in Chicago, which shows the sunlight casting. You can use Auto-CAD's built-in Sun Angle Calculator to calculate the exact position of the sun at any location at any time of the day of the year. The Sun Angle Calculator is shown as Figure 12.18. It is very useful to create a sunlight cast for an exterior architectural model. The AutoCAD program recognizes three types of light: distant light, point light, and spotlight. Light from these sources passes through faces and by default, does not cast shadows. To create shadows, you will have to specify shadow on or off options in the Properties dialog box.

The procedure of creating sunlight is demonstrated as the following:

1. Open up the drawing Falling-Water.dwg. Refer to Figure 16.35 and Figure 16.36 (pages 290 and 291) for dimension information. However, these dimensions only serve as a reference. You will have to use your judgment when dimensions are not available. You also may

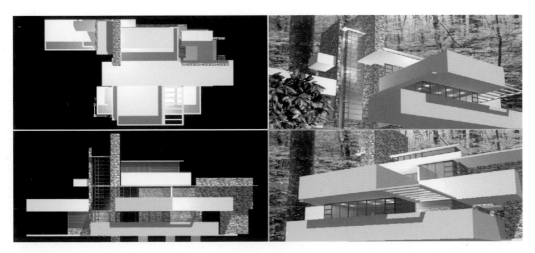

FIGURE 12.16A Rendered perspective, elevation, and top view of Falling Water House

FIGURE 12.16B Perspective of Falling Water House

go to the website to find more information regarding the dimensions.

2. Make the drawing in a plan view setting. Click the Visual Style list to 2D Wireframe. Switch to Top View by select clicking on floating tool bar shown as Figure 9.3a.

3. Click on the New Distant Light command button, shown as Figure 9.24, and then follow the prompt at the command line.

Command: _distantlight

Specify light direction From 0,0,0> or [vector]: **.xy and ENTER**

of **(Pick point at the southeast corner of the building)** (needZ): **40'**

Specify light direction 1,1,1> : **.xy and ENTER**

of **(pick point closer to the building at the southeast corner of the building) (need Z): 20'**

Enter an option to change [Name/Intensity/Status/Hotspot/Falloff/ShadoW/Attenation/Color/eXit] <eXit> : **N**

Enter light name Distant1> : **SUN**

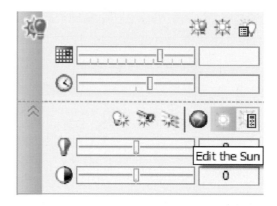

FIGURE 12.17 Dashboard (edit the sun)

Enter an option to change [Name/Intensityfactor/Status/Photometry/ShadoW/Attenation/filterColor/eXit] <eXit> : **ENTER**

4. Click on the Edit the Sun button in the Dashboard, as shown in Figure 12.17. You will be prompted with the Sun Properties dialog box as shown in Figure 12.18.

5. Adjust all lighting design settings in the Sun Properties dialog box. Make the intensity as 1.00. Check the Shadow On box.

6. In the Sun Properties dialog box, you will have a Sun Angle Calculator dialog box, shown in Figure 12.18.

7. Click on the Geographic Location button in the Dashboard (Figure 12.19a), and then you will be promoted with the Geographic Location dialog box (Figure 12.19b). Select Pittsburgh, PA, or Chicago, IL, and click OK to close the dialog box.

FIGURE 12.19B Graphic location dialog box

8. Click the Render button to begin rendering the model. You will get a model with sun cast light, shown in Figure 12.16a and Figure 12.16b.

Scene Command

In an older version of AutoCAD, such as AutoCAD 2006, there is a command called Scene. It controls the scenes in Model Space. The following procedure demonstrates how to use the Scene command.

A scene represents a particular view of all or any portion of the drawing. You can set up a scene with or without lighting. A drawing can have an unlimited number of scenes. You can use SCENES to create rendering with different lighting especially for lighting studies. You can exclude lighting from the current scene. To ensure that you do not create lights with duplicate names, do not copy the light. The procedure of using SCENES to create different rendering with different lighting is demonstrated as the following:

1. Open up the drawing Vase-Lighting.dwg and render the perspective view as shown in Figure 12.1.

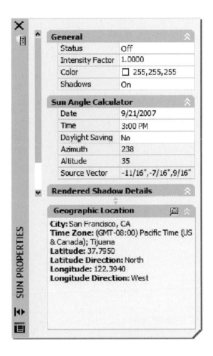

FIGURE 12.18 Sun properties

FIGURE 12.19A Dashboard—graphic location

2. Click on the Scenes command button on the floating toolbar as shown in Figure 12.20. Then you should get a dialog box, shown as Figure 12.21.

FIGURE 12.20 Render floating tool bar (AutoCAD 2006 Version)

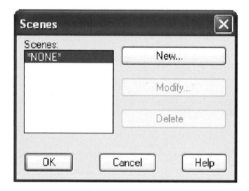

FIGURE 12.21 Scene dialog box (AutoCAD 2006 Version)

3. Click on the New button, and then you will have a dialog box as shown in Figure 12.22. Type "Point" for the scene name. Hold the shift key and highlight all point lights. Click on OK to close the window.

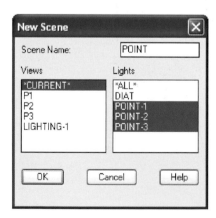

FIGURE 12.22 New Scenes dialog box (AutoCAD 2006 Version)

4. Click on OK to close the Scenes window.

5. Render the perspective by clicking on Point scene to render. Your rendering will look like Figure 12.23, which is just with all the point lights.

6. Click on SCENES command on the floating toolbar again.

7. Click on the New button. Type "Spot" for the scene name. Hold the shift key and highlight all spotlights. Click on OK to close the window.

8. Click on OK to close the Scenes window.

9. Render the perspective by clicking on "Spot" scene to render. Your rendering will look like Figure 12.24, which is just with all of the spot lights.

SUMMARY

Lighting design is a very important component in design. It can add more interest to an interior space or an architectural setting. In this chapter, AutoCAD lighting design settings and types of lighting were introduced. AutoCAD provides three types of lightings: Distance light, spot light, and point light. Hotspot and Falloff are two settings that control the spotlight. The greater the difference between the Hotspot and Falloff angle, the softer the edge of the light beam. A default light that gives an overall appearance of lighting is also provided. Ambient light is the overall brightness of the scene. It controls background light that provides constant illumination of all the surfaces in the model. Intensity controls the brightness or darkness of the light. You can set it to zero to turn off the light. You also can assign a different color to each light in the scene in order to generate dramatic effects. You must use the Shadow option in the Properties dialog box to render your drawing to create shadow casts.

FIGURE 12.23 Point light scene rendering

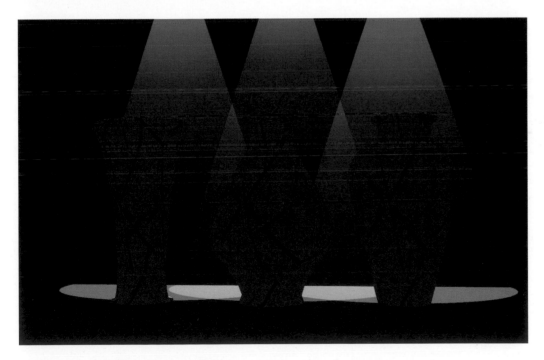

FIGURE 12.24 Spot light scene rendering

You can use Distant Light to create sunlight for an architectural model. AutoCAD provides the built-in Sun Angle Calculator to calculate the exact position of the sun at any location at any time of the day of the year.

In older versions of AutoCAD, the Scenes command controls the scenes in Model Space. You can set up a scene with or without lightings. You can use the Scene command to create a rendering with different lighting especially for lighting studies.

KEY TERMS

default light	point light
distance light	scene command
geographic location	spotlight
intensity	

PROJECTS

1. Create a 3-D model of a display case using spot light and point light to illuminate the display objects. The display objects could be any objects of your choice.

2. Use the Scene command to create different renderings with different light settings for the 3-D model of a display case.

3. Create an exterior architecture model and add sunlight to the model to create sunlight cast effect.

4. Create a 3-D model of the Sears Tower with sunlight cast effect (Figure 12.25). Use the dimensions in Figure 12.26 and Figure 12.27.

5. Use Surface modeling to create a 3-D model for an existing conference room. The requirement for this project is to create an attractive and appealing interior space which is facilitated by a tele-conference screen, a refreshment counter, a display case for trophies, and a conference table with at least 10 chairs.

FIGURE 12.25 Sears Tower rendering

Possible architectural components such as coffer ceiling, coved ceiling or dome ceiling with different lighting designs may be used in your design. There is no display case in the existing conference space. The ceiling is comprised of ordinary acoustical ceiling tiles. The interior lighting and wall paint are very simple. You are required to design a space, which is appealing, with the following design requirements:

- A conference table with at least 10 chairs

- A countertop for serving refreshment and drinks

- A display case for display

- A screen for tele-conferences

- Ceiling could be a dome, curved ceiling; coffer ceiling; floating ceiling or any other type of ceilings.

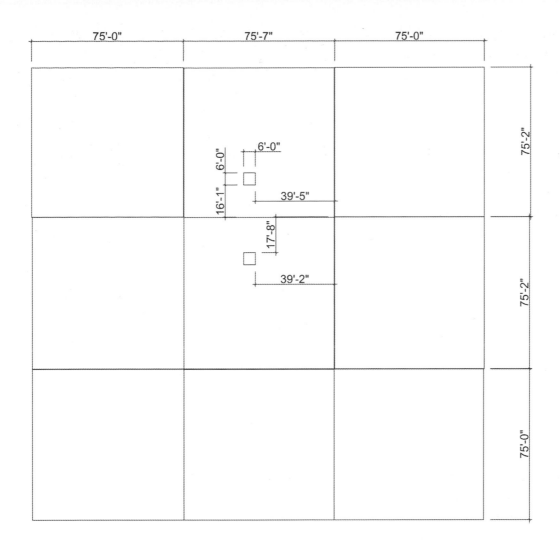

FIGURE 12.26 Floor plan of Sears Tower with dimensions

- Use 3-D AutoCAD to create a 3-D rendering for this space.

- You may choose appropriate finishes for this interior space. Design lighting for this room also.

- Refer to the following floor plan and section for dimensions (Figure 12.29 and Figure 12.30). Sample student works are presented for reference (Figure 12.30, Figure 12.31, Figure 12.32, and Figure 12.33).

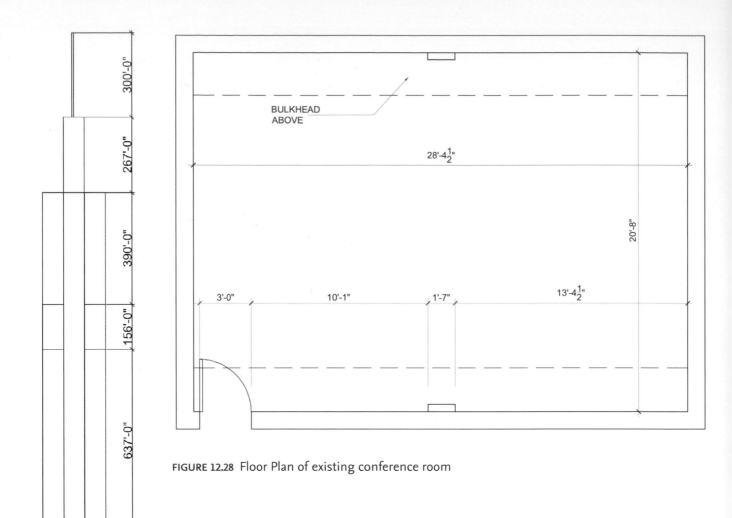

FIGURE 12.28 Floor Plan of existing conference room

FIGURE 12.27 Elevation of Sears Tower with dimensions

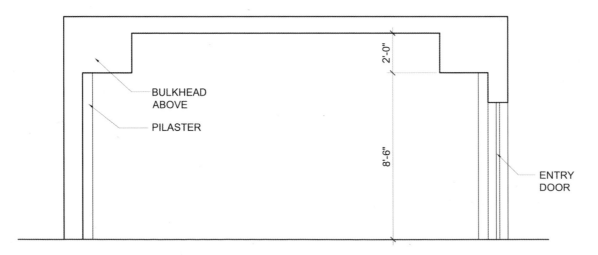

FIGURE 12.29 Section of existing conference room

FIGURE 12.30 Sample of student work (3-D model of conference room)

FIGURE 12.31 Sample of student work (3-D model of conference room)

FIGURE 12.32 Sample of student work (3-D model of conference room)

FIGURE 12.33 Sample of student work (3-D model of conference room)

Chapter Thirteen

Solid Modeling

Objectives

Solid modeling is an important technique in AutoCAD to generate three-dimensional forms. A tutorial for creating a 3-D model of a Gallery Lobby is presented. After completing this chapter, you will be able to:

- Create primitives.

- Work with EXTRUDE and REVOLVE commands.

- Work with one of the Boolean Operation commands—SUBTRACT (the other two Boolean Operation commands UNION and INTERSECT will be introduced in Chapter 14).

- Apply lighting design to the interior space with an in- depth exercise.

- Create multiple perspective views.

- Change the background.

- Apply digital images on the surface of object.

INTRODUCTION TO SOLID MODELING

A solid object represents the entire volume of an object. Complex solid shapes are easier to construct and edit than wireframes and meshes. Solid modeling consists of creating fundamental three-dimensional elements, such as boxes, spheres, cones, cylinders, wedges and tours (donuts). These basic three-dimensional forms are called primitives, which are predefined in the AutoCAD system. They are very easy to access.

Once you have created solid primitives, you can then combine and manipulate those primitives into more complex objects by joining or subtracting them or finding their overlapping volume. The joining, subtracting, and overlapping are also called Boolean Operations. You can also create solid objects by sweeping a 2-D object along a path or revolving it about an axis, which is called **Revolve**. You also can use the **Extrude** command to extrude a 2-D object along a path. A 3-D solid model can be further modified by using FILLET, CHAMFER, SECTON, and SLICE.

You will be able to create a 3-D interior space of a Gallery Lobby as shown in Figure 13.1, Figure 13.2, Figure 13.3, and Figure 13.4 after this tutorial. Floor plans and interior elevations with dimensions are available for your reference. You may start a new drawing and name it 3D-lobby.dwg.

The floor plan (Figure 13.5), interior elevations (Figures 13.6a, 13.6b, and Figures 13.7a, 13.7b, 13.7c, 13.7d) and reflected ceiling plan (Figure 13.8) show the major dimensions of this interior space. You can refer to these drawings while you go through this tutorial process. This gallery lobby is a 40' × 50' × 20' height space with a cathedral ceiling. It is an open two story contemporary looking interior space with simple and sophisticated decorations. You will draw a solid north side wall, half solid and half glass wall as an east wall, as well as an open glass wall at the south side. When you first start your drawing, don't be intimidated by all kinds of shapes and all the

FIGURE 13.1 Gallery lobby interior perspective

FIGURE 13.2 Gallery lobby interior perspective

dimensions. The entire model building process can be blocked into several zones. The following tutorial will walk you through this 3-D model creating a step-by-step process in each zone. In the meantime, you will explore and apply the new commands to create the solid 3-D models. The following list shows the major zones you may consider when you create this gallery lobby.

Zone One: The shell of the interior space

Zone Two: Waiting area sofas

Zone Three: Grid partition with the column and three recessed decorative elements (red color)

Zone Four: Curved display wall with five columns

FIGURE 13.3 Gallery lobby interior perspective

FIGURE 13.4 Gallery lobby interior perspective

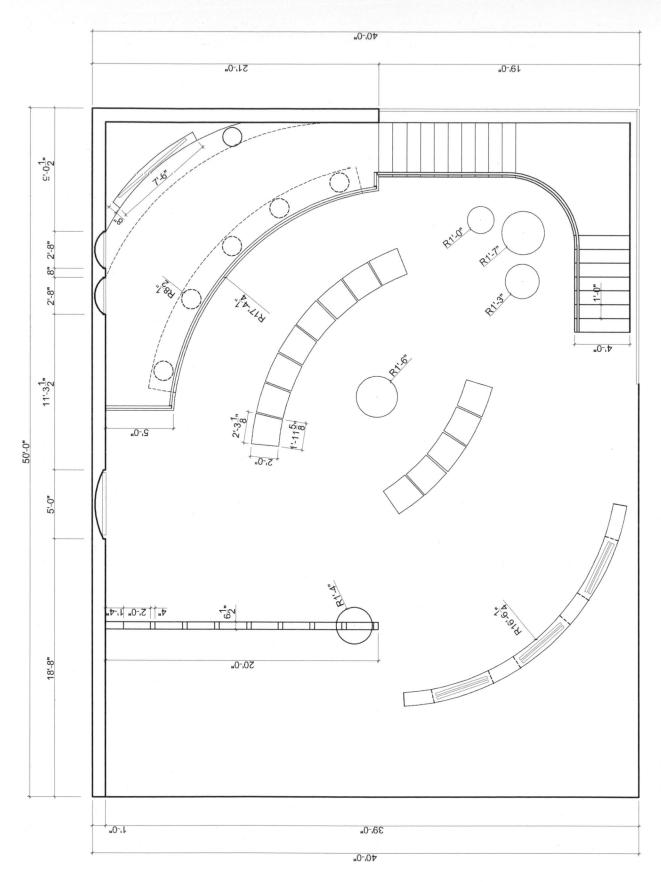

FIGURE 13.5 Gallery lobby floor plan

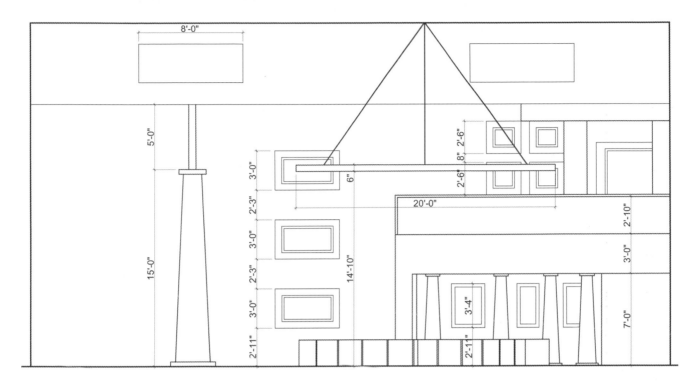

FIGURE 13.6A Gallery lobby interior elevation

FIGURE 13.6B Rendered interior elevation

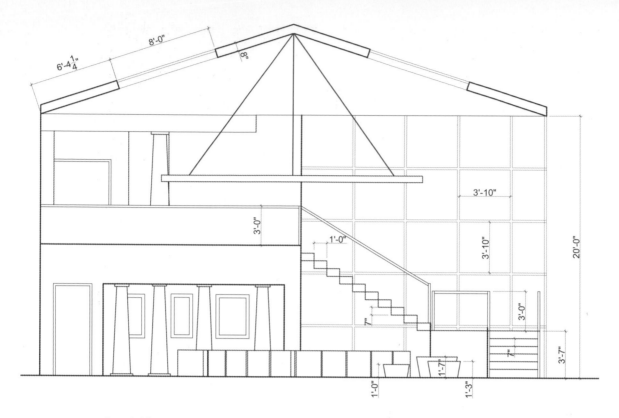

FIGURE 13.7A Gallery lobby interior elevation

FIGURE 13.7B Rendered interior elevation

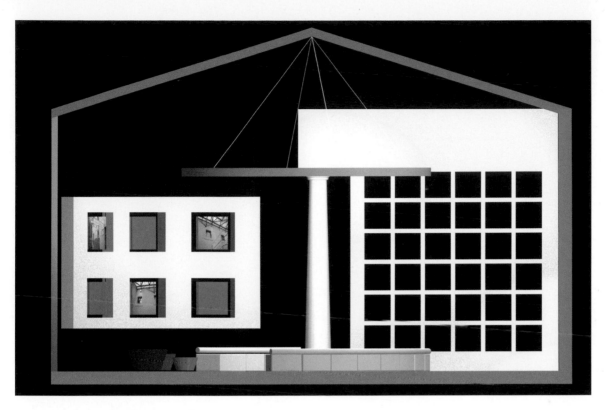

FIGURE 13.7C Rendered interior elevation

FIGURE 13.7D Rendered interior elevation

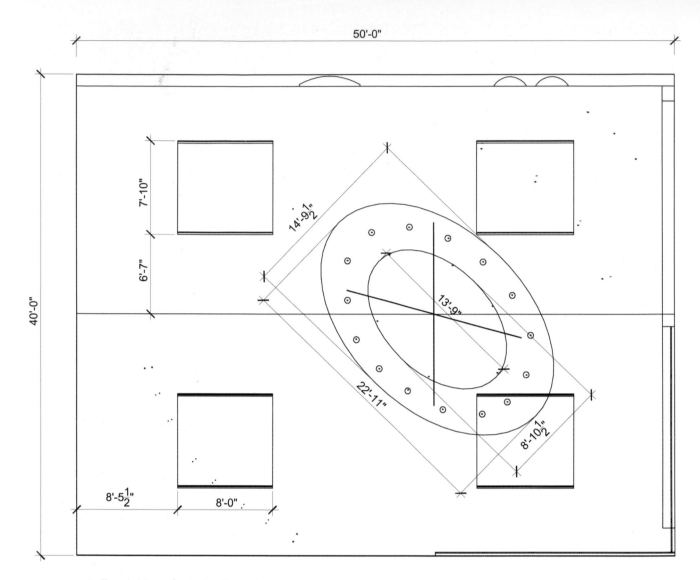

FIGURE 13.8 Gallery lobby reflected ceiling plan

Zone Five: Stairs with three benches

Zone Six: Display loft with framed pictures

Zone Seven: Curved void display panel with metal black cables

Zone Eight: Oval shape dropped ceiling

Zone Nine: Roof with skylights

Rendered interior elevations provide reference information for your model-building process. These drawings are also used a lot in the schematic design process for professional presentations.

Tutorial Project 13-1

GALLERY LOBBY

As mentioned before, to start a new drawing you always have to set up the right UNITS and LIMITS, as well as appropriate layers.

UNITS	Architectural
LIMITS	upper right corner 500', 500'

1. Save your drawing file and name it 3D-Lobby.dwg.

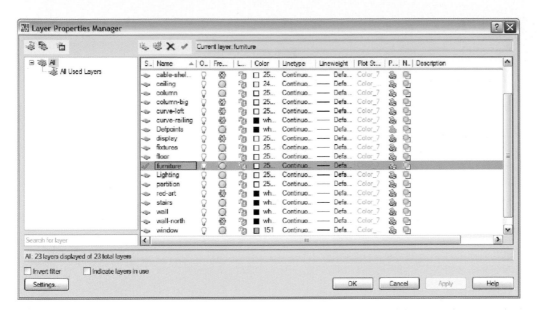

FIGURE 13.9 Layer properties manager

2. Click the Visual Style list to select 2D Wireframe.

3. Switch to Top View through the View floating tool bar.

4. Make the following layers and assign colors as shown in Figure 13.9.

ZONE ONE: THE SHELL OF THE INTERIOR SPACE

The first step is to start with Zone One to build the lobby shell. The command used is the solid Box command. The reason that you have to use the solid Box command rather than the surface Box command is that you will use the Boolean Operations command—**SUBTRACT**—in this tutorial. Boolean Operations only can be used on solid objects. Therefore, only solid commands will be used in this tutorial.

The solid Box command was introduced in Chapter 9. You can refer to that chapter for more detailed information. The steps of building the shell of the lobby are:

1. Use BOX to create the floor, which is 40' × 50' × 1' (H).

2. Use BOX to create north side wall, which is 50' × 1' × 20' (H).

3. Use BOX to create part of east wall (solid part), which is 21'-0" × 1' × 20' (H), and part of east wall (glass curtain wall), which is 19'-0" × 2" × 20' (H).

4. Use BOX to create south side glass curtain wall, which is 20' × 2" × 20' (H).

5. Use BOX to create window mullions (2" (W) × 1" (D) × 20' (H)).

6. Use WEDGE to create a triangular shape portion of east wall. (You may use EXTRUDE command to create this object also.)

Remember to put floor and walls on the right layers. The colors that are associated with layers are white and light beige. After you finish these steps, you can put several lightings in the room. You may choose distance light at this point to generate a daylight look. You may add other types of lighting, such as spotlight and point light later. You can apply clear glass material from the Mate-

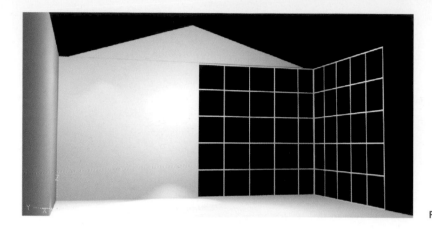

FIGURE 13.10 The shell of gallery lobby

Wedge

FIGURE 13.11 Modeling floating tool bar (Wedge)

rial Library to be glass curtain wall. The shell of this lobby should look like Figure 13.10.

The key point for creating the shell of the gallery lobby is to set up the right elevation. You will have to remember that the floor thickness is 1'. Therefore, the elevation is 1' before you create all the walls.

The following is the detailed procedure to create window mullions and triangular shape portions of the back wall.

> **Command: BOX (or click on solid BOX on the floating tool bar, Figure 9.7, page 87, or go to the Dashboard as shown in Figure 9.2b, page 91)**
>
> Specify corner of box or [Center]: **(Click on a point at the bottom of glass curtain wall)**
>
> Specify corner or [Cube/Length]: **L**
>
> Specify length: **19'**
>
> Specify width: **1**
>
> Specify height or [2points]: **2**

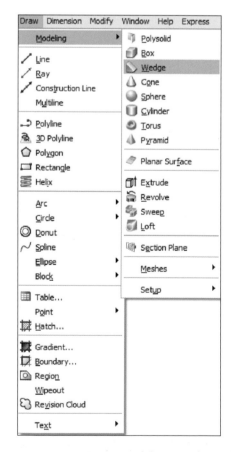

FIGURE 13.12 Draw-Modeling-Wedge pull-down menu

After you finish the first window mullion, you can copy it on the rest of the glass curtain wall. Before you use the Copy command, draw 4' apart from reference lines. Then, you can use solid BOX to create vertical window mullion. Copy it on the rest of glass curtain wall. Repeat these procedures for the other glass curtain wall.

WEDGE Command—Building Triangular Portion of East Wall

The triangular portion of the east wall can be built by using the Wedge command. It also can be built by using the Extrude command, which will be introduced later in this chapter. WEDGE can be found from the drop-down menu or floating tool bar (Figure 13.11 and Figure 13.12). You may also use the Dashboard to access this command.

You can use WEDGE to create a solid wedge with specified length, width, and height values. The base of the wedge is parallel to the XY plane of the current UCS. The length corresponds to the X axis, the width to the Y axis, and the height to the Z axis. You can enter a positive value to draw the length, width, and height along the positive X,Y, and Z axes of current UCS. You also can enter a negative value to draw them along the negative axes. Its height is parallel to the Z axis.

Make drawing 3D-lobby.dwg a plan view.

Command: ELEV

Specify new default elevation: <0'-0"> : **21'** (wall height plus 1' floor thickness)

Specify new default thickness: <0'-0"> : **ENTER**

Command: click on WEDGE on the Dashboard

Command: _wedge

Specify first corner or [Center]: **pick the midpoint of the back wall**

Specify corner or [Cube/Length]: **L**

Specify Length 0'-1"> : **17' 8-¹/₂"**

Specify width 19'-1"> : **1'**

Specify height [2point] 0'-2"> : **5'7- ¹/₂"**

ENTER

1. Rotate the object you just created 90.

2. Mirror the object and make it look like Figure 13.13.

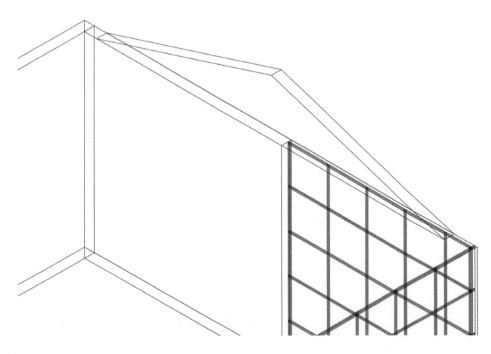

FIGURE 13.13 Isometric view of a portion of the gallery lobby

ZONE TWO: WAITING AREA SOFAS

Sofas in the waiting area will be built by using the Extrude command. You only need to build one sofa. Then you can copy it for the rest of the sofas. But you may need to adjust the sofa location by rotating each single one because the sofas are arranged in a curve.

EXTRUDE Command—Building Sofas

As mentioned before, solid primitives, such as box, cylinder, wedge, sphere, cone, and torus are frequently used in combination to produce new solid shapes. In addition to primitives, AutoCAD provides two powerful commands that produce more complex forms from closed 2-D curves or closed straight lines. These two powerful commands are Extrude and Revolve. The Revolve command will be introduced later in this chapter. With the Extrude command; you can give thickness to a 2-D object. You also can extrude along a path, or you can specify a height and change the taper angle. The 2-D object has to be "closed" in order to extrude. You can extrude closed plotlines, polygons, closed splines, circles, and ellipse. You cannot extrude 3-D objects contained within a block with polylines that have crossing or self-intersecting segments, or polylines that are not closed (CAD help menu).

Lines, circles, arcs, ellipses, polylines or splines can be paths. You can select the extrusion path based on a specified object. The profile of the selected object is extruded along the chosen path to create solid objects. If you enter a positive value, the object will be extruded along the positive Z axis. If you enter a negative value, the object is extruded along the negative Z axis.

If you create a profile using lines or arcs, use the join option of PEDIT to convert them to a single polyline object or make them into a region before you EXTRUDE.

1. Draw sofa's plan view shown in Figure 13.14. And make the 2-D plan view a polyline by using PEDIT command.

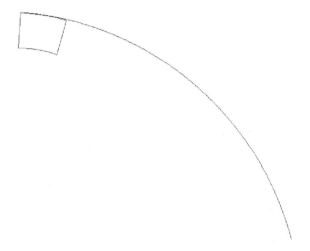

FIGURE 13.14 Reference lines for EXTRUDE

Command: **PEDIT**

Select polyline or [Multiple]: **M**

Select objects: pick four lines or cross-window four lines

Convert lines and Arcs to polylines [Yes/No]? <Y> **ENTER**

Enter an option [Close/Open/Join/Width/Fit/Spline/Decurve?Ltype gen/Undo]: **J**

Join Type = Extend

Enter fuzz distance or [Jointype] <0'-0"> : **ENTER**

3 segments added to polyline

Enter an option [Close/Open/Join/Width/Fit/Spline/Decurve?Ltype gen/Undo]: **ENTER**

2. Choose EXTRUDE from the floating tool bar (Figure 13.15a) or from the Dashboard (Figure 13.15b).

Command: _ extrude

Current wireframe density: ISOLINES =4

Select objects: **1 found (click on the polyline)**

FIGURE 13.15A
Modeling float-
ing tool bar
(EXTRUDE)

Select object to extrude: **ENTER**

Specify height of extrusion or [Direction/Path/
Taper angle] 5'-7 ½">: **1'4**

ENTER

You just completed the Extrude command. Your
drawing should look like Figure 13.16. You will
use EXTRUDE again for building other objects
for this gallery lobby.

3. Use the Fillet command to make the edges
rounded (Radius = 1-½") and copy the object
along the curve line. You may want to use
ROTATE to adjust the sofa location. Your
drawing should look like Figure 13.17.

In addition to extruding straight up or down,
with or without a taper, you can extrude a closed
2-D object along a path. Using the Path option
creates the back of sofas, which is a continued
pipe-looking object.

4. Use EXTRUDE to build the back of sofa. First,
you need to make a left side view (left elevation) current and draw a circle with 3" radius
as shown in Figure 13.18a. And set SW isometric view current as shown in Figure 13.18b.

Command: _ extrude

Current wire frame density: ISOLINES =4

Select objects to extrude: **1 found (click on the
polyline)**

Select object: **ENTER**

Specify height of extrusion or [Direction/Path/
Taper angle] <1'- 4">: **P**

Select extrusion path or [Taper angle]: **click on
the curve line**

FIGURE 13.15B Dashboard
(EXTRUDE)

FIGURE 13.16 Reference lines for EXTRUDE

FIGURE 13.17 Isometric view of sofas

FIGURE 13.18A Reference Lines for EXTRUDE

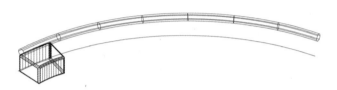

FIGURE 13.18A Reference Lines for EXTRUDE

FIGURE 13.18B EXTRUDE with Path option for sofa

You just completed EXTRUDE command with path option. Your drawing should look like Figure 13.18c.

CYLINDER Command—Building Ottoman

You can use **CYLINDER** to create a solid cylinder with a circular or an elliptical base. The base of the cylinder lies on the XY plane of the current UCS. If you want to create a cylinder with special detail, such as grooves along its side, you may create a 2-D profile of its base with a closed PLINE and EXTRUDE to define its height along Z axis.

Use CYLINDER to build the ottoman. You can find the command on the floating tool bar as shown in Figure 13.19.

Command: _cylinder

Specify center point for base or [3P/2PElliptical]: **click on screen**

Specify base radius or [Diameter]: **1'4**

Specify height or [2Point/Axisendpoint] <1'-4"> : **1'4**

You just completed CYLINDER procedure. Use FILLET to make the edges rounder (Radius = 1-½"). Your drawing should look like Figure 13.20.

FIGURE 13.20 Isometric view of ottoman

You can RENDER your drawing and make a perspective view like Figure 13.22a. You can change the background from solid to image. The background image is a photo, which has been modified by Microsoft Photo Editor (or Photoshop). The image has been made softer because you want your interior space to be clear and focused. The background should be a little blurry with lower resolution. Figure 13.21 is the photo used for background. Figure 13.22b and Figure 13.22c show the close images of the waiting area after all the objects are built. These images will give you a better idea about the interior space of the gallery lobby. They will help you in the tutorial process, as well.

FIGURE 13.19 Modeling floating tool bar (cylinder)

FIGURE 13.21 Background of gallery lobby

FIGURE 13.22A Perspective of the gallery lobby

FIGURE 13.22C
Perspective of the
gallery lobby

ZONE THREE: GRID PARTITION WITH COLUMN AND THREE RECESSED DECORATIVE ELEMENTS (RED COLOR)

The following is the procedure for creating a grid partition with columns and recessed decorative elements (red color). The commands that will be used are Revolve, Extrude, Solid Box, Subtract Boolean Operation, and Array. The steps of building the objects in zone three are:

1. Use REVOLVE to create the column, which is 15' high. The dimensions are shown as Figure 13.23.

2. Use EXTRUDE to create a solid partition first. Refer to Figure 13.24 for dimensions. The thickness of the partition is 6 ½".

FIGURE 13.23 Dimensions of the column

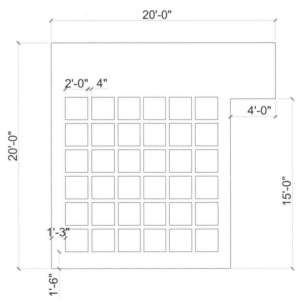

FIGURE 13.24 Dimensions of the grid partition

3. Use BOX to create solid box first. Then use ARRAY to place solid boxes on the solid partition.

4. Use SUBTRACT Boolean Operation to create the grid partition.

5. Use SUBTRACT Boolean Operation to create alcoves for decorative elements on the north wall.

6. Use the Box command to create recessed decorative elements (red color). Refer to floor plan Figure 13.5 and interior elevation Figure 13.6 for dimensions.

7. Add spot lightings and point lightings in alcoves.

REVOLVE Command—Creating Column

The Revolve command produces solid objects from 2-D profiles, much like the Extrude command. With REVOLVE, you can create a solid by revolving a closed object about the X or Y axis of the current UCS, using a specified angle. The 2-D profiles must be a polyline. You can create the profiles with lines and arcs first. Then use PEDIT to join all the segments together as a single closed polyline object before you use REVOLVE, just like EXTRUDE. With REVOLVE, an axis of revolution is specified. Therefore, the 3-D form produced with the REVOLVE has a radial axis of symmetry. You also can revolve any number of degrees about the axis of revolution, but full 360-degree revolutions are the most common. You can revolve closed polylines, polygons, circles, ellipses, closed splines and donuts. But you cannot revolve polylines that have crossing or self-intersecting segments.

The following is the procedure for creating a column by using the Revolve command. REVOLVE can be accessed in floating tool bar (Figure 13.25a) and pull-down menu (Figure 13.25b) or click on the command button on the Dashboard.

Complete half of the column elevation as shown in Figure 13.23. Use PEDIT join option to convert lines into a single polyline.

Command: _ revolve

Current wire frame density: ISOLINES =4

Select objects to revolve: **1 found (click on the polyline)**

Select object to revolve: **ENTER**

Specify axis start point or define axis by [Object/X/Y/Z] Object> : **pick the center point of the column at the bottom**

Specify axis endpoint: **pick the center point of the column at the top**

Specify angle of revolution or [Start angle] <360> : **ENTER**

You just complete REVOLVE command. Your drawing should look like Figure 13.25c.

EXTRUDE Command—Create a Solid Partition

1. Use PLINE to draw the profile of the solid partition. Dimensions can be found from Figure 13.24.

2. Use EXTRUDE to extrude the Polyline 6 ½" shown as Figure 13.26.

ARRAY Command—Creating Grid Partition

You can create copies of objects in a rectangular or polar (circular) pattern called an array. For rectangular arrays, you control the number of rows and columns and distance between each. For polar arrays, you control the number of copies of the object and whether the copies are rotated (CAD help menu).

You can use BOX to create a solid box with dimension 2'-0" (Width) × 2'-0" (Height) × 1'-0" (Thickness). Place the first solid box at lower left corner, 1'-3" away from left side edge and 1'-6" away from the floor on the solid partition.

Use ARRAY to place the solid boxes on the solid partition as shown in Figure 13.29. ARRAY

FIGURE 13.25A Modeling floating tool bar (Revolve)

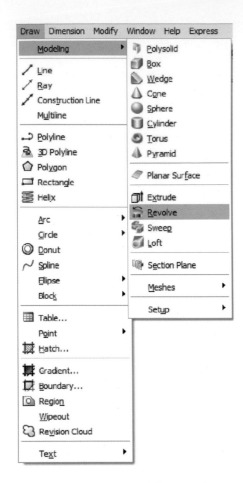

FIGURE 13.25C Isometric view of column

FIGURE 13.25B Draw-modeling-revolve pull-down menu

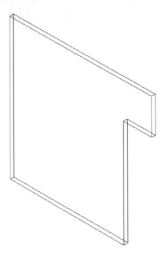

FIGURE 13.26 Isometric view of grid partition

FIGURE 13.27A Modify floating tool bar (array)

can be found on floating tool bar as shown in Figure 13.27a and Figure 13.27b. With 3D Array, you can create a rectangular array or a polar array of objects in 3-D. In addition to specifying number of columns (X direction) and rows (Y direction), you also specify the number of levels (Z direction, CAD help menu). In this case of creating the partition, you can just use 2-D array because number of levels (Z direction) is 1.

1. Click on the floating tool bar to get ARRAY.

2. You will get a dialogue box as shown in Figure 13.28.

3. Check the Rectangular Array box. Enter number six for both rows and columns. Enter 2'-4" for both row offset and column offset.

4. Click on "Select Object" button.

5. Select the first solid box on the solid partition, which you just placed.

6. You can "Preview" the box layout. Then click on the Accept button. Now your drawing should look like Figure 13.29.

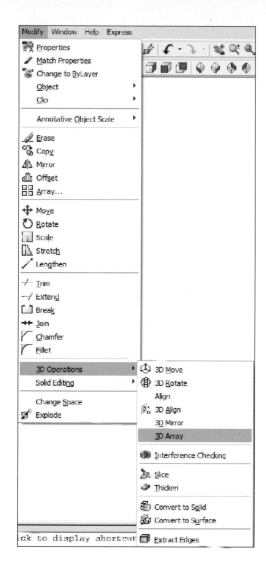

FIGURE 13.27B Modify 3D operations pull-down menu (3D array)

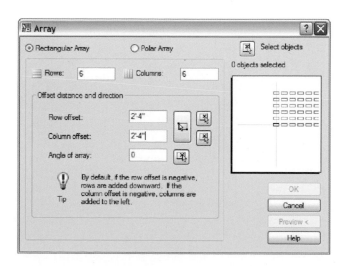

FIGURE 13.28 Array dialog box

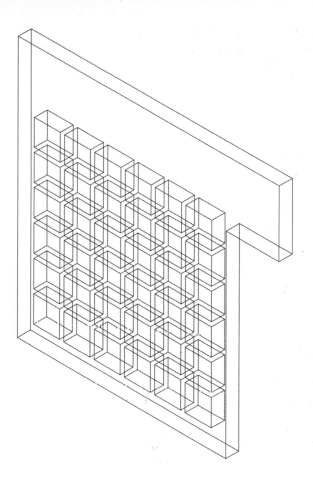

FIGURE 13.29 Isometric view of grid partition

SUBTRACT Boolean Operation— Creating Grid Partition

SUBTRACT Boolean Operation is a powerful modeling tool. 3-D Boolean commands enable you to quickly and easily create complex forms from simple primitives. There are three Boolean Operations you can use: Union, Intersect, and Subtract. UNION and INTERSECT will be introduced in Chapter 14. Subtract operation means that objects in the second selection set are subtracted from objects in the first selection set.

Click on SUBTRACT (Boolean Operations) the on floating tool bar as shown in Figure 13.30a, or pull-down menu (Figure 13.30b) or click the command button on Dashboard.

FIGURE 13.30A Modeling floating tool bar (SUBTRACT)

FIGURE 13.30B Modify-solid-editing pull-down menu (SUBTRACT)

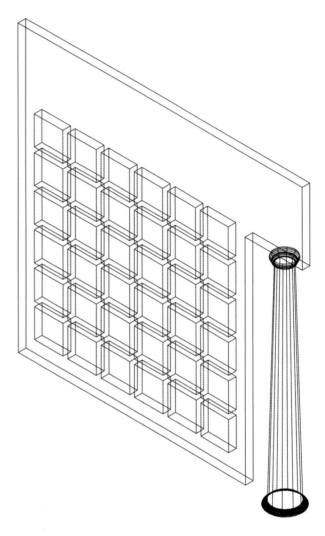

FIGURE 13.31 Isometric view of grid partition

Command: _subtract select solids and regions to subtract from.

Select objects: **(click on the partition) 1 found**

Select objects: **ENTER**

Select solids and regions to subtract.

Select object: **(click on solid boxes) 1 found**

Select object: **ENTER**

Your drawing should look like Figure 13.31.

SUBTRACT Boolean Operation—Create Alcoves for Decorative Elements

1. Refer to floor plan (Figure 13.5) and interior elevation (Figure 13.6) for dimensions to create a solid object 5'-0"(Arc Length) × 3'-0" (Height) by using EXTRUDE.

2. Copy this solid object twice and place them on the west sidewall, shown as Figure 13.32. Setting up the right elevation is the key for this step.

3. Use the Subtract Boolean operation to subtract these three solid objects from the west wall. Your drawing should look like Figure 13.32.

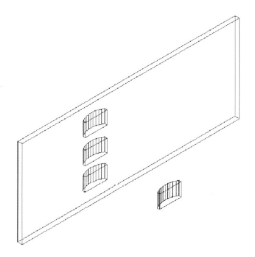

FIGURE 13.32 Art alcove on wall

BOX Command to Create Recessed Decorative Elements (Red Color)

1. Use BOX to create a solid box, which is 4'-0" (Width) × 2'-0" (Height) × 4" (Thickness).

2. Use BOX to create another solid box, which is 3'-8" (Width) × 1'-8" (Height) × 1½" (Thickness).

3. Use SUBTRACT (Boolean command) to subtract the second solid box from the first solid box. It is the frame of the decorative element. Your drawing will look like Figure 13.33.

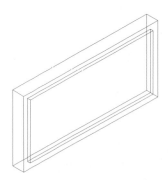

FIGURE 13.33 Decorative element

4. Use BOX to create another solid box, which is 3'-8" (Width) × 1'-8" (Height) × 1½" (Thickness), and insert it into the frame. Copy it for the rest of two decorative elements and place each one in the alcoves on the west wall. Then you will have a drawing that looks like Figure 13.34.

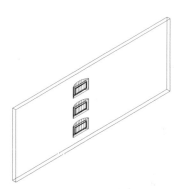

FIGURE 13.34 Decorative element in art alcove

5. Add spot lighting and point lighting in alcoves.
   - Add one-spot lighting in each alcove and one point light in each alcove. You can refer to Chapter 12 for lighting design.
   - Apply red color from material library for decorative elements. Apply black color for the frames.

The following figures show different perspectives of a grid partition with the column and decorative elements in alcoves on the north wall (Figure 13.35). Figure 13.36 and Figure 13.37 represent the completed perspectives with other objects.

ZONE FOUR: CURVED DISPLAY WALL WITH COLUMNS

In zone four, there is a curved display wall with five columns. There are also four framed pictures (Figure 13.46 and Figure 13.47). To build 3-D models for these objects, you will need use EXTRUDE, SUBTRACT (Boolean Operation),

FIGURE 13.35 Interior perspective of gallery lobby

FIGURE 13.36 Interior perspective of gallery lobby

FIGURE 13.37 Interior perspective of gallery lobby

BOX and REVOLVE. You also will need to modify the Materials Library to create framed pictures. Lighting design, such as spot lighting and point lighting will be reinforced in this tutorial. The steps of building the objects in zone four are:

1. Use EXTRUDE to create a curved display wall with two doors on both sides. The dimensions are shown in Figure 13.5a and Figure 13.7a.

2. Use SUBTRACT (Boolean command) to create two recessed door spaces, which are 3'(W) × 7' (H) × 2" (TH).

3. Use BOX to create two doors and place them in the recessed niches.

4. Use SUBTRACT to create recessed curved displace space.

5. Use REVOLVE to create columns.

6. Use BOX and SUBTRACT to create picture frames on the curved display wall.

7. Modify the Materials Library and apply photos to the picture frames. Refer to Chapter 15 for details about material modification.

8. Add spot lightings and point lightings on soffit of recessed display wall.

EXTRUDE Command—Create a Curved Display Wall with Two Doors

1. Draw the base profile of curved display wall. Refer to floor plan (Figure 13.5) for dimensions.

2. Use PEDIT to join all lines and arc as a single entity.

3. Use EXTRUDE command to extrude the polyline to 10'. Your drawing should look like Figure 13.38.

4. Use BOX to create two doors, which are 3' (W) × 7' (H) × 2" (TH) as the second set of objects.

5. Use SUBTRACT to subtract two doors from the first solid object shown as Figure 13.38

to create two recessed door niches, which are 3'(W) × 7' (H) × 2" (TH). After SUBTRACT, the object should look like Figure 13.39.

6. Use BOX to create two doors and place them in the recessed niches. Your drawing should look like Figure 13.39.

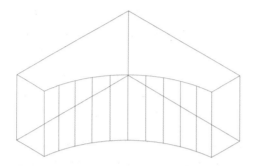

FIGURE 13.38 Isometric view of loft

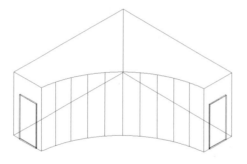

FIGURE 13.39 Isometric view of loft with doors

SUBTRACT Boolean Operation—Create Recessed Curved Display Space

1. Draw the base profile as shown in Figure 13.40.

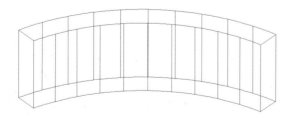

FIGURE 13.40 Isometric view of the second object for subtract

2. Use PEDIT to join all lines and two arcs and make a single polyline.

3. Use EXTRUDE to extrude polyline to 7' high to make a solid object as shown in Figure 13.40. It is the second object, which will be subtracted from the first object as shown in Figure 13.39.

4. Use SUBTRACT (Boolean command) to subtract this object (Figure 13.40) from the curved wall you just created, as shown in Figure 13.39. You should have a drawing like Figure 13.41.

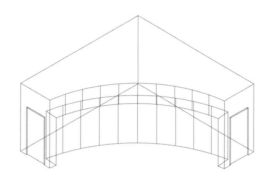

FIGURE 13.41 Display loft

5. Use REVOLVE to create columns shown in Figure 13.25c (page 188). Refer to interior elevation in Figure 13.6a for dimensions.

6. Copy the column and lay out the columns as in Figure 13.42.

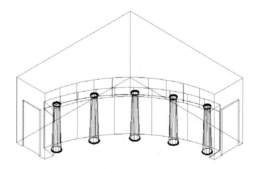

FIGURE 13.42 Display loft with columns

7. Use BOX command and SUBTRACT Boolean Operation to create picture frames on the curved display wall. Refer to floor plan and

interior elevations for dimensions. The procedure is similar to the one for creating recessed red art works in the previous tutorial.

8. Modify material library and apply photos to the picture frames. Your picture frame should look like Figure 13.43 and Figure 13.44. You can refer to Chapter 15 for more details of modifying material library.

9. Add spot lightings and point lightings on soffit of recessed display wall.

The following figures above (Figure 13.45 and Figure 13.46) show different perspectives of a curved display wall with columns and picture frames. Figure 13.47, Figure 13.48, and Figure 13.49 represent the completed perspectives with other objects. You can refer to these images for more visualized information in this tutorial process.

ZONE FIVE: STAIRS WITH THREE BENCHES

Zone five in this tutorial will include stairs with a landing and handrails, as well as a curved railing at the landing. There are three benches by this stair. The commands that you will use are EXTRUDE, BOX, and REVOLVE. Again, the key point is to set up the right elevation. The steps of building the objects in zone five are:

1. Use EXTRUDE to create a curved landing for the stairs. The dimensions are shown in Figure 13.5a and Figure 13.7a.

FIGURE 13.43 Perspective of gallery lobby

FIGURE 13.44 Perspective of gallery lobby

FIGURE 13.45 Perspective of gallery lobby

FIGURE 13.46 Perspective of gallery lobby

FIGURE 13.47 Perspective of gallery lobby

FIGURE 13.48 Perspective of gallery lobby

2. Use BOX to create steps, which are 4'-0" (Width) × 12" (Depth) × 7" (Height).

3. Use COPY to create stairs.

4. Use EXTRUDE to create a curved railing at the landing.

5. Use EXTRUDE with Path option to create handrails.

6. Use REVOLVE to create three benches.

EXTRUDE Command—Create a Curved Landing

1. Draw the base profile of the landing according to the dimensions shown on floor plan and interior elevations. Use PEDIT to join all the lines and arc together and make it a polyline.

2. Use EXTRUDE to extrude the polyline 4'-2". The object you just created should look like Figure 13.50.

BOX Command—Create Steps

Figure 13.52 shows the steps with the landing.

1. Use BOX to create steps, which is 4'-0" (width) × 12" (depth) × 7" (height).

2. Use COPY to create stairs like in Figure 13.51.

FIGURE 13.49 Perspective of gallery lobby

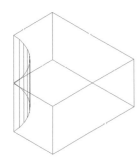

FIGURE 13.50 Isometric view of stair landing

EXTRUDE Command—Create a Curved Railing at the Landing

1. Draw the base plan view of the curved railing according to the dimensions shown on the floor plan and interior elevations. Use PEDIT to join all lines and arcs together and make it a polyline.

2. Use EXTRUDE to extrude the polyline 3'-0". You should get a curved screen. Apply "blue glass" from the Materials Library. You also can use clear glass in the Materials Library and modify the color to blue. Set up the elevation

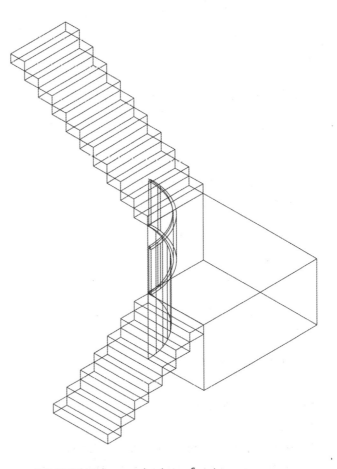

FIGURE 13.51 Isometric view of stairs

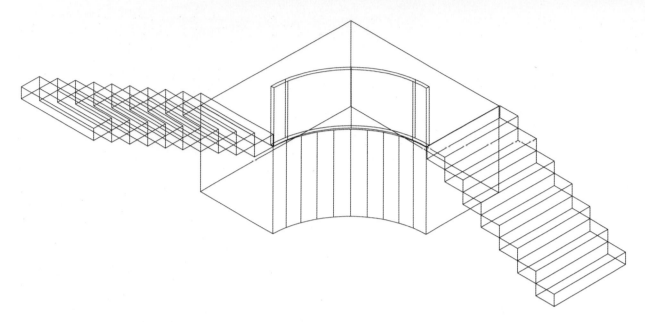

FIGURE 13.52 Isometric view of stairs

to 5'-2" because the landing height is 4'-2" and floor thickness is 1', and place the curved railing on top of the landing. Your drawing should look like Figure 13.52.

EXTRUDE Command with Path Option— Create Hand Rails

1. Draw a circle on top of the curved railing and a curved line along the curved railing shown as Figure 13.53.

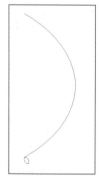

FIGURE 13.53 Reference lines for the Extrude Command

2. Use EXTRUDE with Path Option to extrude the circle. The procedure is the same as the one you created for the sofa back; you should get a drawing like Figure 13.54.

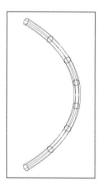

FIGURE 13.54 Stair railing

3. Use EXTRUDE with Path Option to create the rest of the hand railings. The rest of the handrails are straight lines with the path option.

REVOLVE Command—Create Three Benches

1. Create the section profile of three benches. Dimensions are shown on the floor plan and interior elevations.

2. Use PEDIT to join all lines together as a single polyline.

3. Use REVOLVE to create the benches.

The following figures show different perspectives of the stairs with three benches.

FIGURE 13.55 Perspective of stair area

ZONE SIX: DISPLAY LOFT

Zone six includes a display loft. It is at 10' high level. You will have to set the elevation at least 10' when you create another object, such as a column. In this display loft, there is a curved railing with hand rails, a column to support the soffit, a big picture display alcove, and four recessed picture alcoves on north wall. The commands that you will use are EXTRUDE, SUBTRACT, BOX, and REVOLVE. The steps of building the objects in zone six are:

1. Use EXTRUDE to create a curved railing. The dimensions are shown in Figure 13.5 and Figure 13.7a.

2. Use EXTRUDE with Path option to create the hand railings.

3. Use SUBTRACT to create picture alcoves.

4. Use BOX and SUBTRACT to create picture frames.

FIGURE 13.56 Perspective of gallery lobby

FIGURE 13.57 Perspective of gallery lobby

5. Use EXTRUDE to create curved wall.

6. Use SUBTRACT to create the big picture alcove

7. Use BOX and SUBTRACT to create the big picture frame.

8. Use REVOLVE to create the column or copy the column from the first floor.

9. Use EXTRUDE to create soffit.

10. Add spot lighting and point lighting.

EXTRUDE Command—Create a Curved Railing

1. Draw curves as shown in Figure 13.58. Refer to floor plan for dimensions.

FIGURE 13.58 Curves for railing

2. Use PEDIT to join all lines together as a single polyline.

3. Use EXTRUDE to extrude the polyline 3' high to create a curved railing as shown in Figure 13.59.

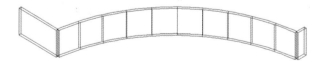

FIGURE 13.59 Isometric view of railing at loft

4. Use BOX to create two panels on both sides of curved railing and apply "Blue Glass" material from the Materials Library.

5. Use CYLINDER to create black posters. The dimensions for the poster are 2" (Diameter) × 3'-0" (Height).

6. Use EXTRUDE with Path option to create handrails on top of the curved railing and two panels. The procedure is as same as for the stair hand railing (Figure 13.60).

FIGURE 13.60 Isometric view of railing at loft

SUBTRACT Boolean Operation—Create Picture Alcoves

1. Refer to floor plan (Figure 13.5) and interior elevation (Figure 13.7a) for dimensions to create a solid object by using EXTRUDE. (Figure 13.61a).

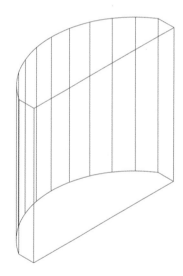

FIGURE 13.61A The second object for Boolean Operation

2. Copy this solid object three times and place them on the north sidewall.

3. Use SUBTRACT (Boolean operation) to subtract these four solid objects from the north wall. Your drawing should look like Figure 13.61b.

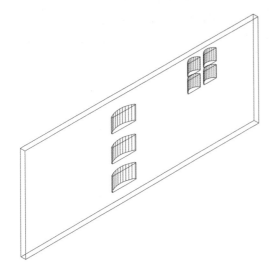

FIGURE 13.61B Isometric view of art alcove wall

BOX Command and SUBTRACT Boolean Operation—Create Picture Frames

1. Use BOX to create a solid box, which is 1'-10" (Width) × 1'-10" (height) × 4" (Thickness).

2. Use BOX to create the second solid box, which is 1'-6" (Width) × 1'-6" (Height) × 2" (Thickness).

3. Use SUBTRACT (Boolean command) to subtract the second solid box from the first solid box. It is the frame of the decorative element. Your drawing will look like Figure 13.62.

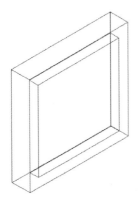

FIGURE 13.62 Picture frame

4. Use BOX to create the third solid box, which is 1'-6" (Width) × 1'-6" (height) × 1" (Thickness).

5. Use BOX to create the fourth solid box,

which is 1'-2" (Width) × 1'-2" (Height) × ½" (Thickness).

6. Use SUBTRACT (Boolean command) to subtract the fourth solid box from the third solid box. It is the frame of the picture. Your drawing will look like Figure 13.63.

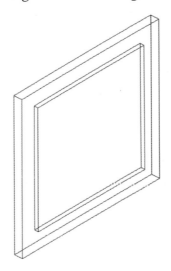

FIGURE 13.63 Picture frame

7. COPY the fourth solid box and insert it into the recessed area and it is the picture, which you will attach modified material to. You need to insert the object shown as Figure 13.63 into the object shown as Figure 13.62. Then your drawing should look like Figure 13.64. COPY this object and insert them in the picture alcoves.

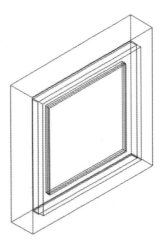

FIGURE 13.64 Picture frame

8. Add spot lighting and point lighting in alcoves.
   - Add one spot lighting in each alcove and one point light in each alcove. You can refer to Chapter 12 for lighting design.
   - Apply modified materials from material library for pictures. Apply black color for the frames.

The following figures (Figure 13.65, Figure 13.66, and Figure 13.67) show different perspectives of picture frames in alcoves on north wall.

EXTRUDE Command—Create Curved Wall

1. Use EXTRUDE to create a solid object for curved wall at the display loft. Refer to floor plan and interior elevations for dimensions.

2. Use EXTRUDE to create the second solid object, which is for picture alcove subtraction.

3. Use SUBTRACT (Boolean command) to subtract the second solid object from the first solid object. It is a big picture alcove. Your drawing will look like Figure 13.68.

FIGURE 13.65 Perspective view of framed picture

FIGURE 13.67 Perspective view of framed picture

FIGURE 13.66 Perspective view of framed picture

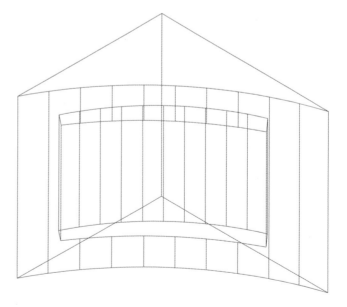

FIGURE 13.68 Picture alcove at loft

BOX and SUBTRACT Command—Create the Big Picture Frame

1. Use BOX to create a solid box, which is 7'-6" (Width) × 5'-4" (height) × 4" (Thickness).

2. Use BOX to create the second solid box, which is 4'-0" (Width) × 4'-0" (Height) × 1½" (Thickness).

3. Use SUBTRACT (Boolean command) to subtract the second solid box from the first solid box. It is the frame of the picture.

4. Use BOX to create the third solid box, which is 4'-0" (Width) × 4'-0" (Height) × 1 ½" (Thickness).

5. Use BOX to create the fourth solid box, which is 4'-0" (Width) × 4'-0" (Height) × 1" (Thickness).

6. Use SUBTRACT (Boolean command) to subtract the fourth solid box from the third solid box. Your drawing should look like Figure 13.69.

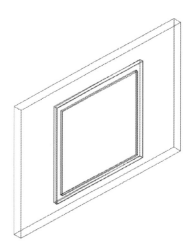

FIGURE 13.69 Picture frame at loft

7. Apply red modified materials from material library for pictures. Apply orange color for the frame.

EXTRUDE Command—Create Soffit

1. Use EXTRUDE to create a solid object for curved soffit at the display loft. Refer to floor plan and interior elevations for dimensions.

2. Your drawing should look like Figure 13.70.

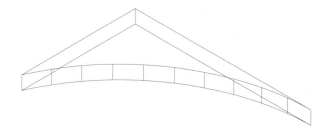

FIGURE 13.70 Isometric view of the soffit at loft

The following figures (Figure 13.71 and Figure 13.72) show different perspective views of the big picture alcoves.

FIGURE 13.71 Perspective of picture frame at loft

FIGURE 13.72 Perspective of picture frame at loft

ZONE SEVEN: CURVED DISPLAY PANEL WITH METAL BLACK CABLES

There is a curved display panel with metal black cables in zone seven. It is a panel with void display windows for picture display. The commands that you will use to create the objects in this zone are EXTRUDE, SUBTRACT, and CYLINDER. The procedures of building the objects in zone six are:

1. Use EXTRUDE to create a curved display panel. The dimensions are shown as Figure 13.5 and Figure 13.7a.

2. Use EXTRUDE to create a solid object for SUBTRACT (Boolean Operation) to create void windows.

3. Use SUBTRACT to create void picture windows.

4. Use BOX to create an object for attaching picture.

5. Modify materials from Material Library to create pictures.

6. Use EXTRUDE or CYLINDER to create vertical cables and apply "black plastic" material to them.

7. Use EXTRUDE or CYLINDER to create short picture hanger for each picture (each picture has four short hangers).

EXTRUDE Command—Create a Curved Display Panel

1. Use EXTRUDE to create a solid object as a curved display panel at the southwest corner. Refer to floor plan and interior elevations for dimensions. A solid object is shown in Figure 13.73.

2. Use EXTRUDE to create the second solid object, which is for void picture window

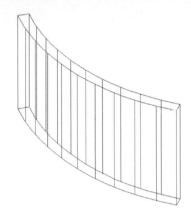

FIGURE 13.73 Isometric view of curved display panel

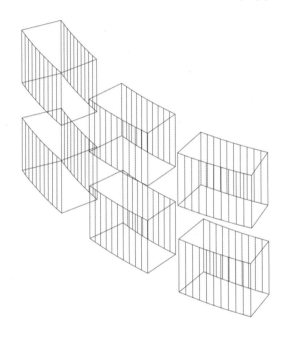

FIGURE 13.74 Objects for Boolean Operations at curved display panel

subtraction (Figure 13.74). You can place these solid objects for subtraction as shown in Figure 13.74.

3. Use SUBTRACT (Boolean Operation) to subtract solid objects as shown in Figure 13.74 from the first solid object (Figure 13.73). It is a curved display panel with void windows. Your drawing will look like Figure 13.75.

4. Use EXTRUDE or CYLINDER to create cables and short picture hangers. Also use BOX command to create pictures (Figure 13.76).

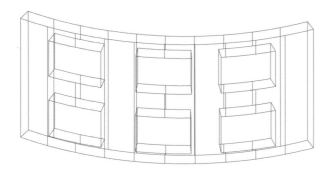

FIGURE 13.75 Curved display panel

FIGURE 13.77 Perspective view of gallery lobby

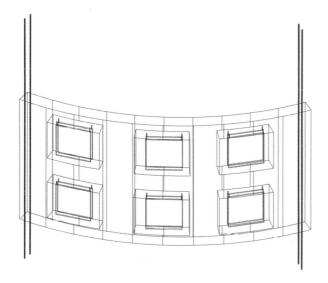

FIGURE 13.78 Perspective view of gallery lobby

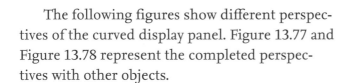

FIGURE 13.76 Curved display panel

The following figures show different perspectives of the curved display panel. Figure 13.77 and Figure 13.78 represent the completed perspectives with other objects.

ZONE EIGHT: OVAL SHAPE DROPPED CEILING

In zone eight, an oval shape dropped ceiling is the only object. You will use EXTRUDE and SUBTRACT to create it. The hanging cables can be created by CYLINDER or EXTRUDE. The procedures of building the objects in zone eight are:

1. Use EXTRUDE to create an oval shaped dropped ceiling. The dimensions are shown as Figure 13.5 and Figure 13.7a.

2. Use EXTRUDE or CYLINDER to create a solid object for subtraction of recessed can light.

3. Use SUBTRACT to create recessed can lights.

4. Use SUBTRACT to make a recessed area in the center of the dropped ceiling.

5. Use EXTRUDE to create ½" diameter cable and rotate 45 degrees. Add four cables for the dropped ceiling.

6. Add point lights in each recessed can light. Your drawing should look like Figure 13.80. You will need to adjust the value of lighting brightness or darkness.

The following figures shows the perspective view of the completed ceiling (Figure 13.80 and Figure 13.83).

ZONE NINE: ROOF WITH SKYLIGHTS

Zone nine consists of a roof with skylights. The roof is a cathedral ceiling with four square shaped skylights. You will need to use EXTRUDE to create the cathedral ceiling and use SUBTRACT to create skylights. The procedures of building the objects in zone eight are:

1. Use EXTRUDE to create a slopped ceiling. The dimensions are shown as Figure 13.5 and Figure 13.7a. You can start with profile as shown in Figure 13.81. Then use EXTRUDE to extrude the profile 40'.

2. Use BOX to create the skylight. The dimension is 8'-0" × 7'-10".

3. Use SUBTRACT to create the void square for the skylight. Now your roof should look like Figure 13.82.

4. Add a box-shaped skylight to the roof and apply blue glass material from the Materials Library.

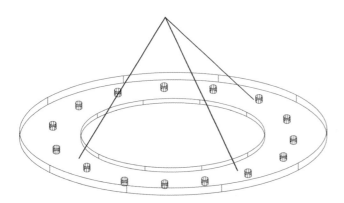

FIGURE 13.79 Isometric view of ceiling lighting fixture

FIGURE 13.81 Profile of the roof

FIGURE 13.80 Perspective view of gallery lobby

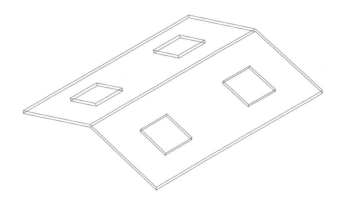

FIGURE 13.82 Isometric view of the roof

Your drawing should look like Figure 13.83. Figure 13.82 shows the perspective view of the cathedral ceiling. Figure 13.84a and Figure 13.84b are perspectives generated by the Hide command.

SUMMARY

The tutorial in this chapter is to create a 3-D model of a Gallery Lobby, which is focused on solid modeling. Basic solid modeling commands, such as BOX, WEDGE, and CYLINDER were

FIGURE 13.83 Perspective view of the gallery lobby

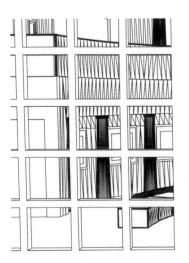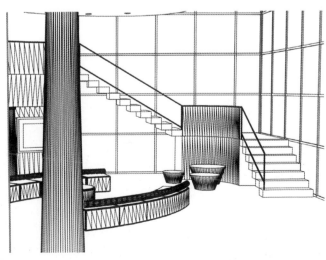

FIGURE 13.84A Perspective view of the gallery lobby with HIDE

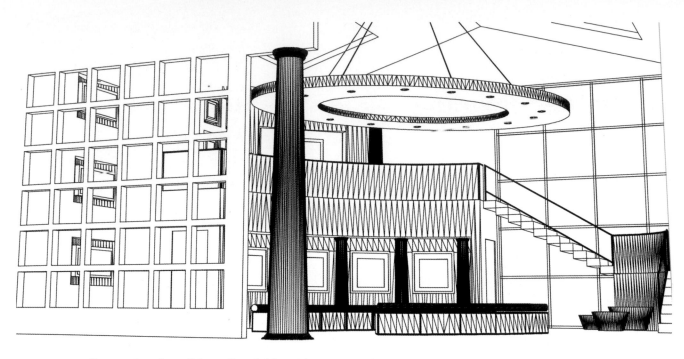

FIGURE 13.84B Perspective view of the gallery lobby with HIDE

introduced by creating primitives. REVOLVE and EXTRUDE are two powerful commands to create complex 3-D forms. They were used extensively in this tutorial. You can create each component individually or you can follow the sequence of this tutorial. You have to extrude or revolve the 2-D object, which is a single entity. You cannot extrude or revolve a 2-D object that has crossing segments or unclosed polylines. Using PEDIT with join option can make 2-D profile become a single entity.

In addition to the normal Extrude command, AutoCAD provides path option that allows you to select the extrusion path based on a specified object.

Boolean operation is another powerful technique in solid modeling. It will be introduced in details in Chapter 14. The Subtract operation was demonstrated in this chapter. It allows you to subtract the second solid object from the first solid object. You can create a more complex object with EXTRUDE and REVOLVE, as well as Boolean Operations.

KEY TERMS

CYLINDER	REVOLVE
EXTRUDE	SUBTRACT

PROJECTS

1. Create several pieces of furniture and apply different materials on the object surface. Use modified materials of your choice.

2. Create several recessed picture frames of your choice, and then arrange them on the wall with point lights and sport lights.

3. Complete project 13-1 if you only finished part of the gallery lobby project. You may use different color and materials for your design. The following are samples of student work.

FIGURE 13.85 Sample of student work (3-D model of the gallery lobby)

FIGURE 13.86 Sample of student work (3-D Model of the gallery lobby)

FIGURE 13.87A Sample of student work (3-D Model of the gallery lobby)

FIGURE 13.88 Sample of student work (3-D Model of the gallery lobby)

FIGURE 13.87B Sample of student work (3-D Model of the gallery lobby)

FIGURE 13.89 Sample of student work (3-D Model of the gallery lobby)

FIGURE 13.90 Sample of student work (3-D Model of the gallery lobby)

Chapter Fourteen

Development of Architectural Components

Objectives

A 3-D model may look complex with all kinds of forms, materials, colors, and different perspective views, but if you look at the model and think that the 3-D model can be built by individual architectural components, you will find it is not hard at all. All you need to do is to create each individual piece and assemble them together. This chapter will emphasize how to develop different architectural components.

After completing this chapter, you will be able to:

- Use REVOLVE and EXTRUDE to create 3-D architectural components, such as columns, triangular pediments, domes, barrel vaults and other forms.

- Use Boolean Operations UNION, SUBTRACT, and INTERSECT to create more complex objects.

- Use the SLICE command to cut a section through the building.

- Use solid modeling method with Boolean Operations to create more complex architectural models, such as reconstruction of ancient ruins.

Some of the following concepts have been introduced in previous chapters. But you will use them again for building architectural components to reinforce these concepts. In addition, several new commands will also be introduced in this chapter.

FORMS

By using 3-D AutoCAD, designers and architects can create different forms to build architectural components and more complex three-dimensional architectural models. In the AutoCAD system, there are a series of predefined 3-D forms, which can be generated by specifying particular parameters such as length, width, height, radius, etc. These 3-D forms are located on the tool bar on the screen, such as Figure 13.15a and it is very easy to access and use. The typical forms are box, cylinder, cone, wedge, and sphere. Using these simple predefined 3-D forms with other operations such as Boolean Operations can also create more complex forms. Therefore, Boolean Operations are very important techniques and will be introduced in more detail in this chapter.

These simple solid geometric forms are the most basic 3-D objects. They are called primitives, as mentioned before. They also can be used in various combinations to produce more complex solid geometric shapes. In addition to REVOLVE and EXTRUDE, you also can use Boolean Operations, UNION, SUBTRACT, and INTERSECT to create all kinds of forms. The following example is the reconstruction of the Baths of Caracalla in Rome, Italy (Figure 14.1a, Figure 14.1b, Figure 14.1c, and Figure 14.1d).

Digital media enables researchers and designers to derive better processes and methods in solving problems of historical architectural restoration and ancient ruins reconstruction. There are many ways to reconstruct ruins and represent the past with digital applications. AutoCAD is one of these approaches. Tracing the past and discovering hidden treasures will provide designers and researchers with inspirations for creating a sustainable future. Figure 14.2a and Figure 14.2b are photos showing existing conditions of the ruined baths of Caracalla. Figure 14.3 is a sketch drawn by Giovanni Iopolo (1899) to represent the natatio in Baths of Caracalla. Many researchers have used CAD to reconstruct ruins to represent the past. Perspective view in Figure 14.1a was generated based on Figure 14.3. It is not difficult to reconstruct an ancient building as long as you know how to use basic commands and operations.

When you look at these images, do not be intimidated by their complexity. Actually, they are very simple because many architectural components are exactly the same; for instance, columns, triangular pediments, and domes. You just need to build one model for each of these objects, and then you can copy it over for the rest of these architectural components. Let us start with the architectural components, such as columns,

FIGURE 14.1A Perspective of Baths of Caracalla

FIGURE 14.1B Perspective of Baths of Caracalla

FIGURE 14.1C Perspective of Baths of Caracalla

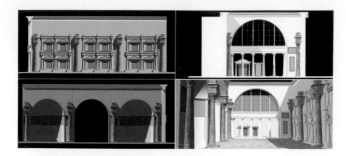

FIGURE 14.1D Exterior elevations and perspective of Baths of Caracalla

FIGURE 14.2A Baths of Caracalla

FIGURE 14.2B Baths of Caracalla

triangular pediment, and domes, etc. Then put these pieces together and apply authentic materials. Finally, you will get the 3-D model. Boolean Operation is one of the most important command operations to create more complex forms. The first step in this chapter is to introduce Constructive Solid Geometry (CSG) method and Boolean Operations.

Constructive Solid Geometry (CSG) and 3-D AutoCAD

Constructive Solid Geometry, or CSG for short, is another way of representing solid objects. It provides a unique opportunity to make form transformations and space interlocking. Constructive Solid Geometry systems allow the defined complex three-dimensional objects using a combination of simpler objects. CSG is used to build solid models by combining primitive objects with Boolean Operations. Solid primitive objects, such as spheres, cubes, and cylinders, can be manipulated with Boolean Operations to produce new objects based on union, subtraction, and intersection of primitive objects. In addition to Boolean Operations, 3-D AutoCAD also has the ability to create complex solid geometry form by sweeping two-dimensional shapes and projections. The commands are REVOLVE and EXTRUDE. Most of the architectural components can be created by these two commands and Boolean operations. Therefore, 3-D AutoCAD with the CSG method will be a powerful tool to generate complex forms and achieve the goals of form and space interchange and manipulation.

Boolean Operations

Boolean Operations are powerful capabilities of solid modeling in AutoCAD. Three-dimensional Boolean Operations enable you to create complex forms from simple primitives quickly and easily. You also can use Boolean Operations on different forms, which are created by using EXTRUDE or REVOLVE. There are three types of Boolean Operations: UNION, SUBTRACT, and INTERSECT. A Boolean operation typically affects two objects at a time. Boolean operations are absolutely fundamental in AutoCAD, allowing the creation of complex forms. Learning how to use Boolean Operations to generate a particular form is essential for a designer. Figure 14.4 illustrates Boolean Operations UNION, SUBTRACT, and INTERSECT for Form A and Form B.

FIGURE 14.3 Drawing of Natatio in Baths of Caracalla

- **UNION**—Union combines form A and form B and deletes line segments in the overlapping area.

- **SUBTRACT**—Subtract the second solid form, B, from the first solid form, A. Or, subtract solid form A from solid form B. Subtraction is useful for making holes in walls for windows and doors.

- **INTERSECT**—Intersection deletes all but the overlapping portions of the two solid forms. Using the intersection between the two objects can create a new object.

After you have two or more solid objects, you can use a number of Boolean Operations to create complex shapes. The Union command can be used to weld two or more objects into one. The opposite of UNION is SUBTRACT. This com-

mand removes the volume of selected solids from a selection of other solids. For example, this command could be used to create a hole in a box—subtracting a cylinder from a box. The Intersect command reduces any number of selected solids to only the shared volume.

Boolean Operations commands can be found in the floating tool bar on top of your screen, shown in Figure 13.30a and Figure 13.30b (page 190). You also can access Boolean Operations through the Dashboard. The typical command procedures are shown as the following:

1. Build the first solid geometric form (such as cube, cylinder or dome, etc.).

2. Build the second solid geometric form.

3. Use Boolean Operation commands to create the form you want.

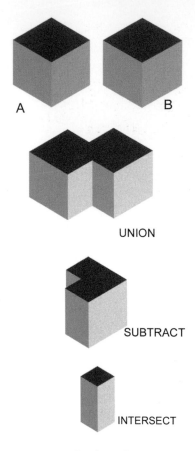

A   B

UNION

SUBTRACT

INTERSECT

FIGURE 14.4 Boolean Operations

Command: _UNION (or click on the button on the floating tool bar in Figure 13.30)

Select object: **(click on form A)** 1 found

Select objects: **(click on form B)** 1 found, 2 total

Select objects: **(press ENTER or right click)**

Command: _SUBTRACT Select solids and regions to subtract from...(or click on the button on the floating tool bar in Figure 13.30)

Select object: **(click on form A)** 1 found

Select object: **(press ENTER or right click)**

Select solids and regions to subtract.....

Select objects: **(click on both form A and form B)** 1 found, 2 total

Select objects: **(press ENTER or right click)**

Command: _INTERSECT (or click on the button on the floating tool bar in Figure 13.30)

Select object: **(click on form A)** 1 found

Select objects: **(click on form B)** 1 found 2 total

Select objects: **(press ENTER or right click)**

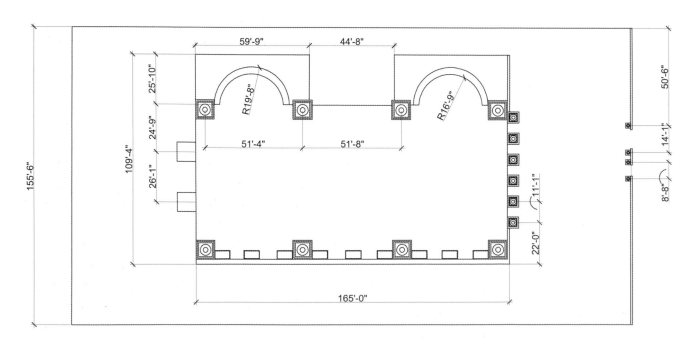

FIGURE 14.5 Floor plan of the Baths of Caracalla

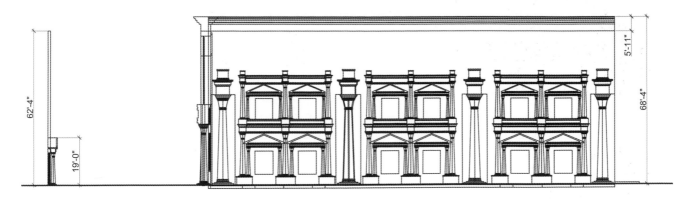

FIGURE 14.6 Exterior elevations of the Baths of Caracalla

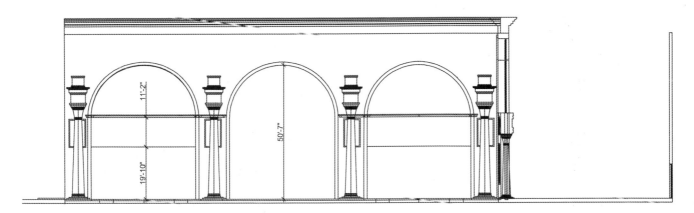

FIGURE 14.7 Exterior elevations of the Baths of Caracalla

BUILDING ARCHITECTURAL COMPONENTS

All of the architectural components, such as columns, domes, arch windows, triangular pediments, and cornices can be built by using the Constructive Solid Geometry method, which are Boolean Operations.

Case Study One

RECONSTRUCTION OF BATHS OF CARACALLA, ROME, ITALY

The following figures present a floor plan and elevations with dimensions of the Baths of Caracalla. These dimensions come from existing documents and drawings. You can refer to these drawings when you create the 3-D model of the

Baths of Caracalla. A typical procedure for building basic architectural elements will be described in detail.

Column

To build a 3-D model for the column, you can use REVOLVE, just like you created the column in Chapter 13. You also can refer to Figure 14.8 for dimension information. It is not intended to show all the detailed dimensions. You can use your judgment and come up with an approximate dimension. For the column base, you can use BOX to create it. The real column in the Baths of Caracalla has a Corinthian capital. It has been simplified here. The cap of the column is created with EXTRUDE and INTERSECT (Boolean Operation). The procedure and the command are described as the following:

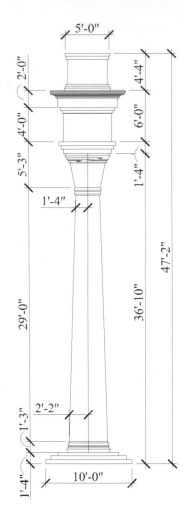

FIGURE 14.8 Column elevation with dimensions

1. Draw elevation as Figure 14.9.

2. Use PEDIT to join all segments together and make it a single Polyline.

3. Use the Extrude command and extrude it with 5'-1". You should get an object shown as Figure 14.10. Copy it over and rotate it 90 degrees.

4. Move one object to the other one and make them perpendicular. Make sure they are at the same elevation.

5. Use INTERSECT to join two objects together. You should get an object as shown in Figure 14.11.

   Command: _INTERSECT (or click on the button on the floating tool bar in Figure 13.30)

Select object: (**click on object A**) 1 found

Select objects: (**click on object B**) 1 found, 2 total

Select objects: (**press ENTER or right click**)

The rest of the portions of the column can be built by using BOX and REVOLVE. After you finish all individual pieces, you also can use UNION to put them together. The final column should look like Figure 14.12.

You can use BOX to create the floor and the pool area. Pay attention to half circles at the pool

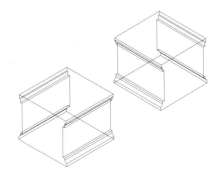

FIGURE 14.9 Column detail dimensions

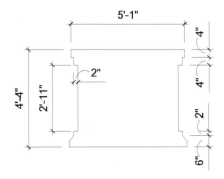

FIGURE 14.10 Column detail isometric view

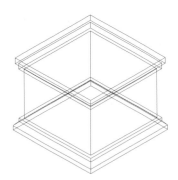

FIGURE 14.11 Column detail isometric view

area. Dimensions can be obtained from the floor plan. Import water image (Figure 14.13a) to the Materials Library. Use a blue-sky photo (Figure 14.13b) as the image background. Copy the column several times and locate them as shown in floor plan. SCALE the column down and locate the column at the back wall. Copy it several times. You can get a perspective view shown as Figure 14.13c.

FIGURE 14.13A Water image

FIGURE 14.13B Sky image for the background. A low-resolution image is recommended

FIGURE 14.12 Isometric view of 3-D column

FIGURE 14.13C Perspective of the Baths of Caracalla

Arch Window

1. Use EXTRUDE to create the stone beam above shorter columns. You should use PEDIT to join all of the single segments together and make it a polyline before you extrude it, and then extrude the polyline to 60'-0". Dimensions can be obtained from Figure 14.14a. The stone beam should look like Figure 14.14b.

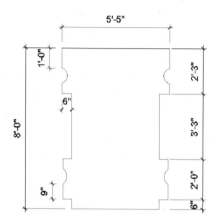

FIGURE 14.14A Side elevation of stone beam

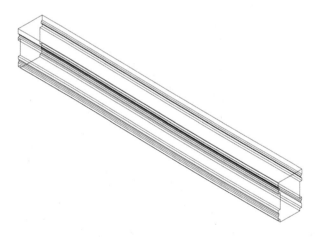

FIGURE 14.14B Isometric view of stone beam

2. Draw elevation as shown in Figure 14.15a. Use PEDIT to join all single lines together to a single entity, and then use EXTRUDE to extrude the polyline 4'. It is the solid portion of the arch window on top of the stone beam you just created.

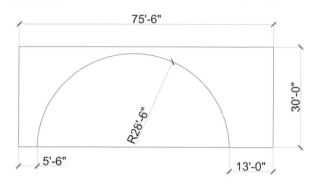

FIGURE 14.15A Elevation of the arch

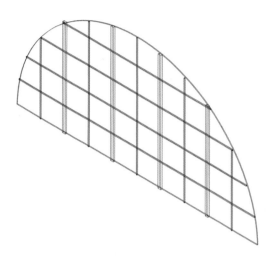

FIGURE 14.15B Isometric view of arch window

3. Use EXTRUDE to create arched window glass (the thickness is 2" and draw its elevation first). Use BOX to create arched window mullions shown as Figure 14.15b.

4. Insert arched window glass in the void arch wall shown as Figure 14.15c.

5. Use BOX to create a piece of solid wall on the right side of the back wall. Also use SUBTRACT to create decorative alcoves on the back wall. The procedure is similar to the one of creating recessed art works in Chapter 13. You can make a perspective view as shown in Figure 14.16.

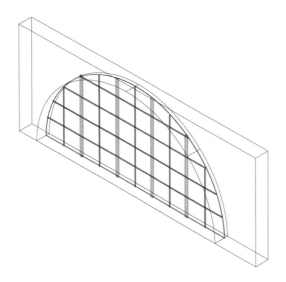

FIGURE 14.15C Isometric view of arch window

Triangular Pediment

1. COPY the column you have created and scale it down according to the dimensions shown in Figure 14.17 for outer column of the triangular pediment.

2. Use EXTRUDE to create a solid triangular object according to the dimensions in Figure 14.17. Use EXTRUDE to create the second solid triangular object, which will be subtracted from the first object. The final triangular object should look like Figure 14.18. Use the same method to create another triangular object for the top triangular pediment. Another method you can use is using the triangular object just created and scaling it down according to the dimensions shown in Figure 14.17. The dimension does not need to be precise. It just needs to be approximate.

FIGURE 14.16 Perspective of the Baths of Caracalla

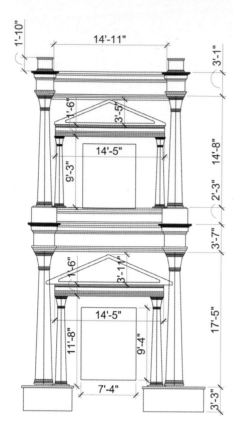

FIGURE 14.17 Triangular pediment elevation

4. Use EXTRUDE to create the decorative lintels on top of the triangular pediments. Figure 14.19a shows the lintel on the top of the lower triangular pediment (extrude it 14'-11"). Figure 14.19b shows the lintel above the top two small columns (extrude it 14'-5"). Figure 14.19c shows two decorative lintels between top and bottom triangular pediments.

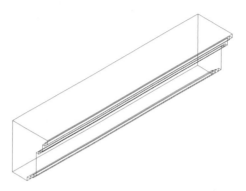

FIGURE 14.19A Isometric view of decorative lintel

FIGURE 14.19B Isometric view of decorative lintel

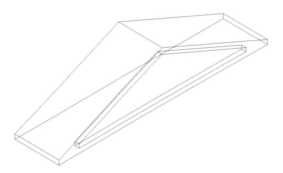

FIGURE 14.18 Isometric view of triangular pediment

3. Again, use SCALE to scale down the columns. You do not have to recreate each column. Refer to Figure 14.17 for dimension information. Here, you should be careful that the top columns are smaller than the bottom columns. The inner column is smaller than the outer column.

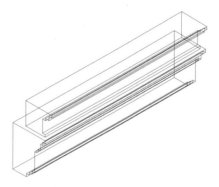

FIGURE 14.19C Isometric view of decorative lintel

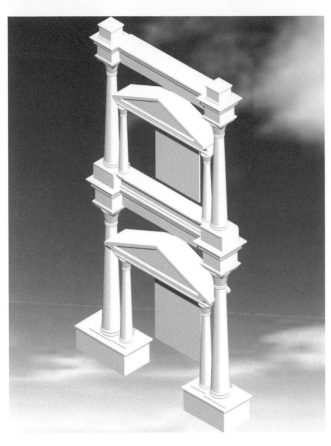

FIGURE 14.20 Isometric view of triangular pediment

FIGURE 14.21 Fresco of the Baths of Caracalla

FIGURE 14.22 Fresco of the Baths of Caracalla

5. Use SUBTRACT to create the alcove for the decorative art. The dimensions are shown in Figure 14.17.

6. Use BOX to create a thin object for attaching materials. The digital images are imported into the AutoCAD Materials Library. This image is the fresco on the wall of the Baths of Caracalla. (Figures 14.21 and 14.22).

7. The key for creating the east sidewall is to make sure that the elevation is correct. You can create one for the top triangular pediment and one for the bottom (Figure 14.20). Copy it for the rest and apply materials to the decorative arts. The colors of the column are very light beige and light yellow. You can assign colors to each layer.

8. The following images (Figure 14.23, Figure 14.24, and Figure 14.25) are the perspective views at the back wall and east wall.

FIGURE 14.23 Perspective of the Baths of Caracalla

FIGURE 14.24 Perspective of the Baths of Caracalla

FIGURE 14.25 Perspective of the Baths of Caracalla

Dome Alcove

1. Use EXTRUDE to create a solid object, as shown in Figure 14.26. Refer to the floor plan for dimensions. Extrude 50'-11" high. You will use SUBTRACT to create recessed decorative alcove. It is only recessed 3" to 4" when you complete step 3.

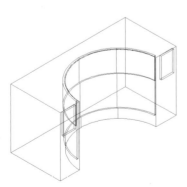

FIGURE 14.26 Decorative alcove

2. Use SUBTRACT to create recessed decorative art alcoves on both sides.

3. Use EXTRUDE to create a solid object as shown in Figure 14.27.

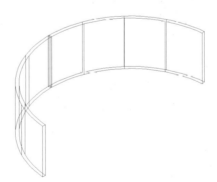

FIGURE 14.27 Thin piece on decorative alcove

4. Use SUBTRACT to subtract the second object (Figure 14.27) from the first object (Figure 14.26).

5. Use BOX and the Solid Sphere command to create two objects as shown in Figure 14.28.

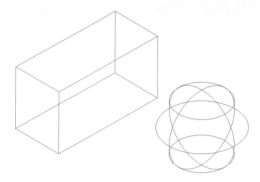

FIGURE 14.28 Objects for Boolean Operations

6. Use SUBTRACT to subtract the solid sphere from the solid box. You should get a half dome as shown in Figure 14.29.

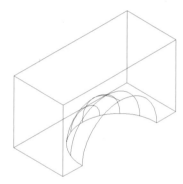

FIGURE 14.29 Isometric view of half dome

7. Since you are going to apply materials on the inner side of the half dome, you have to create a thin layer, which is attached to the inner side the half dome (Figure 14.30).

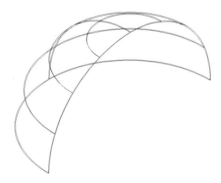

FIGURE 14.30 Isometric view of thin piece of half dome

8. To create an object shown as Figure 14.30, you need to create a sphere first and use the Slice command to cut the sphere to a quarter of a sphere. The radius of the sphere is 19'-6". The following is the procedure to use SLICE. You can access SLICE from the pull-down menu as shown in Figure 14.31.

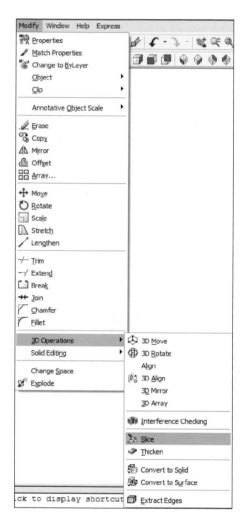

FIGURE 14.31 Modify-3-D operation—Slice pull-down menu

Command: _ slice

Select objects to slice: **(click on the sphere)**

Select objects to slice: **ENTER**

Specify start point of slicing plane or [Planar Object/Surface/Zaxis/View/XY/YZ/ZX/3points] 3points > : **ZX then ENTER**

Specify a point on the ZX-plane 0,0,0> : **(snap to the center of the sphere)**

Specify a point on desired side or [Keep Both Sides}: **(click on top of the sphere)**

Now you should get half of the sphere as shown in Figure 14.32.

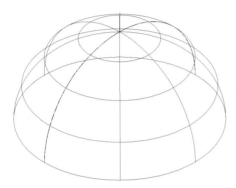

FIGURE 14.32 Isometric view of half sphere

9. Use SLICE again to cut the half sphere to quarter sphere. You should get an object like Figure 14.33.

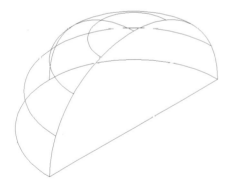

FIGURE 14.33 Quarter sphere

10. Copy the object in Figure 14.33 and use SCALE to scale it down 2" smaller. This smaller half dome is the second object for you to subtract.

11. Use SUBTRACT to subtract the second object from the first object. Your drawing should look like Figure 14.30.

12. Place the object shown in Figure 14.30 inside the half dome (Figure 14.29). It is ready for you to apply materials to it.

13. The key point here to use SLICE is to identify the right XY, ZX, YZ, which is parallel with the slicing plane.

14. Place the object shown in Figure 14.29 on top of the object shown in Figure 14.26. Your drawing should look like Figure 14.34.

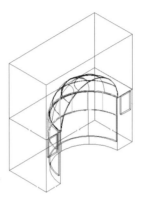

FIGURE 14.34 Isometric view of half dome

15. Use EXTRUDE to create the arch doorway in the center of the west sidewall. You have to draw a 2-D elevation first, and then use PEDIT to join all lines together and make it a polyline, and then extrude it 25'- 10". The object is shown in Figure 14.35.

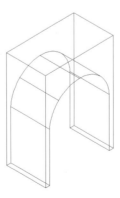

FIGURE 14.35 Isometric view of arch

16. Use MIRROR to mirror the object in Figure 14.34 to the other side of the object in Figure 14.35. The west sidewall is symmetrical.

17. Use EXTRUDE with the Path option to create the trim around the arch.

18. The following images (Figure 14.36 and Figure 14.37) are different perspective views for the west sidewall.

19. You can apply authentic materials to the surface of the dome. Figure 14.38 is a fragment of the fresco on the wall and Figure 14.39 is a fragment of the floor mosaic. These materials are digital files imported in the Materials Library.

20. You also can copy the triangular pediment from the east sidewall and scale it to the appropriate size and build a wall behind the arch window wall and colonnade shown in Figure 14.41. Figure 14.40 and Figure 14.41 are perspectives with authentic materials

Cornice

1. Draw a cornice side view as shown in Figure 14.42. Use PEDIT to join all segments to a single polyline.

2. Use EXTRUDE to create a cornice as shown in Figure 14.43.

FIGURE 14.36 Perspective of the Baths of Caracalla

FIGURE 14.37 Perspective of the Baths of Caracalla

FIGURE 14.38 Fresco of the Baths of Caracalla

FIGURE 14.39 Floor Mosaic of the Baths of Caracalla

Now you have explored how to build basic architectural components through this case study. You also have explored how to use Boolean Operations on solid objects. In addition to this, REVOLVE and EXTRUDE are very powerful commands in solid modeling. The following images are different perspective views for the Baths of Caracalla generated by solid modeling. Figure 14.44b is a perspective without RENDER. Figure 14.46 is a perspective without RENDER, but with HIDE. You can use different techniques for your final drawing presentations.

FIGURE 14.40 Perspective of the Baths of Caracalla

FIGURE 14.41 Perspective of the Baths of Caracalla

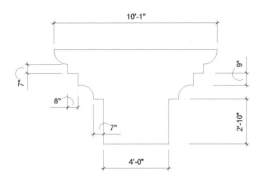

FIGURE 14.42 Cornice side view with dimensions

FIGURE 14.43 Isometric view of Cornice

FIGURE 14.44A Perspective of the Baths of Caracalla

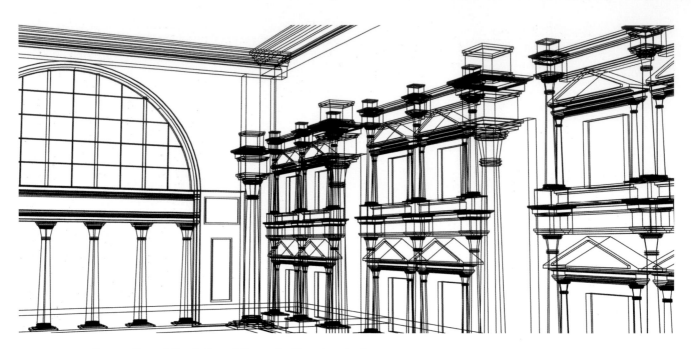

FIGURE 14.44B Perspective of the Baths of Caracalla (line drawing)

FIGURE 14.45 Perspective of the Baths of Caracalla

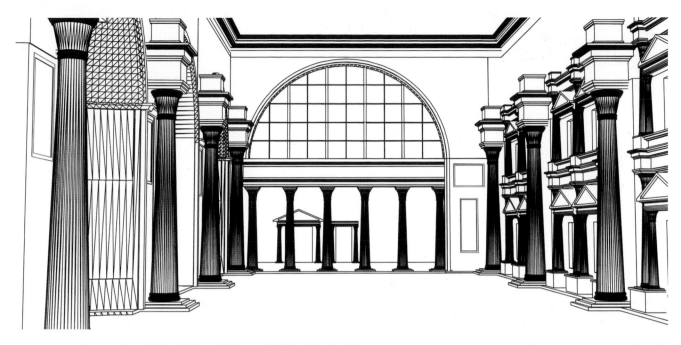

FIGURE 14.46 Perspective of the Baths of Caracalla (line drawing)

Case Study Two

FLORENCE CATHEDRAL

The second case study is to build a 3-D model of Florence Cathedral. The construction method used for the cathedral was geometric construction. It makes the model building process easier and quicker because there are many squares and rectangles. Many architectural components are repetitive, such as columns and barrel vaults. Another characteristic of the building is its symmetry. You do not have to create every single object. You just need to mirror the objects to be productive. The following images are floor plans and building sections of the Cathedral with graphic scales. You can refer to the floor plan and building section when you create the model. The process is to create each individual architectural piece first and then put them together.

1. **Column**—Use the Revolve command. First, draw half of the column elevation in 2-D based on the dimensions. Use PEDIT to join all single segments together to get a single entity before using REVOLVE.

2. **Triangular Pediment**—Use the Extrude command. Draw a triangle in 2-D, and then use PEDIT to join all segments together to make it a single entity, and then extrude the polyline. Use SUBTRACT to create a recessed area on the triangular pediment.

3. **Dome**—Use the Revolve command. The process is similar to creating the column. The differences are that you need to draw half of the section of the dome to present the thickness of the dome. The revolve axis can be offset from the edge of the section in order to create a void dome with open oculus, the unglazed opening on top of the dome.

4. **Barrel vault**—Use the Extrude command. Draw the section of the barrel vault in 2-D elevation, and then use PEDIT to join all segments together to make it a single entity. Then EXTRUDE the single entity. For an

intersected barrel vault, copy the barrel vault just created and rotate it 90 degrees and place it on top of the first one. Use UNION Boolean operation to create an intersected barrel vault.

5. These are the typical architectural components in classical architecture. If some special forms need to be created, CSG method, in other words, Boolean operations are very powerful to achieve these goals.

The following images (Figure 14.47, Figure 14.48) show the floor plan and cross-section of the cathedral with graphic scales. You can refer to these two drawings for dimensions. Figure 14.49a shows exterior elevations and roof plan of the cathedral with the Render command.

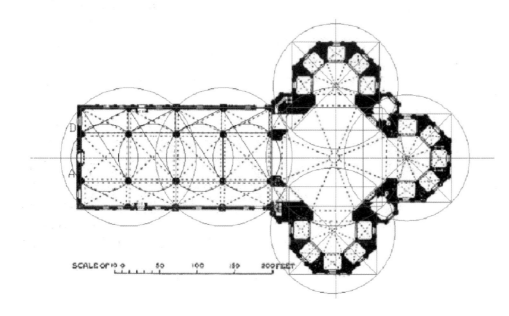

FIGURE 14.47 Floor Plan of Florence Cathedral

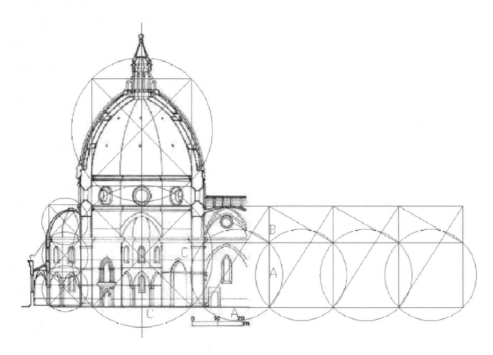

FIGURE 14.48 Section of Florence Cathedral

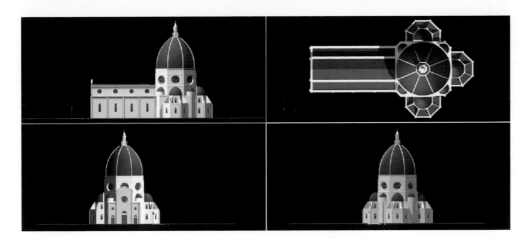

FIGURE 14.49A Exterior Elevations of Florence Cathedral

You also can use geometric analysis on floor plans and elevations. This step serves as verification for uncertain data such as dimensions and missing portions of the structure. It also can be used as the rationale for completion of floor plans and elevations when some of the structure was missing. When a floor plan or elevation was retrieved from the Internet or obtained from a book, not all dimensions are typically shown. It is necessary to use a geometric analysis to calculate unknown dimensions. As long as the drawings are presented in a graphic scale, it is not difficult to measure and get all of the dimensions. The following is an example of the geometric analysis for the Florence Cathedral. Figure 14.47 is the floor plan and Figure 14.48 is the cross section of the cathedral.

Literature review shows that squares and rectangles were used extensively in Roman geometric construction. Circles on the floor plan and section indicate that the shapes inside circles are squares. It is obvious that many spaces were constructed that follow the rule of height, equal to the side length. If one side of the dimension is known, then the height will be found out easily.

The other characteristic of Roman architecture is using rectangles. By using golden ratio or golden section, it is not hard to calculate the height of a rectangular in a section of the

Cathedral (Figure 14.48). The golden ratio can be described as if one divides a line into two unequal segments so that the ratio of the first short segment to the long segment equals the ratio of the long segment to the total line length (the short segment plus the long segment). To apply golden section to this case in Figure 14.48, A is a longer segment and B is a shorter segment. The formula used for calculation the value for B is:

$$B : A = A : (A+B)$$

A value can be found from the floor plan with graphic scales. It is also the height for that square. B is the height of the rectangular, which is unknown. The C value can be found from the floor plan and C is equal to A + B. With a simple mathematic calculation, it is easy to find out the value for B, which is about 3'-10". The other way that can be used is to use the number 0.618 along with the formula B: A = 0.618 to calculate the B value. The same process can be done on the cathedral floor plan to calculate the value for D. The formula is D: A = A : (A + D).

The third characteristic in Roman architecture geometric construction is symmetry. Because of this, it makes the calculation and modeling process easier and quicker. In Figure 14.48 of the section of the cathedral, portions on the right side are missing. But with the geometric analysis and Golden section theory, it is not hard to figure out all the dimensions and reveal the missing structure portions.

The following images are exterior perspectives and interior views of the Cathedral (Figure 14.49b through Figure 14.49e). It is obvious that the dome and barrel vaults are two major architectural components of this building. The procedure of the model building process will be demonstrated in the following instructions. The emphasis has been put upon the dome and barrel vaults because other architectural components have been introduced in previous chapters. The methods of creating the model for column and cornice are the same as the model of the Baths of Caracalla.

FIGURE 14.49B Isometric View of Florence Cathedral

FIGURE 14.49C Isometric View of Florence Cathedral

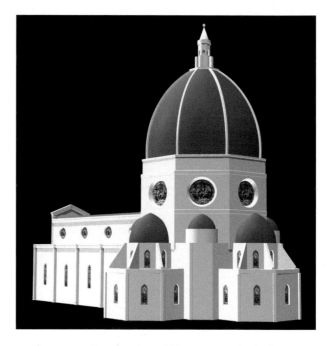

FIGURE 14.49D Perspective of Florence Cathedral

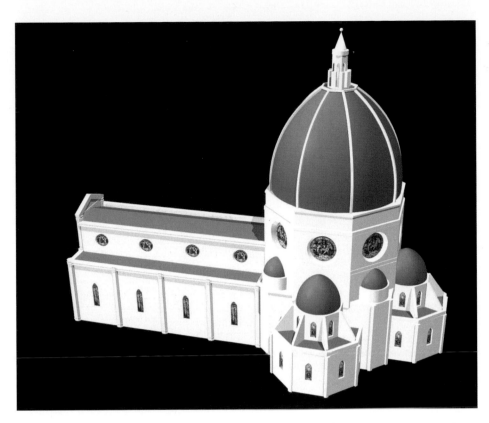

FIGURE 14.49E Perspective of Florence Cathedral

FIGURE 14.49F Line Drawing Perspective of Florence Cathedral (hidden)

FIGURE 14.49G Line Drawing Perspective of Florence Cathedral (hidden)

FIGURE 14.49H Line Drawing Interior Perspective of Florence Cathedral (hidden)

FIGURE 14.49I Line Drawing Interior Perspective of Florence Cathedral (hidden)

FIGURE 14.50 Perspective of Florence Cathedral

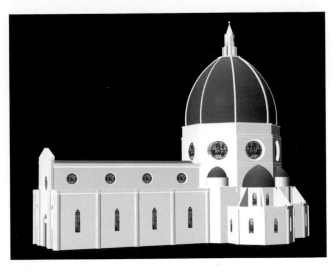

FIGURE 14.51 Perspective of Florence Cathedral

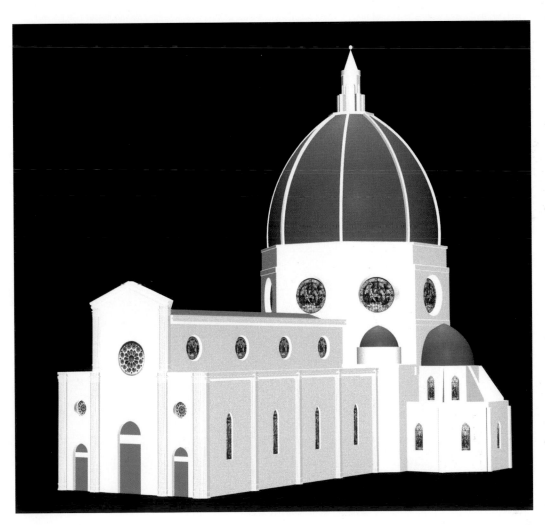

FIGURE 14.52 Perspective of Florence Cathedral

FIGURE 14.53 Interior Perspective of Florence Cathedral

FIGURE 14.54 Interior Perspective of Florence Cathedral

FIGURE 14.55A Interior Perspective of Florence Cathedral

FIGURE 14.55B Interior Perspective of Florence Cathedral

FIGURE 14.55C Interior Perspective of Florence Cathedral

FIGURE 14.56A Perspective of Florence Cathedral

FIGURE 14.56B Exterior Perspective of Florence Cathedral

Dome

Dome is a very popular architectural form and can be found in many famous architectural structures. Dome is used widely in classical architecture and can be generated by revolving curves of any shape about a vertical axis. Revolving an arc can generate a simple dome. However, domes can be generated with other curved profiles, such as an ellipse or random curves. If there is an oculus on top of the dome, the revolving axis can be offset from the elevation.

FIGURE 14.57 Section of the dome

1. Draw a section of the dome as shown in Figure 14.57. Offset an axis from the section. The offset width is the radius of the oculus.

2. Use REVOLE to complete the revolving process. The drawing should look like Figure 14.58.

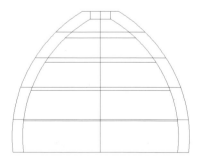

FIGURE 14.58 Dome after using the Revolve command

3. Use EXTRUDE with Path option to create white ribs on the dome (refer to Chapter 13 for more detailed information), and then use Boolean Operations (UNION, SUBTRACT) to create the decorative portion on top of the dome. The final isometric view is shown in Figure 14.59.

FIGURE 14.59 Isometric view of dome

The typical procedure to create a more complex profile and dome by using REVOLVE is described in the following steps:

Command: PLINE (draw the profile you want according to the dimensions)

Specify start point: **pick a point on screen**

Specify next point or [Arc/Halfwidth/Length/Undo/Width]: **(pick the point on screen)**

Current line-width is 0'-0"

Specify next point or [Arc/Halfwidth/Length/Undo/Width]: **(pick the point on the screen)**

Specify next point or [Arc/Close/Halfwidth/Length/Undo/Width]: **ENTER**

Command: PEDIT

Select polyline [multiple]: **M**

Select objects: **(cross window)**

Select objects: **specify opposite corner**

Select objects: **ENTER**

Enter an option[Close/Open/Joint/Width/Fit/Spline/Decurve/Ltype/Gen/Undo]: J

Enter fuzz distance or [jointype] <0'-0"> : **ENTER**

Command: REVOLVE

Current wire frame density: ISOLINES =4

Select objects to revolve: **(pick on Polyline)**

Select objects to revolve: **ENTER**

Specify axis start point or define axis by [object/X/Y] Object> : **(pick the point on vertical axis)**

Specify axis endpoint: **(pick the point on vertical axis)**

Specify angle of revolution 360> : **ENTER**

Barrel Vaults

Barrel vaults are the typical shapes for a vault ceiling. It can be found in a lot of classical architecture, especially Romanesque and Gothic. The curve of the cross-section of a barrel is usually a semicircle or a pointier semicircle. The following steps show the procedure for building barrel vaults.

1. Draw vault cross-section (in elevation) with PLINE (Figure 14.60).

FIGURE 14.60 Cross-section of barrel vaults

2. Use the Extrude command to extrude the vault cross-section, then you will have a barrel vault as shown in Figure 14.61.

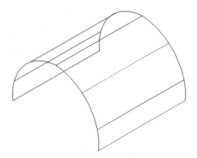

FIGURE 14.61 Isometric view of barrel vaults

Barrel Vaults Intersection

Intersected barrel vaults as shown in Figure 14.62a are generated by Boolean Operations. Figure 14.62b is a rendered intersected barrel vault.

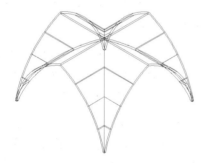

FIGURE 14.62A Barrel vaults intersection

FIGURE 14.62B 3-D model of intersected barrel vaults

The creation process is shown as the following:

1. Create a box and use that box as object two. Use SUBTRACT to subtract the box from object one, which is the barrel vault shown as in Figure 14.61.

2. Use SUBTRACT twice and you will get a quarter portion of the vault as shown in Figure 14.63, and then use UNION to generate the vault ceiling as shown in Figure 14.62a. When using SUBTRACT (Boolean Operation), start from plan view and draw cross lines from each opposite corner. Use SUBTRACT first to get half of the barrel vault, and then use SUBTRACT again to get the quarter portion of the barrel vault. The procedure can be illustrated as in Figure 14.64.

FIGURE 14.63 Isometric view of intersected barrel vaults

FIGURE 14.64 Illustration of procedure of intersected barrel vaults

Cutting Through the Building by SLICE Command

The Slice command is used to divide a solid object on either side of a plane. A section can be cut through a complex 3-D model by using SLICE. You can retain one or both halves of the sliced solids. The sliced solids retain the layer and color properties of the original solids. The default method of slicing a solid is to specify three points that define the cutting plane and then select which side to retain.

You either can cut through a portion of the building to reveal some interior structure as shown in Figure 14.65, or you can cut through the entire building. The difference between these two procedures is that you have to use UNION to make the entire building a single entity before you cut through the entire building. For cutting through a small portion of the building, you do not have to do so. Figure 14.66 shows a cross-section of the Florence cathedral created by using the Slice command. After using UNION, the color associated with each layer has been changed. There are five methods you can use to define the slicing or cutting plane:

- **3 points**—Defines the slicing plane using three points. If the desired plane is not parallel with the current XY, YZ, or ZX plane, the 3-points method is usually the best choice (CAD help menu).

- **Object**—Aligns the cutting plane with a circle, ellipse, circular or elliptical arc, 2-D spline, or 2-D polyline. The object needs not be separated from the volume of the solid (CAD help menu).

- **View**—Aligns the cutting plane with the current viewport's viewing plane. Specifying a point defines the location of the cutting plane along the Z-axis of the viewing plane.

- **Z-axis**—Defines the cutting plane by specifying a point on the plane and another point on the Z-axis (normal) of the plane.

- **XY, YZ, and ZX**—Aligns the cutting plane with the XY, YZ, or ZX plane of the current UCS. Specifying a point defines the location of the cutting plane (CAD help menu).

The typical procedure can be described as the following:

1. Set the 3-D object in southwest isometric view. The section will be cut through south-north axis.

2. Choose SLICE from solid toolbar.

3. When prompted, select the point on the 3-D model and press ENTER.

4. Type YZ and press ENTER to indicate that you want to define the slicing plane parallel with the current YZ plane.

5. When prompted to specify a point on the YZ plane, snap to either of the end point of the line defining the axis of revolution.

6. When prompted to specify a point on the desired side of the plane, pick a point at the side you want to keep. You also can choose to keep both sides, and then delete the one you do not want to keep. Then AutoCAD completes the Slice command.

7. One important thing to remember is to use UNION before you use SLICE when the 3-D model is created by many solid objects. For example, many solid objects, such as dome, column, and barrel vaults were created for the Florence Cathedral 3-D model. It is important to UNION all the objects into a single entity, that way, it will be able to be sliced.

Command: _SLICE

Select object to slice: **pick a point on 3-D model and ENTER**

Select object to slice: **ENTER**

Specify start point on slicing plane or [planar Object/ Surface/Zaxis/View/XY/YZ/ZX/3Points]3 points> : **YZ**

Specify a point on the YZ-plane 0.0.0> : **Pick a point on YZ plane**

Specify a point on desired side of the plane or [Keep Both Sides]: **Click on the side you want to keep the object**

The SECTION Command

The Section command works almost exactly the same way as the Slice command except with one major difference. The Section command generates a region that is representative of a cross-section of the selected plane instead of slicing the object like SLICE normally does. You can create a cross-section through a 3-D solid. The result can be a two-dimensional object representing the shape of the section, or it can be a 3-D solid divided in half (CAD help menu).

The default method is specifying three points to define the plane. Other methods define the cross-sectional plane by another object, the current view, the Z axis, or the XY, YZ or ZX plane. The cross-sectional plane is placed on the current layer (CAD help menu). Enter SECTION at the command line.

The following exercise shows how to create a section of a solid object.

1. Load the file Florence-Cathedral. dwg.

2. Use UNION to make the model a single entity.

3. Enter SECTION at the command line.

Command: **_section**

Select Objects: **Click on the solid model, 1 found**

Select objects: **ENTER**

Specify first point on Section plane by [Object /Zaxis/View/XY/YZ/ZX/3 points] 3 points> : **ZX and ENTER (ZX is parallel to the section plane)**

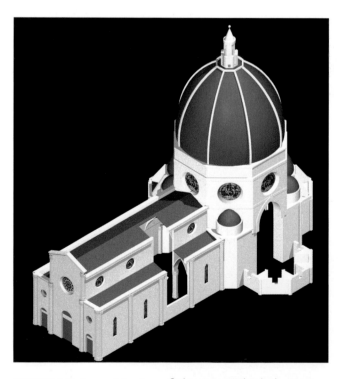

FIGURE 14.65 Isometric view of Florence Cathedral using the Slice command

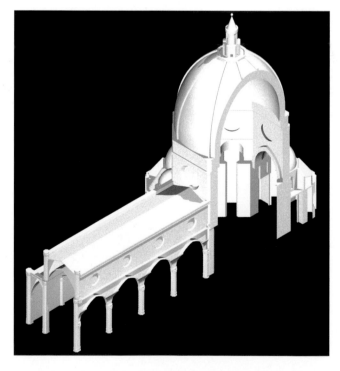

FIGURE 14.66 Isometric view of Florence Cathedral with SLICE

Specify a point on the ZX-plane 0,0,0> : **Pick mid point of the front wall**

As this exercise shows, the way SLICE and SECTION are used is very similar. The difference between the two is one generates a 2-D region and the other one cuts through the model and makes the model into pieces. The Section command generates a line drawing, which can be exploded and further edited. You also can use it to develop new solids by extruding it (Figure 14.67a and Figure 14.67b).

The INTERFERENCE CHECKING Command

The last important command that is addressed here is **INTERFERENCE CHECKING**. You can access this command through the pull-down menu as shown in Figure 14.68.

INTERFERENCE CHECKING performs the same operation as INTERSECT. But INTERFERENCE CHECKING keeps the original two objects. INTERFERENCE CHECKING is used to determine whether two solids overlap, or interfere,

with each other. If they do, you can generate a new solid that is the volume of the area where the two solids interfere. INTERFERENCE CHECKING allows you to calculate how much volume is interfering between the two solids. The red area in Figure 14.69 shows the interfering volume between the two solids.

SUMMARY

The methods and procedures of building architectural components have been demonstrated with two case studies in this chapter. Typical architectural components, such as column, triangular pediment, cornice, dome, and vault ceiling have been demonstrated by examples and detailed procedures. Constructive Solid Geometry (CSG) is a method that provides opportunity to make form transformations with Boolean operations. Boolean operations include UNION, SUBTRACT, and INTERSECT. It is a procedure of generating more complex forms from simple objects, such as box, sphere, and wedge, etc. These

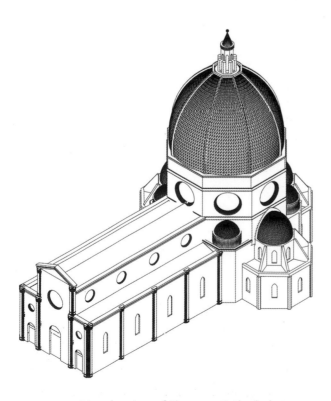

FIGURE 14.67A Line drawing of Florence Cathedral

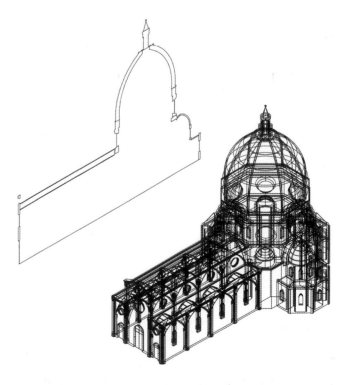

FIGURE 14.67B Line drawing of Florence Cathedral

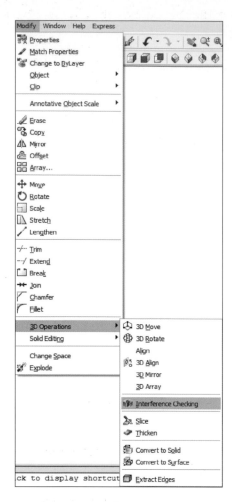

FIGURE 14.68 Modify pull-down menu (INTERFERENCE CHECKING)

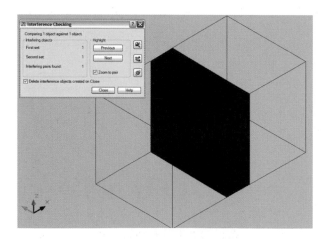

FIGURE 14.69 Isometric view of INTERFERENCE CHECKING

simple objects are called primitives, which can be easily created with AutoCAD commands. In addition to Boolean operations, REVOLVE and EXTRUDE are two useful commands to generate more complex forms with different profiles. Virtual reconstruction of archeological sites is a topic that many scholars and researchers have explored. Three dimensional AutoCAD solid modeling is a powerful tool that can be used to reconstruct ancient ruins and accomplish historical building restorations. The procedures have been described, which is to build the architectural component individually.

SLICE is another powerful command, which can be used to cut through the building to reveal interior structure components.

KEY TERMS

INTERFERENCE CHECKING	SLICE
	SPHERE
INTERSECT	UNION
SECTION	WEDGE

PROJECTS

1. Use Internet search or literature review to collect data, such as dimensioned floor plan, elevation or section of a famous architecture and create a 3-D model for that.

2. Practice creating architectural models and sunlight to generate rendering.

3. Design a small project, such as a gate with the masonry for a safari park or botany park or a special monumental sculpture at a famous square. Use 3-D AutoCAD to create digital models and apply materials and lightings.

Chapter Fifteen

Apply and Modify Materials

Objectives

AutoCAD Materials Library provides many predefined materials. Rather than create a material from scratch, you can use or modify a predefined material imported from the library supplied with the program. You also can create a new material from a digital image. The digital image could be a scanned graphic or a digital photo. You can assign either predefined materials or new materials to your 3-D model. Materials make your model look more realistic. You can manipulate digital images and create all kinds of surface materials for your digital model. After finishing this chapter, you will be able to:

- Modify materials in the Materials Library and apply it to a 3-D model.

- Import digital images to the library and apply modified materials to a 3-D model.

- Create a digital image in Photoshop or other software and import digital images to the Materials Library and apply this material to a 3-D model.

The following figures show the perspective views of a gallery lobby, which has been created in Chapter 13. Figure 15.1a and Figure 15.1b demonstrate the use of a red fabric material on a curved sofa. The red color repeats the red artwork on the north sidewall. Figure 15.1c and Figure 15.1d present different surface materials for the curved sofa. The material is a blue abstract fabric pattern, which picks up the color in the blue glass loft railing panel and stair railing panel. Figure 15.2 shows a vase with the surface material, which is created from scratch. It was drawn by Photo-shop and imported into the Materials Library. The procedure will be introduced in this chapter.

APPLYING MATERIALS TO THE INTERIOR SPACE

After you accomplish a 3-D model, you can begin assigning materials to the model's surfaces. The very basic Materials Library concept and applying procedure was introduced in Chapter 9. In this chapter, the materials application will be intro-

FIGURE 15.1A Perspective of gallery lobby with created new material

FIGURE 15.1B Perspective of gallery lobby with created new material

FIGURE 15.1C Perspective of gallery lobby with created material

FIGURE 15.1D Perspective of gallery lobby with created material

FIGURE 15.2 Perspective of vases

duced in depth. Materials are handled through the Materials and Materials Tool Palettes dialog boxes (Figure 9.20b and Figure 9.21b, page 105). The Materials dialog box is used to assign, create, or modify materials and their associated set of attributes. Materials Tool Palettes is used to store a group of predefined materials or materials you created.

Use the Materials Tool Palettes to choose materials that you want to import into your model for assignment as surfaces or for use as the basis for creating a modified or new material. You can access the Materials Library (Material Tool Palettes) by clicking on the materials button from the Dashboard (Figure 9.20a). Then you will be prompted with Material Tool Palettes, which contains many predefined materials, such as flooring, windows and doors, masonry, and so on. (Figure 9.20b).

As mentioned earlier, you will have to import materials from the Materials Library (Material Tool Palettes) to your drawing first before you can apply these materials to your model. Material

Editor Palette (Figure 9.22 and Figure 9.23) allows you to bring materials from the Materials Library and change the attributes of the materials. To bring the Material Editor Palette to the screen, you need to click on the materials button on the Dashboard as shown in Figure 9.21a. The Material Editor Palette contains the following sections and buttons.

- Available Materials in Drawing (Figure 15.3a): This section displays the available materials in the current drawing. The material swatches geometry can be a cube, a sphere or a cylinder. In this section, there are several command buttons that you can use. These buttons are:
  - Create New Material
  - Purge from Drawing
  - Indicate Material in Use
  - Apply Material to Object
  - Remove Material from Selected Object

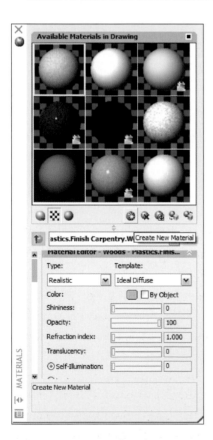

FIGURE 15.3A Materials palette

- **Material's Name:** Right underneath the Available Materials in Drawing section is the Material's name, which is highlighted in Available Materials in Drawing section. Figure 15.4b displays Wood-Plastics. Finish Carpentry. Wood. Maple.

- **Materials Editor (Figure 15.3b):** This section allows you to change the attributes of the materials, such as color, shininess, and translucency.

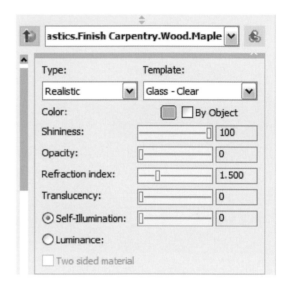

FIGURE 15.3B Material palette

- **Maps (Figure 15.3c):** In the center of Material Editor is the material Map section. You may change the value of Diffuse map, Opacity map, and Bump map in order to create the special effect you desire.
  - **Diffuse Map:** Provides a pattern of colors for a material.
  - **Opacity Map:** Creates the illusion of opacity and transparency.
  - **Bump Map:** Simulates a bumpy or irregular surface.

- **Material Scaling & Tiling (Figure 15.3d):**
  - **Scale Units:** Specifies the units to use in scaling:
    - § None: Specifies a fixed scale

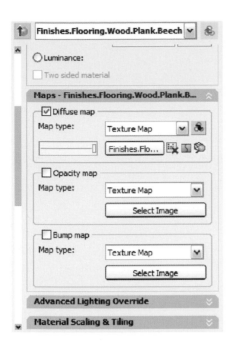

FIGURE 15.3C Materials editor palette (maps)

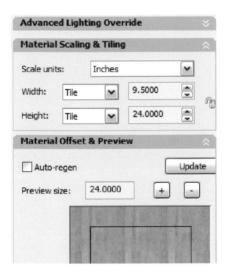

FIGURE 15.3D Materials editor palette (scaling & tiling)

§ Fit to Gizmo: Fits the image to the face of the object
- **Width and Height:** there are three options:
  § **None:** Controls the map to not be tiled within the material; just one tile will appear across the object it is applied to.
  § **Tile:** Controls the map to be tiled within the material. This affects real-world scale.

§ **Mirror:** Controls the map to be tiled, but each tile will be a mirror of the adjacent one.

- **Material Offset & Preview (Figure 15.3e):** It specifies the offset and preview properties of maps on materials.

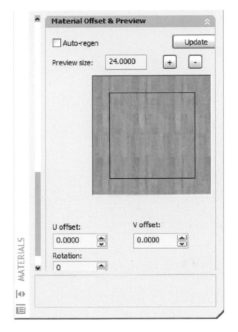

FIGURE 15.3E Materials editor palette (material offset & preview)

- **Preview:** Displays a preview of the map on the face or object that updates as you change settings. Click and drag inside the square to adjust the U and V offsets (CAD help menu).
- **U Offset:** Moves the starting point of the map along the U axis. You can set this value interactively by moving the square inside the preview (CAD help menu).
- **V Offset:** Moves the starting point of the map along the V axis. You can set this value interactively by moving the square inside the preview (CAD help menu).
- **Rotation:** Rotates the map around the W axis of the UVW Coordinate system. Rotation is not available for spherical and cylindrical mapping (CAD help menu).

There are lots of predefined materials in the AutoCAD Materials Library, which are ready for use, such as glass, marble, wood, and so on. However, you also can modify these materials by changing their attributes. In addition to that, you can import a material's digital file to the Materials Library. For instance, you can import a digital image to the material library and apply this digital image as material to the model you have created. The tutorials in this chapter will demonstrate how to assign materials, modify materials, and create new materials.

Basic Materials and Mapped Materials

Materials can be roughly divided into two categories: basic materials and mapped materials. **Basic materials** can be obtained from the Materials Library without the use of bitmaps. **Mapped materials** make use of a bitmap, or image to represent the color, texture or other attributes of a material. Defining mapped materials requires more effort. However, mapped materials can generate more realistic results with materials that display textures or patterns.

Basic Materials

Generally speaking, basic materials can be modified by changing values in Materials Editor in Materials Tool Palettes (Figure 9.22).The following are the attributes you can modify:

- **Color:** It displays the Select Color Dialog Box when you double click on the small color swatch.

- **Shininess:** It sets the shininess of the material. The highlight on the face of a very shiny solid is smaller and brighter. A face that is less shiny reflects the light in more directions, creating a large, softer highlight (CAD help menu).

- **Opacity:** It sets the opacity of the material. A completely opaque solid object does not allow the passage of light through its surface. An object with no opacity is transparent (CAD help menu).

- **Reflection Index:** It sets the refraction index of the material. It controls how light is refracted through an object with a partially transparent material attached (CAD help menu).

- **Translucency:** it sets the translucency of the material. A translucent object transmits light, but light is also scattered within the object. The translucency value is a percentage: at 0.0, the material is not translucent; at 100.0 the material is as translucent as possible (CAD help menu).

- **Self-illumination:** When set to a value more than 0, it makes the object appear to give off light. When self-illumination is selected, luminance is unavailable.

- **Luminance:** It is the value of light reflected off a surface. It is a measure of how bright or dark the surface is perceived. When selecting luminance, the self-illumination is unavailable. Luminance is specified in real lighting units (CAD help menu).

Mapped Materials

You can find the Maps section in the Material Editor Palette, as shown in Figure 15.4c. If you click on the Select Image button, you can browse to any directory on your computer and select a bitmap file for use in the materials library. AutoCAD supports any bitmap file format, which includes the JPG, TIF, TGA, PCX, and GIF formats.

You can shrink or stretch an image, repeat it on the surface of an object, or scale the image to create the special effects that you want. You can map materials to fit the object or a fixed scale. In the Material Scaling & Tiling section, under Scale Units—Fit to Gizmo, you map the material according to the boundaries of the rendered surface; therefore, the material image is stretched or shrunk to fit the object. In Scale Units- None mapping, you map the material according to a fixed scale, thus the material image is tiled to the surface boundaries, rather than being stretched.

You use None and Fit to Gizmo mapping methods for different rendering purposes. You can use Fit to Gizmo for rendering landscapes or objects whose material is based on a single graphic image (such as billboards or wall paintings). The framed pictures you created in Chapter 13 were created by using the Fit to Gizmo option. You can use the None option for rendering materials built from images containing multiple repeated patterns (such as bricks, stone work, tile, and wall paper). The 3-D model of the Falling Water House was created by using the None option for the imported stone image. When you are using the None option, the scale values you enter in UV fields control the scale values manually.

Tile or Mirror Material Map

In Figure 15.4d, you see the Material Scaling & Tiling section; follow U tile and V tile; there are two drop-down menus, which contain tile and mirror options for material mapping. Tiling is the effect of applying an image and repeating the image as a pattern. This effect is used to represent a tiled floor. For example, in the following tutorials of Beach House and Falling Water House, the bricks on the back wall and the stones on the staircase chase are created using the Tile option. Tiling is adjustable to obtain different tiling values along the mapping axes, U and V. With cropped projection, you can place an image in a single location on an object. Mirroring is an effect related to tiling. It doubles the map and flips the doubled copy. As with tiling, you can mirror the U dimension, the V dimension or both.

Tutorial Project 15-1

CHANGING PREDEFINED MATERIALS

Figure 15.4a and Figure 15.4b shows the perspectives of a beach house. The back wall is a brick wall. In Figure 15.4b, the clear glass was modified with blue color and reflections.

1. Open beach house.dwg

2. You can access the Materials Library in the Dashboard and get Material Tool Palette dialog box as shown in Figure 9.20b.

FIGURE 15.4A Perspective view of beach house (with brick wall)

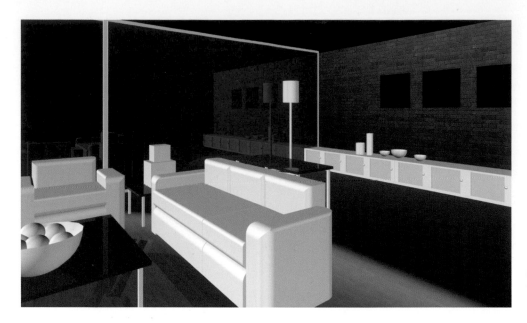

FIGURE 15.4B Perspective view of beach house (with blue glass)

3. In the Material Tool Palette, go to the Masonry tab and drag Masonry.Unit.Masonry.Brick.Modular.English to the Material Editor palette, as shown in Figure 9.21b.

4. Click on the Bump Map button to show bumpy surface.

5. In the Material Editor Palette (Figure 15.4c), you can change the object size and scale by choosing different UV values to make the materials look appropriate after you render the drawing.

6. Double click on the Masonry.Unit material swatch in the Material Editor Palette, and then use paint brush to choose the object that will be attached with this material.

In this tutorial, you used basic materials from the Materials Library and modified them by changing some attributes, such as bump map and Width and Height in the Material Scaling & Tiling section for the brick on the back wall. You also can modify the glass material in the Material Editor Palette by changing the color to blue and by changing the value of the refraction so that

the interior scene is reflected on the glass wall. The attributes of the clear glass are shown in the Material Editor Palette, as shown in Figure 15.5b.

Tutorial Project 15-2

CREATING SURFACE MATERIALS FOR VASES

Figure 15.2 shows three vases with graphic patterns on their surfaces. These graphic patterns can be created by paint draw in MS Word or Photoshop. It is created in JPG format and imported into the materials library. The first step is to build the models for these three vases. To recap the command Revolve, let's go through one procedure to build one vase. The other two should be pretty easy. Figure 15.6 shows the dimensions for three vases.

1. Use ARC and LINE to create a profile (half of the vase) as shown in Figure 15.7 according to the dimensions in Figure 15.6.

2. OFFSET all lines $1/4$" to show the thickness of the vase.

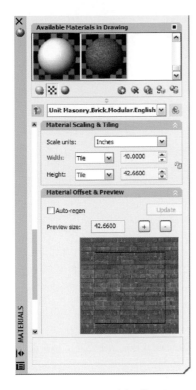

FIGURE 15.4C Material editor palette (brick)

FIGURE 15.5A Material editor palette (brick)

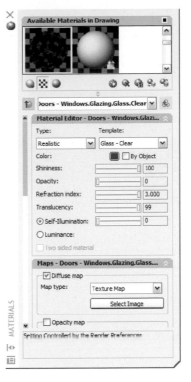

FIGURE 15.5B Material editor palette (brick)

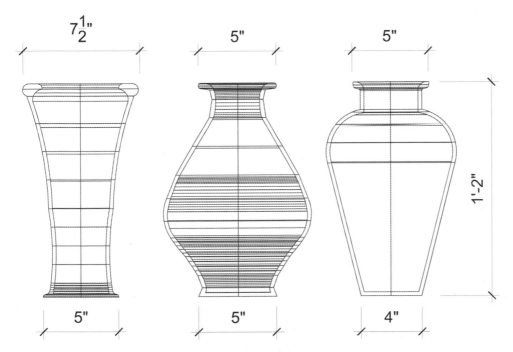

FIGURE 15.6 Vase elevations with dimensions

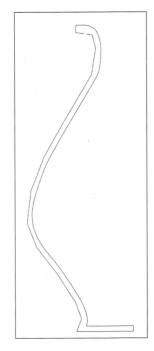

FIGURE 15.7 Vase profile

3. Use PEDIT to join all segments together to get a polyline, which is a single entity.

4. Use REVOLVE to create the entire vase.

Command: _revolve

Current wire frame density: ISOLINES = 4

Select objects to revolve: **click on the profile** 1 found

Select objects to revolve: **ENTER**

Specify axis start point or define axis by [Object/ X/Y/Z] Object> : **Click on the centerline start point.**

Specify axis endpoint: **click on the centerline end point**

Specify angle of revolution or [STart angle] <360> : **ENTER**

Now your drawing should look like Figure 15.8.

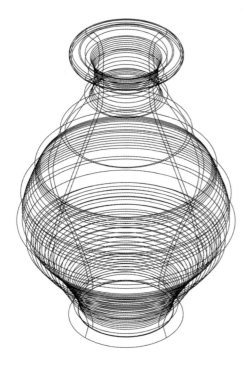

FIGURE 15.8 Isometric view of vase

5. You can draw something up, such as Figure 15.9. It is the material, which will be applied to all the vases.

6. Click on Create New Material button in Material Editor Palette, you should have a screen that looks like Figure 15.10a. Give a name for the material, such as Graphic.

7. Click on the Select Image button in the Map section and browse the JEP file from your computer. Your screen should look like Figure 15.10b.

8. In the Material Scaling & Tiling section, adjust the width and height value for the material until it looks like Figure 15.11a.

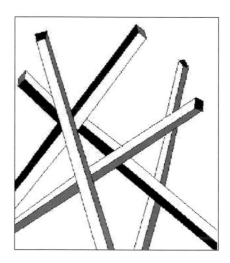

FIGURE 15.9 Graphic on vase

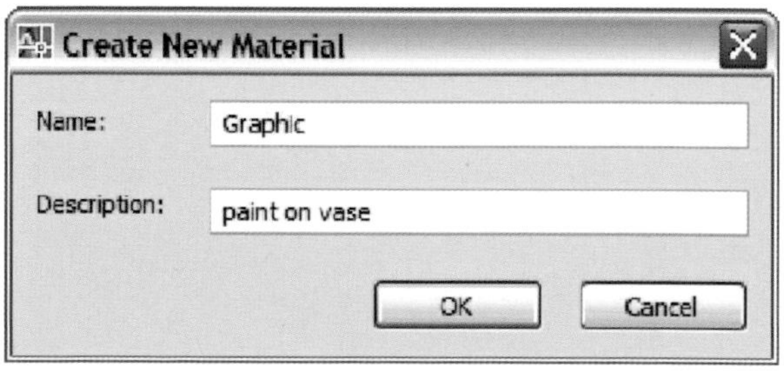

FIGURE 15.10A Create new material dialog box

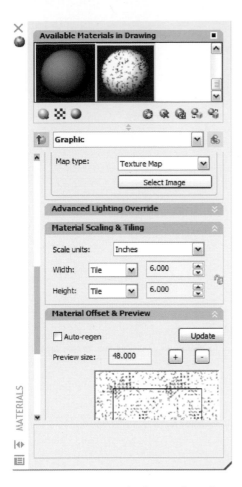

FIGURE 15.10B Material editor palette (new materials)

FIGURE 15.11A Perspective of vases

Tutorial Project 15-3

IMPORTING CUSTOMIZED MATERIALS

Figure 15.1a to Figure 15.1d demonstrates the examples of importing customized materials to the surface of a curved sofa. The following is the procedure of creating this specific effect.

1. Open 3D-lobby.dwg.

2. You can access the Dashboard and get the Material Editor Palette as shown in Figure 9.22.

3. Click on the Create New Material button and name the new material as Fabric-1; you should have a dialog box like Figure 15.11b.

4. Click on the Select Image button in Figure 15.11b, and then browse the file for a bitmap image (Figure 15.11c or Figure 15.11d).

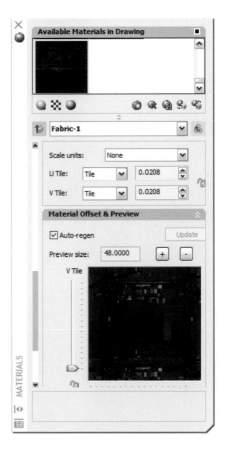

FIGURE 15.11B Material Editor Palette (new material)

FIGURE 15.11C Image of material in gallery lobby

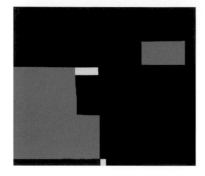

FIGURE 15.11D Image of material in gallery lobby

5. Click on the Select Image button; you should have a dialog box, as shown in Figure 15.11b.

6. In this dialogue box, you can adjust the width and height of Fabric-1.

7. Double click on the Fabric-1 swatch in the Material Editor Palette, and then use the paint brush to attach the fabric to the surface of the sofa.

8. You should have a rendered image like the one shown in Figure 15.1a.

Case Study Three

APPLYING AUTHENTIC MATERIALS —FALLING WATER HOUSE

Figure 15.12a, Figure 15.12b, and Figure 15.12c shows a 3-D model of Frank Lloyd Wright's world-famous masterwork, designed in 1936. Figure 15.12c is a photo showing the real Falling Water House. The stones on the chase of staircase are imported from a digital image (Figure 15.12d).

FIGURE 15.12A Perspective of Falling Water House

FIGURE 15.12B Perspective of Falling Water House

FIGURE 15.12C Photo of Falling Water House

FIGURE 15.12D
Photo of stone
at Falling
Water House

Figure 15.12d is a photo of stone on Falling Water House that has been modified by Microsoft Photo Editor. The procedure of importing the digital image is:

1. Access the Material Editor Palette from the Dashboard. You should get the Material Editor Palette as shown in Figure 9.22.

2. Click on the Create New Material button.

3. Then you will have a dialog box like Figure 15.10a. Type in the material name "stone" and click OK.

4. Click on the Select Image button to browse the file from your computer.

5. In the Map section, adjust the value of width and height of the material.

6. Click on Preview.

7. Double click on the stone material swatch, and then use the paint brush to attach the material to the object.

8. Render a scene to see the results.

Case Study Four

APPLYING AUTHENTIC MATERIALS— REBORN OF POMPEII

This case study demonstrates how to create a digital 3-D model to represent the ruined House of Vettii in Pompeii. Pompeii is the world's oldest archaeological dig. It has been under excavation more or less continually since 1748, and two-thirds of the town has been stripped of the Vesuvian ash that buried it on August 24, 79 AD. Researchers have searched beneath Pompeii's mosaic floors for evidence of its origins and early development.

Representing Pompeii's hidden past has become a task for architects, designers and archaeologists. Using 3-D software to reconstruct this famous Roman resort is not a new task, but has become more and more feasible and promising by the revolution of computer technology. The following shows how to construct a 3-D model of the House of The Vettii—one of the finest and most luxurious in Pompeii. The decoration of the rooms is still in excellent condition. Three dimensional AutoCAD has the power to undertake this task. The authentic materials can be imported into the CAD library. Lighting applications can be used in the interior space to present this "Reborn of Pompeii" project.

Figure 15.13a and Figure 15.13b is a 3-D model that shows the corner of the House of Vettii. Authentic material has been applied to the interior surface. Figure 15.14 is a photo that shows the existing condition of the House of Vettii. You can see that part of the frescos are missing. Three dimensional AutoCAD accom-

FIGURE 15.13A Interior perspective of the House of Vetii

plished the task of restoration and represented this famous ancient building. Figure 15.15 is a digital image that shows the frescos in the House of Vettii.

Applying Mapped Coordinates

Usually, when you use materials that are composed wholly or in part of bitmap images, you usually must apply **mapping coordinates** to the object. You can right click on the floating tool bar on top of your screen and highlight Mapping as shown in Figure 15.16a and then you will get a floating tool bar as shown in Figure 15.16b. You

also can type Materialmap or SETUV at the command prompt. You are then prompted to select the object to which you want to apply the mapping coordinates. You need to select the appropriate object at this moment, and then you will be prompted with a material mapper grip tool as shown in Figure 15.17.

AutoCAD system provides four types of mapping: planar mapping, cylindrical mapping, spherical mapping, and box mapping (Figure 15.18). The first three generally refer to how the bitmap is wrapped around the object to which the mapping is applied.

FIGURE 15.13B Interior perspective of the House of Vetii

FIGURE 15.14 Photo of the House of Vetii

FIGURE 15.15 Fresco in the House of Vetii

FIGURE 15.16B Mapping floating tool bar

FIGURE 15.16A Pull-down menu (mapping)

- **Planar Mapping:** Maps the texture onto the object with a one-to-one correspondence, as if you were projecting the texture from a slide projector on to the surface. This does not distort the texture; it just scales the image to fit the object (CAD help menu).

- **Cylindrical Mapping:** Maps an image onto a cylindrical object; the horizontal edges are wrapped together but not the top and bottom edges. The height of the texture is scaled along the cylinder's axis (CAD help menu).

- **Spherical Mapping:** Wraps the texture both horizontally and vertically. The top edge of the texture map is compressed to a point at the "north pole" of the sphere, as is the bottom edge at the "south pole" (CAD help menu).

- **Box Mapping:** Applies the material according to coordinates you specify. It is intended for use with materials such as wood, marble, and granite. They have three mapping coordinates, U, V and W, and can be applied from any angle (CAD help menu).

After you select the type of mapping you want to use, a material mapper grip tool is displayed on the object (Figure 15.17). You can use the grip tools and the representation of the object to

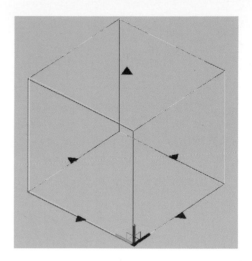

FIGURE 15.17 Material mapper grip tool

adjust the display of the image on the object or the face.

As long as you follow the prompted command line, the procedure is straightforward. By adjusting the offset, rotation, scale, and coordinates of bitmapped materials, you can control over how materials will appear in the rendered model.

SUMMARY

The materials application is a very important component in 3-D rendering. AutoCAD provides predefined materials in its Materials Library. You can import these predefined materials to your

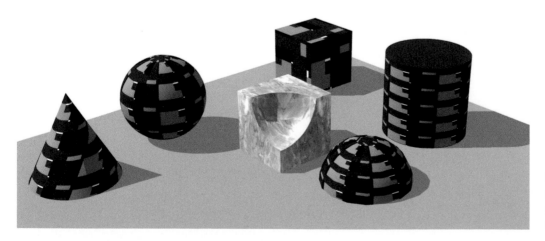

FIGURE 15.18 Objects with different coordinates of bitmapped material

3-D models. You also can make modifications to these predefined materials by changing their attributes. These are the basic materials. The following are the attributes that associate with predefined materials: Color, Shininess, Opacity, Reflection Index, Transparency, Self-illumination, and Luminance.

You also can create new materials and import them into the Materials Library. You can import bitmap images to the Materials Library. These are called mapped materials. You can choose either Fit to Gizmo or the None option to adjust the mapped materials. You can shrink or stretch an image, repeat it on the surface of an object, or scale the image to create the special effect that you want. You just need to adjust U or V values. You also can choose either Tile or Mirror to create special effects. With the tiling option, you can create repeated patterns with different scales. With mirror projection, you can place an image in double mirrored pattern on an object.

KEY TERMS

Basic Materials	Mapping Coordinates
Bump Map	Reflection
Color/Pattern	Refraction
Mapped Materials	Transparency

PROJECTS

1. Use the 3-D model of the gallery lobby and beach house created in previous chapters and apply different materials to the surface and create different framed pictures.

2. Use the 3-D model of a piece of art accessory created in the previous exercise and apply materials to the model.

3. Use the 3-D model of a piece of furniture created in a previous exercise and apply different materials to the model.

4. Create an image by using Photoshop or another software and apply this image as a material on the surface of your 3-D model.

Chapter Sixteen

Solid Editing and Form Transformation

Objectives

Up to this point, major commands and operations in AutoCAD have been introduced and demonstrated with relevant examples. In addition to meshes modeling and solid modeling commands, as well as Boolean Operations, there are several Solidedit commands that are very useful for modifying a 3-D object. After completing this chapter, you will be able to:

- Use the Solidedit command to make changes on a solid geometric form.

- Explore Geometric form transformation.

- Reinforce Boolean Operations UNION, SUBTRACT, and INTERSECT to create a more complex 3-D model.

FORM TRANSFORMATION— COOPER RESIDENCE

In this chapter, Solidedit commands will be demonstrated using an example of a 3-D model of the Cooper Residence in Orleans, Massachusetts designed by Gwathmey-Siegel. The Cooper residence was designed by subtractive and additive transformations to create volumes of spaces. Subtractive transformation means a form can be transformed by subtracting a portion of its volume. Additive transformation means a form can be transformed by the addition of elements to its volume. The Cooper Residence is a good example of using these two form transformations. The 3-D model (Figure 16.1a and Figure 16.1b) was created by SUBTRACT and UNION Boolean Operations. Figure 16.2a and Figure 16.2b show the rough dimensions for the floor plan and elevation. They are derived from the 3-D model's top view and side view. The intention is to provide approximate dimensions and you may alter them based on your judgment.

Francis Ching in his book, *Architecture: Form, Space and Order*, stated about the transformation of form, "all other forms can be understood to be transformations of the primary solids, variations which are generated by the manipulation of one or more dimensions or by the addition or subtraction of elements."

A form can be transformed by changing one or more of its dimensions and still retain its identity. For example, a cube can be changed into a thin plane by compressing its dimensions or can be stretched to a linear form. A form also can be changed by subtracting a portion of its volume and retain its identity or into a totally new form. Addition is another method of transformation. A form can be changed by the addition of elements to its volume. The number and the relative size of the additive objects dictate if the original form will retain its identity or be transformed into a new form.

Constructive Solid Geometry (CSG) is a method of manipulating geometric forms in the CAD environment. In AutoCAD, Boolean Operations are the commands to accomplish these tasks by using UNION, SUBTRACT, and INTERSECT. The Cooper Residence is designed with subtractive and additive form transformations. The 3-D model of the Cooper Residence was started with a cube rather than with each individual wall. Subtracting a solid cube from the large cube created each room. The following is the process of building the 3-D model for the Cooper Residence.

FIGURE 16.1A Perspective of the Cooper Residence

FIGURE 16.1B Perspective of the Cooper Residence

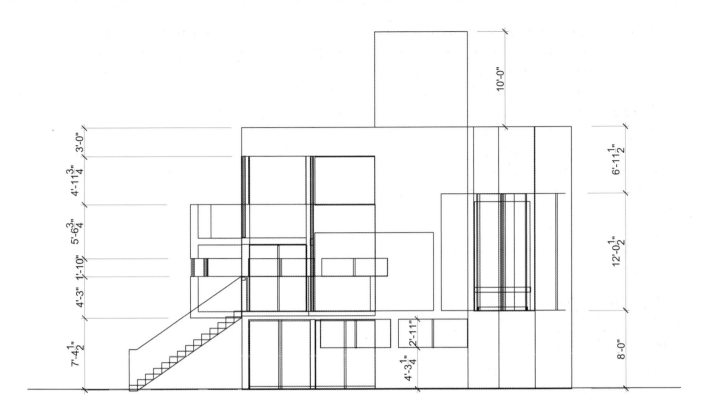

FIGURE 16.2A Exterior elevation of the Cooper Residence.

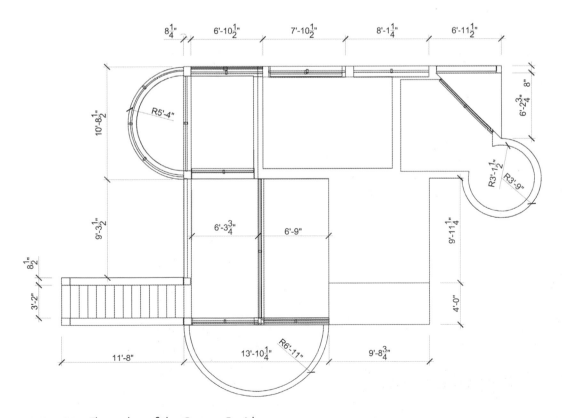

FIGURE 16.2B Floor plan of the Cooper Residence

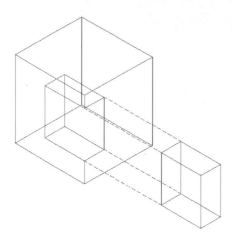

FIGURE 16.3 Subtract cube from the object

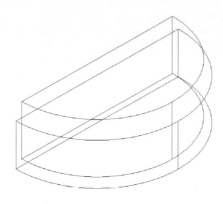

FIGURE 16.4A Two objects for subtract

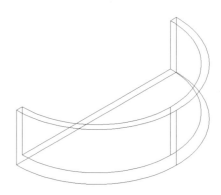

FIGURE 16.4B Object after subtract

1. Start with a solid cube. 23'-7" (Length) × 24'-7" (Width) × 27'-0" (Height).

2. Use BOX to create the second solid cube. 6'-11" (Length) × 13'-11" (Width) × 16'-0" Height).

3. USE SUBTRACT (Boolean Operation) to create an object as shown in Figure 16.3.

4. Use EXTRUDE to create two half cylinders as shown in Figure 16.4a, and then use SUBTRACT to create a half circle balcony (Figure 16.4b). The dimensions for these two half cylinders are 12'-10" (Diameter) × 3'-3"(Height) and 13'-10" (Diameter) × 4'-3" (Height).

5. Use the same method to create another half balcony on the left side. (Figure 16.5). Also use SUBTRACT to create the curved window.

6. Use SUBTRACT to create the Northwest corner of the building. Create a triangle solid object as the second object, and then subtract it from the building (Figure 16.6).

7. The staircase at the Northwest corner of the building was created using the Cylinder command (Figure 16.6).

8. In general, the building components are geometric forms, such as cubes, triangular forms or cylinders. These geometric forms can be

FIGURE 16.5 Perspective of the Cooper Residence

either subtracted or added to the building, which is a big cube. Boolean Operations can be used to achieve the goal of subtraction and addition by using SUBTRACT and UNION. The isometric views of the building in Figure 16.7a, Figure 16.7b, Figure 16.8a, and Figure

FIGURE 16.6 Perspective of the Cooper Residence

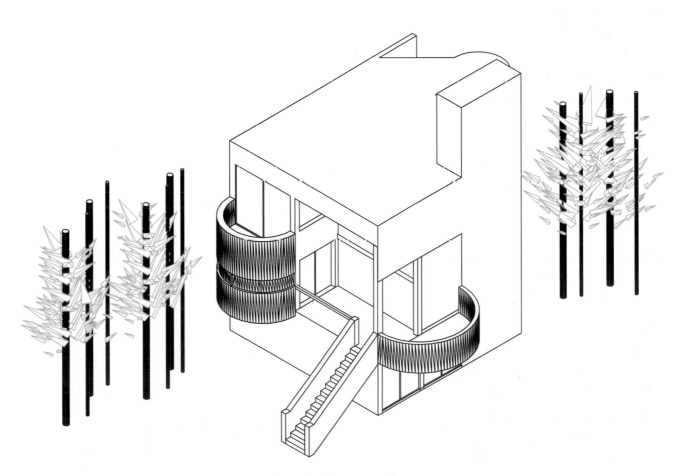

FIGURE 16.7A Isometric view of the Cooper Residence (Hide command)

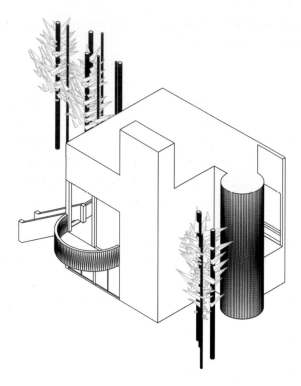

FIGURE 16.7B Isometric view of the Cooper Residence (Hide command)

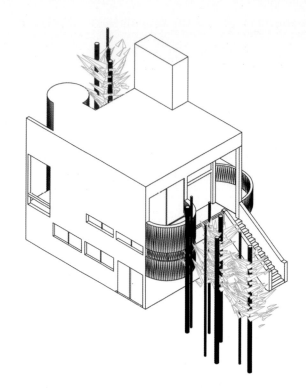

FIGURE 16.8B Isometric view of the Cooper Residence (Hide command)

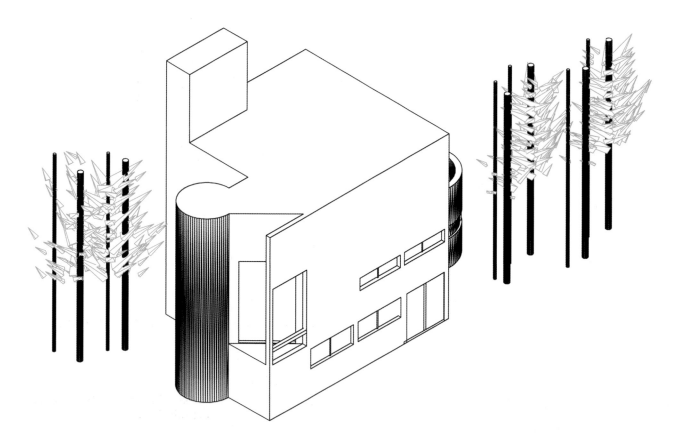

FIGURE 16.8A Isometric view of the Cooper Residence (Hide command)

16.8b show the clear spatial relationship of these geometric forms. These isometric views are created using the Hide command.

SOLIDEDIT COMMAND

Like the editing and modifying commands in 2-D AutoCAD, you can edit your 3-D solid object by using SOLIDEDIT in 3-D AutoCAD. Through SOLIDEDIT, you can extrude, rotate, offset, taper, delete or copy the object. You also can change the color of the face of an object using the Solid-edit command. SOLIDEDIT can be operated for modification in three aspects: Body of the object, Face of the object and Edge of the object. Each aspect includes several options.

- **Face of the object**—Extrude, Move, Rotate, Offset, Delete, Copy, and Change color.

- **Body of the object**—Imprint, Separate, Shell, Clean, and Check.

- **Edge of the object**—Copy and Change color.

You can type the command SOLIDEDIT at the command line and then chose the option. The following is a generic procedure of using SOLIDEDIT command.

Command line: **solidedit**

Solids editing automatic checking: SOLID-CHECK = 1

Enter a solid editing option

[Face / Edge / Body / Undo / exit] <exit> : Enter an option or press Enter

In addition to the command prompt line, you also can use the floating tool bar and click on the command button (Figure 16.9a), or use pull down menu in Figure 16.9b.

Extrude Faces

This command enables you to select planar faces of a 3-D solid object and extrude this object to a specified height or along a path. You can select multiple faces at one time. The following is an example of using the Extrude faces command to modify the 3-D object in the Cooper Residence. You have created a solid model of a balcony in Figure 16.4b. Now you can use the Extrude faces command to modify it and make it a solid model of the second taller balcony shown in Figure 16.5. Remember to scale it down to the right size

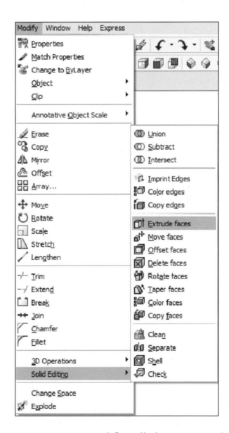

FIGURE 16.9B Modify pull-down menu (Extrude faces)

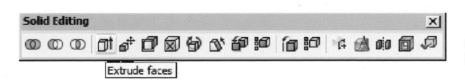

FIGURE 16.9A Solid editing floating tool bar (Extrude faces)

before you use Extrude faces command because the dimension of the diameter is different. In this case, you must select a single face. If you pick an edge of the selected face, you select two faces that share the picked edge and both faces are highlighted. You will have to use the Remove option in order to remove the unwanted face so that you have only the top face selected.

Click on Extrude faces command button on the floating tool bar (Figure 16.9a)

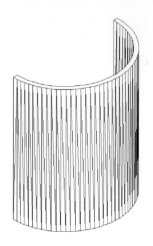

FIGURE 16.10 Object created by Solid Editing command (Extrude faces)

> **Command: extrude**
>
> ---
>
> Select faces or [Undo/Remove]: **Click on top of the half circle**, 2 faces found
>
> ---
>
> Select faces or [Undo/Remove/ALL]: **R**
>
> ---
>
> Remove faces or [Undo/Remove/ALL]: **click on the vertical face,** 2 faces found, 1 removed
>
> ---
>
> Remove faces or [Undo/Remove/ALL]: **ENTER**
>
> ---
>
> Specify height of extrusion or [Path]: **8'9-^{1}/$_2$ and press ENTER**
>
> ---
>
> Specify angle of tape for extrusion 0> : **ENTER**
>
> ---
>
> [Extrude/Move/Rotate/Offset/Taper/Delete/Copy/ Color/Undo/exit] <eXit> : **ENTER**
>
> ---
>
> Solids editing automatic checking: SOLID-CHECK = 1
>
> ---
>
> Enter a solids editing option [Face/Edge/Body/ Undo/exit] <exit> : **ENTER**

Your final drawing should look like Figure 16.10.

Offset Faces

This command enables you to offset faces equally by a specified distance or through a specified point. A positive value increases the size or volume of the solid; a negative value decreases the size or volume of the solid. You can access Offset

faces command by clicking on the floating tool bar (Figure 16.11a) or by using the Modify pull down menu (Figure 16.11b).

Click on the Offset faces command button in the floating tool bar (Figure 16.11a)

> **Command: _ offset**
>
> ---
>
> Select faces or [Undo/Remove]: **Click on inner side of the half circle**, 2 faces found
>
> ---
>
> Select faces or [Undo/Remove/ALL]: **R**
>
> ---
>
> Remove faces or [Undo/Remove/ALL]: **click on outer side of the circle and ENTER,** 2 faces found, 1 removed
>
> ---
>
> Remove faces or [Undo/Remove/ALL]: **ENTER**
>
> ---
>
> Specify the offset distance: **1'6 and press ENTER**
>
> ---
>
> Enter a face editing option
>
> ---
>
> [Extrude/Move/Rotate/Offset/Taper/Delete/Copy/ Color/Undo/exit] <eXit> : **ENTER**
>
> ---
>
> Solids editing automatic checking: SOLID-CHECK = 1
>
> ---
>
> Enter a solids editing option [Face/Edge/Body/ Undo/exit] <eXit> : **ENTER**

Your final drawing should look like Figure 16.12.

FIGURE 16.11A Solid Editing floating tool bar (Offset faces)

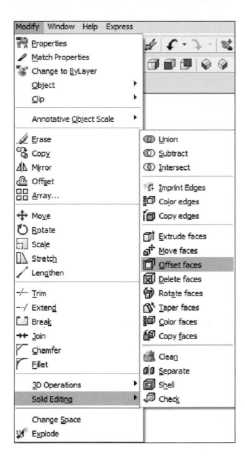

FIGURE 16.11B Modify pull-down menu (Offset faces)

Move Faces

This command enables you to move the selected face on a 3-D solid object to a specified height or distance. You can select multiple faces at one time. You will have to specify two points during this process. The two points you specify define a displacement vector that indicates how far a selected face is moved and in what direction SOLIDEDIT uses the first point as a base point and places a single copy relative to the base point. You can access the Move faces command by clicking on the floating tool bar (Figure 16.13a), or by using the Modify pull down menu (Figure 16.13b). Figure 16.14 is a 3-D object modified by using Move faces command. It is derived from the object in Figure 16.10. The platform of the balcony has been moved up to the third floor. The object can be attached to the main building.

Click on the Move faces command button in the floating tool bar (Figure 16.13a) and you will be prompted:

Command: _ move

Select faces or [Undo/Remove]: **Click on the face of the platform of the balcony,** 2 faces found

Select faces or [Undo/Remove/ALL]: **R and ENTER**

Remove faces or [Undo/Remove/ALL]: **click on the vertical face and ENTER,** 2 faces found, 1 removed

Remove faces or [Undo/Remove/ALL]: **ENTER**

Specify a base point or displacement: **click on the intersection of highlighted line and half circle**

Specify a second point or displacement: **@7'6 and ENTER**

Solid validation completed

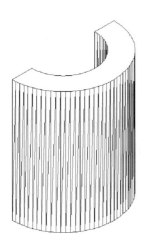

FIGURE 16.12 Object created by Solid Editing command (Offset faces)

FIGURE 16.13A Solid Editing floating tool bar (Move faces)

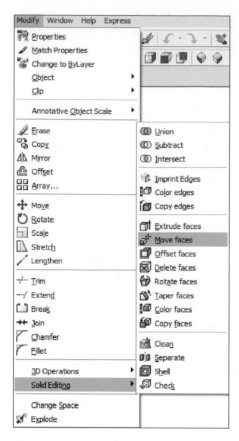

FIGURE 16.13B Modify pull-down menu (Move faces)

FIGURE 16.14 Object created by Solid Editing command (Move faces)

Enter a face editing option

[Extrude/Move/Rotate/Offset/Taper/Delete/Copy/Color/Undo/exit] <eXit> : **ENTER**

Solids editing automatic checking: SOLID-CHECK = 1

Enter a solids editing option [Face/Edge/Body/Undo/exit] <exit> : **ENTER**

Your final drawing should look like Figure 16.14 with HIDE.

Copy Faces

This command enables you to copy faces as a region or a body. If you specify two points, SOL-IDEDIT uses the first point as a base point and places a single copy relative to the base point. If you specify a single point and then press ENTER, SOLIDEDIT uses the coordinate as the new location. This option also creates a two-dimensional copy of a face of the object. Once again, you will have to use Remove option to remove unwanted faces. You can access the Copy faces command by clicking on the floating tool bar (Figure 16.15a), or by using the Modify pull down menu (Figure 16.15b).

Click on the Copy faces command button in the floating tool bar (Figure 16.15a) and you will be prompted:

Command: _ copy

Select faces or [Undo/Remove]: **Click on the top face of half circle,** 2 faces found

Select faces or [Undo/Remove/ALL]: **R and ENTER**

Remove faces or [Undo/Remove/ALL]: **click on the vertical face and ENTER, 2 faces found,** 1 removed

Remove faces or [Undo/Remove/ALL]: **ENTER**

Specify a base point or displacement: **click on the corner of highlighted half circle**

Specify a second point or displacement: **click on the screen**

Enter a face editing option

[Extrude/Move/Rotate/Offset/Taper/Delete/Copy/Color/Undo/exit] <eXit> : **ENTER**

Solids editing automatic checking: SOLID-CHECK = 1

Enter a solids editing option [Face/Edge/Body/Undo/exit] <exit> : **ENTER**

You can also use EXTRUDE to extrude the copy of the 2-D half circle minus three feet (-3'). Your final drawing should look like Figure 16.16 with HIDE.

Delete Faces

This command enables you to delete or remove faces, including fillets and chamfers. Once again, you will have to use the Remove option to remove unwanted faces. You can access the Copy faces command by clicking on the floating tool bar (Figure 16.17a), or by using the Modify pull down menu (Figure 16.17b).

Click on the Delete faces command button in the floating tool bar (Figure 16.17a) and you will be prompted:

Command: _ **delete**

Select faces or [Undo/Remove]: **Click on the face that you want to delete,** 2 faces found (make

sure all the faces you want to delete are highlighted)

Select faces or [Undo/Remove/ALL]: **R and ENTER**

Remove faces or [Undo/Add/ALL]: **click on the outer side of the half circle and two vertical lines and Enter,** 2 faces found, 1 removed

Remove faces or [Undo/Add/ALL]: **ENTER**

Solid validation completed

Enter a face editing option

[Extrude/Move/Rotate/Offset/Taper/Delete/Copy/ Color/Undo/exit] <exit> : **ENTER**

Solids editing automatic checking: SOLID-CHECK = 1

Enter a solids editing option [Face/Edge/Body/ Undo/exit] <exit> : **ENTER**

Your drawing should look like Figure 16.18.

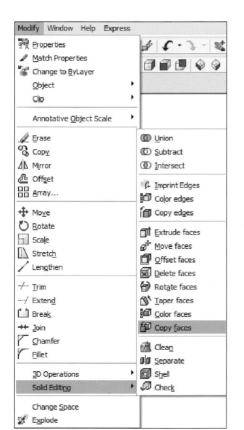

FIGURE 16.15B Modify pull-down menu (Copy faces)

FIGURE 16.15A Solid Editing floating tool bar (Copy faces)

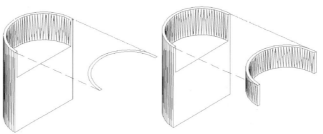

FIGURE 16.16 Object created by Solid Editing command (Copy faces)

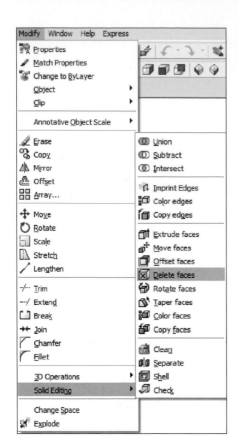

FIGURE 16.17A Solid Editing floating tool bar (Delete faces)

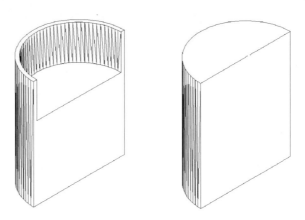

FIGURE 16.18 Object created by using the Solid Editing command (Delete faces)

FIGURE 16.17B Modify pull-down menu (Delete faces)

Rotate Faces

This command enables you to rotate one or more faces or a collection of features on a solid about a specified axis. Remember that you will have to use the Remove option to remove unwanted faces. You can access the Rotate faces command by clicking on the floating tool bar (Figure 16.19a), or by using the Modify pull-down menu (Figure 16.19b).

Click on the Rotate faces command button in the floating tool bar (Figure 16.17a) and you will be prompted:

Command: _ rotate

Select faces or [Undo/Remove]: **Click on all the faces of small cube inside the large cube,** 2 faces found

Select faces or [Undo/Remove/ALL]: **R and ENTER**

Remove faces or [Undo/Add/ALL]: **click on all the faces of large cube and ENTER,** 2 faces found, 1 removed

Specify an axis point or [Axis by object/View/Xaxis/Yaxis/Zaxis] (2 points): **Z ENTER**

Specify the origin of the rotation <0, 0, 0> : **Click on the center of the small cube**

Specify a rotation angle or [Reference]: **R, ENTER**

Specify the reference (starting) angle <0> : **ENTER**

Specify the ending angle: **45**

Solids editing automatic checking: SOLID-CHECK = 1

Enter a solids editing option [Face/Edge/Body/Undo/exit] <exit> : **ENTER**

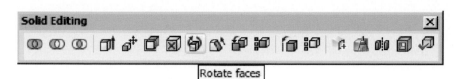

FIGURE 16.19A Solid Editing floating tool bar (Rotate faces)

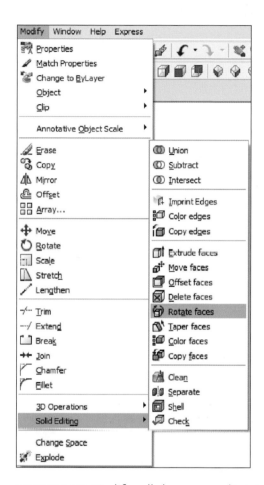

FIGURE 16.19B Modify pull-down menu (Rotate faces)

Your drawing should look like Figure 16.20 with the Render command. The smaller cube inside the large cube was rotated with 45 degrees.

Taper Faces

This command enables you to taper faces with an angle. The rotation of the taper angle is determined by the selection sequence of the base point and second point along the selected vector. Tapering the selected face with a positive angle tapers the face in and a negative angle tapers the face out. All selected faces in the selection set are tapered to the same value. You can access the

Taper faces command by clicking on the floating tool bar (Figure 16.21a), or by using the Modify pull-down menu (Figure 16.21b).

Click on the Taper faces command button in the floating tool bar (Figure 16.21a) and you will be prompted:

Command: _ **taper**

Select faces or [Undo/Remove]: **Click on all the top face of the cube,** 2 faces found

Select faces or [Undo/Remove/ALL]: **R and press ENTER**

Remove faces or [Undo/Add/ALL]: **click on the vertical faces of the cube and press ENTER,** 2 faces found, 1 removed

Remove faces or [Undo/Add/ALL]: **press ENTER**

Specify the base point: **Click on the front upper left corner**

Specify another point along the axis of tapering: **Click on the back upper left corner of the cube**

Specify the taper angle: **-20 and press ENTER**

Enter a face editing option

[Extrude/Move/Rotate/Offset/Taper/Delete/Copy/Color/Undo/exit] <exit> : **ENTER**

Solids editing automatic checking: SOLID-CHECK = 1

Enter a solids editing option [Face/Edge/Body/Undo/exit] <exit> : **ENTER**

Your drawing should look like Figure 16.22 using the Render command. The left side cube was created with negative value 20-degree taper angle, the right side cube was created with positive value 20-degree taper angle. Other steps are exactly the same.

FIGURE 16.20 Object created by using the Solid Editing command (Rotate faces)

FIGURE 16.21A Solid Editing floating tool bar (Taper faces)

Color Faces

This command enables you to change the color of faces on a solid object. Figure 16.24 shows the initial model of the Cooper Residence. A cube has been subtracted from the large cube. You can change the faces of the recessed area to blue color. You can access the Copy faces command by clicking on the floating tool bar (Figure 16.23a), or by using the Modify pull-down menu (Figure 16.23b).

Click on the Color faces command button in the floating tool bar (Figure 16.21a) and you will be prompted:

Command: _ **color**

Select faces or [Undo/Remove]: **Click on the faces that you want to change the color,** 2 faces found

Select faces or [Undo/Remove/ALL]: **R and press ENTER**

Remove faces or [Undo/Add/ALL]: **click on the faces that you don't want to change the color and press ENTER,** 2 faces found, 1 removed

Remove faces or [Undo/Add/ALL]: **press ENTER**

You will be prompted with Select Color dialog box. Select the color there and click OK.

Enter a face editing option

[Extrude/Move/Rotate/Offset/Taper/Delete/Copy/ Color/Undo/exit] <exit> : **ENTER**

Solids editing automatic checking: SOLID-CHECK = 1

Enter a solids editing option [Face/Edge/Body/ Undo/exit] <exit> : **ENTER**

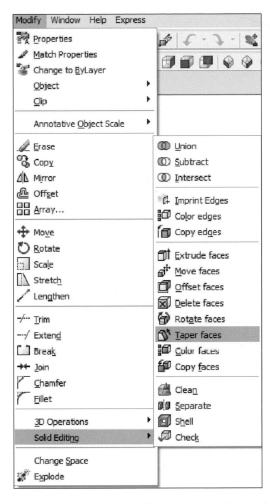

Your drawing should look like Figure 16.24 with the Render command.

Copy Edges

So far, you have explored all Solidedit face options. Now let's look at the edge options in SOLIDEDIT. There are only two edge options, copy and color. The Copy edge command enables you to copy 3D edges. All 3D solid edges can be copied as a line, arc, circle, ellipse, or spline. You can copy more than one edge at one time. The copy option can result in a two-dimensional shape. You can access Copy faces command by clicking on the floating tool bar (Figure 16.25a), or by using the Modify pull-down menu (Figure 16.25b).

Click on the Copy edges command button in the floating tool bar (Figure 16.25a)

Enter an edge editing option [Copy/Color/Undo/eXit] <eXit> : **_ copy**

Select edges [Undo/Remove]: **Click on all four edges of small square and press ENTER**

Specify a base point or displacement: **click on a point on screen**

FIGURE 16.21B Modify pull-down menu (Taper faces)

FIGURE 16.22 Object created by Solid Editing command (Taper faces)

FIGURE 16.23A Solid Editing floating tool bar (Color faces)

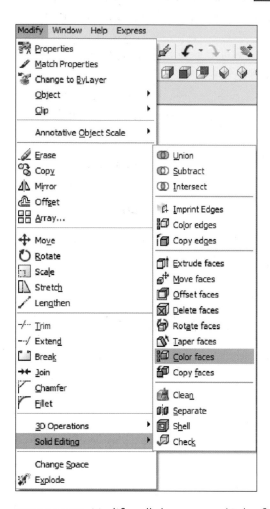

FIGURE 16.23B Modify pull-down menu (Color faces)

FIGURE 16.24 Color change on an object with Solid Editing

Color Edges

The Color edge command enables you to change the color of edges. You can access the Color faces command by clicking on the floating tool bar (Figure 16.27a), or by using the Modify pull-down menu (Figure 16.27b).

Click on the **Copy edges** command button in the floating tool bar (Figure 16.27a) and you will be prompted:

Enter an edge editing option [Copy/Color/Undo/eXit] <eXit> : _ **color**

Select edges [Undo/Remove]: Click on all four edges of small square and press **ENTER**

You will be prompted with the Select Color dialog box. Select a color there and click OK.

Select edges [Undo/Remove]

Enter an edge editing option [Copy/Color/Undo/eXit] <eXit> : **ENTER**

Solids editing automatic checking: SOLID-CHECK = 1

Specify a second point of displacement: **click on another point on screen**

Enter an edge editing option [Copy/Color/Undo/eXit] <eXit> : **ENTER**

Solids editing automatic checking: SOLID-CHECK = 1

Enter a solids editing option [Face/Edge/Body/Undo/exit] <exit> : **ENTER**

Your drawing should look like Figure 16.26 with the Render command.

Enter a solids editing option [Face/Edge/Body/ Undo/exit] <eXit> : **ENTER**

You can change the color of the edges of the bigger cube. Your drawing should look like Figure 16.28.

Shell Option

Until now, you have explored all SOLIDEDIT face options and edge options. Now let's look at the body options in SOLIDEDIT. Body options edit the entire solid object by imprinting other geometry on the solid, separating the solid into individual solid objects, such as shelling, cleaning, or checking the selected solid. The Shell option creates a hollow thin wall with a specified thickness. You can specify a constant wall thickness for all the faces. You can also exclude faces from the shell by selecting them. Three-dimensional solids can have only one shell by offsetting existing ones outside their original positions. A positive value creates a shell from the outside of the perimeter and a negative value creates a shell the inside of the perimeter. You can access the Shell command by clicking on the floating tool bar (Figure 16.29a), or by using the Modify pull-down menu (Figure 16.29b).

Click on the Shell command button in the floating tool bar (Figure 16.29a) and you will be prompted:

[Imprint/seParate solids/Shell/cLean/Check/ Undo/eXit] <eXit> : **_shell**

Select a 3D solid: **click on the cube**

Remove faces [Undo/Add/ALL]: **Click on one edge of the top face,** 2 faces found, 2 removed

FIGURE 16.25A Solid Editing floating tool bar (Copy edges)

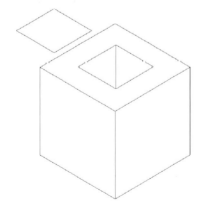

FIGURE 16.26 Copy option in Solid Editing

FIGURE 16.27A Solid Editing floating tool bar (Color edges)

FIGURE 16.25B Modify pull-down menu (Copy edges)

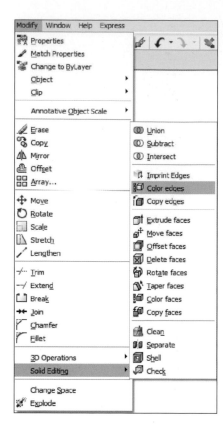

FIGURE 16.27B Modify pull-down menu (Color edges)

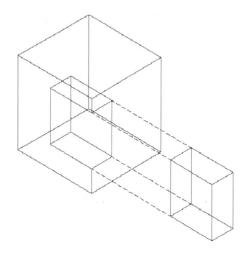

FIGURE 16.28 Edge color change with Solid Editing

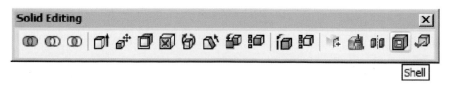

FIGURE 16.29A Solid Editing floating toolbar (shell)

Remove faces [Undo/Add/ALL]: **ENTER**
Enter the shell offset distance: **12 and ENTER**
Enter a body editing option
[Imprint/seParate solids/Shell/cLean/Check/ Undo/eXit] <eXit> : **ENTER**
Solids editing automatic checking: SOLID- CHECK = 1
Enter a solids editing option [Face/Edge/Body/ Undo/exit] <exit> : **ENTER**

Your drawing should look like Figure 16.30 with HIDE.

Imprint Option

The **Imprint option** creates an object on the selected solid. The object to be imprinted must intersect one or more faces on the selected solid in order for imprinting to be successful. Imprinting is limited to the following objects: arcs, circles, lines, 2-D and 3-D polylines, ellipses, splines, regions, bodies, and 3-D solids. You can access the Imprint command by clicking on the floating tool bar (Figure 16.31a), or by using the Modify pull-down menu (Figure 16.31b).

Click on the Imprint command button in the floating tool bar (Figure 16.29a) and you will be prompted:

Command: **_imprint**
Select a 3D solid: **click on the cylinder**
Select an object to imprint: **Click on the cube**
Delete the source object [Yes/No] N> : ENTER
Select an object to imprint: **ENTER**

Your drawing should look like Figure 16.32 using the Hide command.

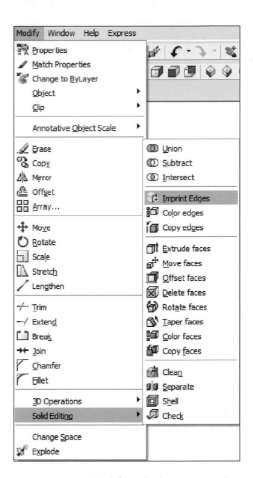

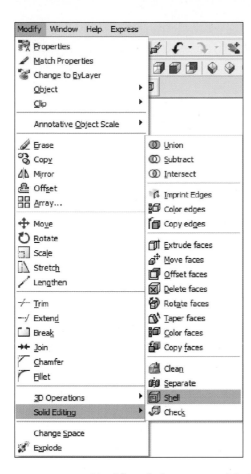

FIGURE 16.29B Modify pull-down menu (shell)

FIGURE 16.31B Modify pull-down menu (Imprint Edges)

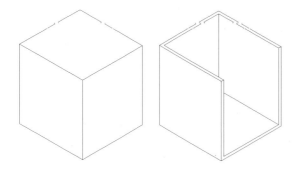

FIGURE 16.30 Object created by Solid Editing command (Shell)

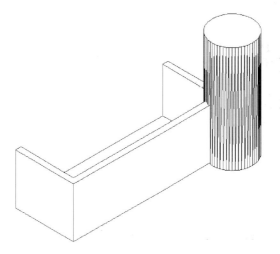

FIGURE 16.32 Object created by using the imprinting option.

FIGURE 16.31A Solid Editing floating tool bar (Imprint Edges)

Case Study

FORM TRANSFORMATION—FALLING WATER HOUSE

The following images are 3-D models of the Falling Water House designed by Frank Lloyd Wright. This model was created by using solid modeling methods with Boolean Operations and Solidedit commands. The overhung platforms were created by using the solid Box command with the SOLIDEDIT Shell option. It is similar to the process in the previous 3-D model of the Cooper Residence. The interior space was created by using the Subtract Boolean Operation command. The dimensions on the floor plan and exterior elevation of the Falling Water House only serve as the reference for your model. You may use your judgment when the dimensions are uncertain or search on the Internet for more information.

SUMMARY

You can edit your solid objects by extruding, moving, rotating, offsetting, tapering, deleting or copying it, or by changing the color of the faces. Solids editing includes the following options: Face, Edge, and Body. Face options include Extrude, Move, Rotate, Offset, Delete Copy, and Change color. Edge options include Copy and Change color. Body options include Imprint, Separate, Shell Clean, and Check. SOLIDEDIT

enables you to copy and modify solid edges and faces after they are created. You can also imprint shapes onto solid objects and create shells from their original solids.

Solid modeling is a very powerful method of creating complex models and transforming forms by combining and editing solid primitives and extruded 2-D shapes. Boolean Operation commands of UNION, SUBTRACT, and INTERSECT, along with EXTRUDE, REVOLVE, SLICE, SECTION, and INTERFERE can be used to accomplish the form transformations.

KEY TERMS

COPY EDGES Option	MOVE FACES Option
COPY FACES Option	OFFSET FACES Option
DELETE FACES Option	SHELL Option
EXTRUDE FACES	TAPER FACES Option
IMPRINT Option	

PROJECTS

1. Create a 3-D model of a conference room with dimensions 15' × 20' × 9' with a meeting table and chairs, as well as built-in shelves and a coffee counter by using SOLIDEDIT.

2. Create a 3-D model of a coffee shop with dimensions 20' × 30' × 10' with tables, checkout computers, and display shelves.

FIGURE 16.33 Perspective of Falling Water House

FIGURE 16.34 Perspective of Falling Water House

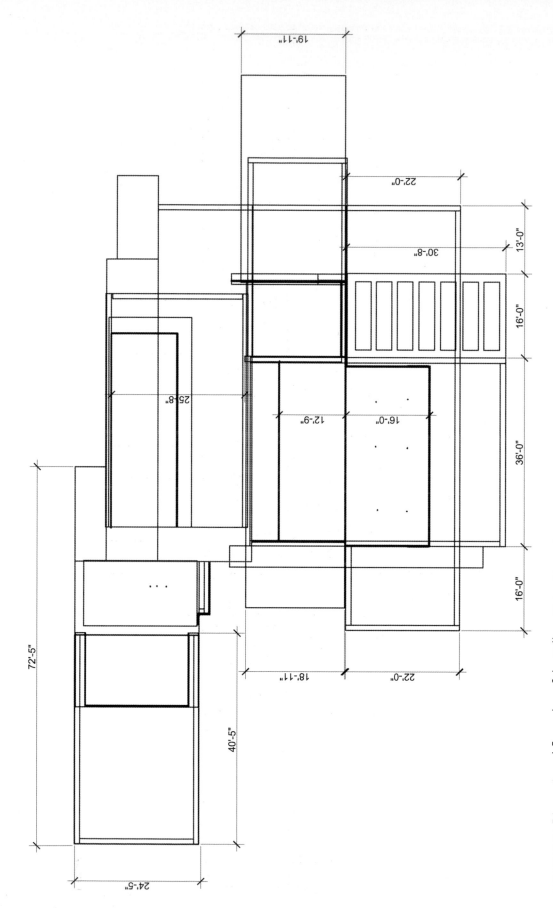

FIGURE 16.35 Dimensioned floor plan of the Falling Water House

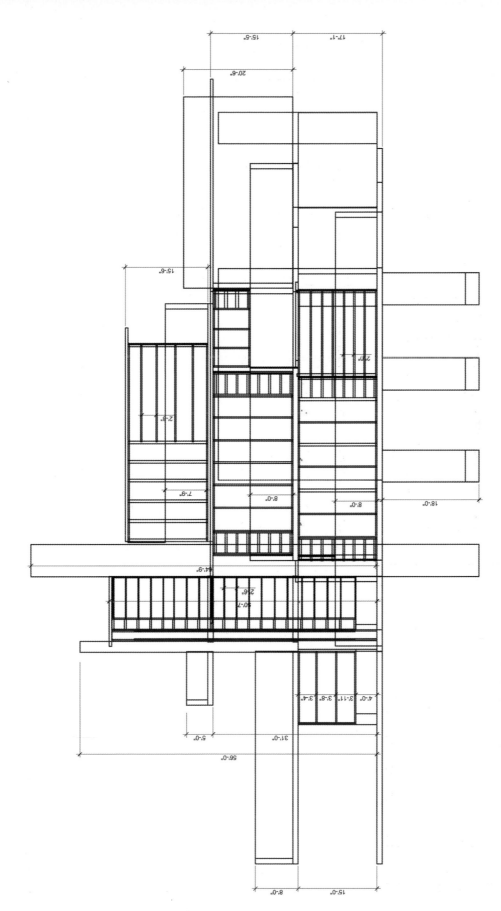

FIGURE 16.36 Dimensioned floor plan of the Falling Water House

A

Aligned Dimension You can create dimensions that are parallel to the locations or objects that you specify. In aligned dimensions, the dimension line is parallel to the extension line origins.

Angular It measures the angle between two or three points.

Arc Length It measures the distance along an arc or polyline arc segment.

Attach/Detach xref Attach and Detach are click buttons in the Xref Manager's dialog box. These click buttons allow users to attach or detach the external reference.

AutoCAD Workspaces The AutoCAD system provides three different workspaces for 2-D drafting and 3-D modeling: AutoCAD Classic Workspace and 2-D Drafting & Annotation Workspace are designed for 2-D drafting, and 3-D Modeling Workspace is for 3-D modeling.

B

Background It is the background of rendered scene, which can be changed.

Baseline Dimension Creates a linear, angular, or ordinate dimension from the baseline of the previous dimension or a selected dimension.

Basic Materials There are predefined materials stored in AutoCAD material library. They can be imported to your drawing.

Bind A click button in the Xref Manager's dialog box. It allows you to bind the external reference with the drawing.

Blipmode Plus-shaped blip markers are on when Blipmode is on.

BLOCK A block is composed of objects drawn on several layers with various colors, linetypes, and line weight properties. It is a single entity and can be inserted into other drawings.

Box The Box command allows you to create a three dimensional solid box.

Bump Map It makes the Bitmap Blend area available to specify the file name of a bump map.

C

Camera Point It is the location where you view the object.

Color/Pattern This setting adjusts the main color of the materials. You can adjust the color using value and the control in the color area.

Color Use RGB values to control the color of the point light. The color swatch shows the current color.

Cone The command creates a 3-D solid with a circular or elliptical base tapering symmetrically to a point.

Continued Dimension Create a linear, angular, or ordinate dimension from the second extension line of the previous dimension or a selected dimension.

Continuous Orbit You can click and drag the 3-D orbit view to start a continuous motion.

Copy edges This command enables you to copy 3D edges. All 3D solid edges can be copied as a line, arc, circle, ellipse, or spline.

Copy faces This command enables you to copy faces as a region or a body.

Crossing face Crossing face object always appears as two triangles intersect at right angles.

Cylinder It creates a 3-D solid similar to an extruded circle or ellipse but without a taper.

D

Dashboard The dashboard is a special palette that displays buttons and controls that are associated with a task-based workspace.

DC Online Opens the DesignCenter Online web page. When you get a web connection, the left pane displays folder containing symbol libraries, manufacturer sites, and additional content libraries. The right side shows more information and symbols enabling you to insert a web-located drawing into your current drawing.

Diameter It measures the diameter of an arc or circle and displays the dimension text with the diameter symbol in front of it.

Delete faces This command enables you to delete or remove faces, including fillets and chamfers.

Dimension This pull-down menu includes the commands used to place dimensions on drawings. You also can access these commands from floating toolbars.

Distance light Emits parallel light beams in one direction. Distant lights have no attenuation.

Draw The Draw pull-down menu has all of the commands used to draw objects in AutoCAD. You can access these commands from floating toolbars.

Drawing Orientation The drawing orientation determines whether the position of the plotted drawing is landscape (the longer edge of the drawing is horizontal) or portrait (the longer edge of the drawing is vertical). This is based on the size of paper selected.

DVIEW It is the command that creates perspective views in 3-D modeling.

E

Edge Copy Option This option allows you to copy individual edges on a 3-D solid object.

EDGESURF Creates a three-dimensional polygon mesh.

Edit This pull-down menu includes the Undo command (allows you to undo or reverse the most recent command) and the Redo command. It also contains the commands of Cut, Copy, and Paste.

ELEV This command sets the elevation and extrusion thickness of new objects.

Explode Use this command if you need to modify one or more objects within a block separately.

Extend Trim and Extend are paired commands. You can learn and memorize them together. You can shorten or lengthen objects to meet the edges of other objects by using the Trim or Extend commands.

Extrude It creates unique solid primitives by extruding existing two-dimensional objects.

Extrude Faces This command enables you to select planar faces of a 3-D solid object and extrude this object to a specified height or along a path.

F

Face Copy Option You can copy faces on a 3-D solid object with this option.

Face Delete Option You can remove faces from a 3-D solid object with this option.

Face Extrude Option You can extrude planar faces of a 3-D solid along a path or you can specify a height value and a tapered angle with this option.

Face Move Option With this option, you can edit a 3-D solid object by moving selected faces of the object.

Face Offset Option You can offset faces by a specified distance on a 3-D solid.

Face Taper Option With this option, you can edit 3-D solid objects. You can taper faces with a draft angle along a vector direction.

FACETRES This command adjusts the smoothness of shaded and rendered objects.

File This pull-down menu includes the commands needed to start a new drawing, open an existing one, save drawings and print, or plot a drawing. It also includes export data and an exit from AutoCAD.

Fillet The Fillet command allows you to round and fillet the edge of an object.

Font Name It lists the font family name for all registered true type fonts and all compiled shape (SHX) fonts in the Fonts folder. When you select a name from the list, the program reads the file for the specified font. The file's character definitions are loaded automatically unless the file is already in use by another text style. You can define several styles that use the same font.

Font Style Specifies font character formatting, such as italic, bold, or regular.

Format This pull-down menu allows you to create layers for our drawing. You may assign different colors, linetypes, and lineweights to layers. You also can change the text style and dimension style from this pull-down menu.

G

Gradient Hatch Gradient fills can be used to enhance presentation drawings, giving the appearance of light reflecting on an object.

Grid Display a dot grid in the current viewport that is not plotted.

H

Hatch You can hatch an area using a predefined hatch pattern, define a simple line pattern using the current linetype, or create more complex hatch patterns.

Height The height of the text should be different because of different scales. It sets the text height based on the value you enter.

Help The AutoCAD Help menu provides information about all program commands and procedures.

Hide This command regenerates a three dimensional wireframe model with hidden lines suppressed.

History Displays the last 20 locations of source objects accessed through the DesignCenter.

I

Imprint Option With this option, you can create new faces on 3-D solids by imprinting arcs, circles, lines, 2-D and 3-D polylines, ellipses, and so on.

Insert This pull-down menu allows you to insert WBLOCKS and attach external references. You also can insert drawing from previous AutoCAD drawings or other drawing programs.

Intensity Adjusts the intensity or brightness of the light. Entering 0 turns off a light.

Interference It creates a composite 3-D solid from the common volume of the two or more solids.

Intersect It creates composite solids or regions from the intersection of two or more solids or regions and removes the areas outside of the intersection.

L

Landscape It is a predefined 3-D model, which can be imported from the Materials Library.

Layer Layers are used to group information in a drawing by function and to enforce linetype, color, and other standards.

Layout Tab Layout tabs access an area called Paper Space. In Paper Space, you place your title block, create layout viewports to display views. Sometimes, you may dimension your drawing and add notes in Paper Space.

Lighting It manages lights and lighting effects in Model Space.

Limits Sets and controls the limits of the grid display in the current Model Space or Paper Space.

Linear Dimension You can create linear dimensions with horizontal, vertical, and aligned dimension lines. These linear dimensions can be stacked or they can be created end to end.

Lines Tab You can control dimension line properties including color, lineweight, and spacing. You also can control the extension of dimension lines and extension beyond the tick marks in the Lines Tab.

M

Mapped Materials This enables you to use Fixed Scale and Fit to Object mapping for different rendering purposes.

Mapping Coordinates You may specify mapping coordinates when you apply materials to the object. The command is SETUV.

Materials Materials can be attached to the object from the Materials Library. It creates a realistic look.

Mirror This command allows you to flip objects about a specified axis to create a symmetrical mirror image.

Model Space When you click on the Model tab, you are in Model Space. In Model Space, you draw your objects at a 1:1 scale and you decide appropriate drawing units, such as Architectural. In Model Space, you can view and edit your objects.

Model Tab The model tab accesses a limitless drawing area called Model Space. In Model Space, you draw, view, and edit your objects.

Modify This pull-down menu allows you to change the position, shape, or number of objects after they are created. The commands to change the text and dimensions are also included in this pull-down menu.

Move faces This command enables you to move the selected face on a 3-D solid object to a specified height or distance.

Multiline Text Used to draw text that is in paragraph form.

MVIEW This command creates and controls layout viewports. You can create a single viewport that fits the entire layout or create multiple layout viewports in the layout. Once you create the viewports, you can change their properties, their size, and move them as needed.

N

North Location Displays the north location dialog box in which you can set the north direction.

O

Offset Offset creates a new object whose shape parallels the shape of a selected object.

Offset faces This command enables you to offset faces equally by a specified distance or through a specified point.

Open Drawings Lists all opened drawings in the current AutoCAD session.

Ortho This option allows you to restrict cursor movement to horizontal and vertical for convenience and precision when creating and modifying objects.

Osnap Use object snaps to specify precision locations on objects.

P

Page Setup When you create a drawing, you specify a plotter and settings such as paper size and plot orientation. These settings are saved in Page Setup. You can control these settings for layouts and for the model tab using the Page Setup manager.

Paper Size In the plot dialog box, select the paper size that you want to use.

Paper Space When you click on the layout tab, you can access an area called Paper Space. In Paper Space, you place your title block and create layout viewports to display views. In Paper Space, one unit represents the paper distance on a plotted sheet. You can view and edit Paper Space objects, such as viewports and titleblocks.

Perspective It presents the object in a three-dimensional view just like a camera.

Plan Displays the plan view of a special user coordinate system.

Pline A polyline is a connected sequence of line segments created as a single entity. You can create straight line segments, arc segments, or a combination of the two.

Plot Area When plotting a drawing, you must specify the area of the drawing to plot.

Plot Offset The plot offset specifies an offset of the plot area relative to the lower-left corner (the origin) of the printable area or the edge of the paper, depending on the X and Y value specified in the options dialog box.

Plot Options In addition to the shaded viewport plotting option, there are several other plot options that can be specified for drawings which affect how objects are plotted, such as Plot Object Lineweights, Plot with Plot Styles, Plot Paper Space Last, and Hide Paper Space Objects.

Plot Scale You have to specify a scale to your final drawing when you start plotting. You can choose from a list of real-world scale, enter your own scale, or select the Fit to Paper to scale option to fit the drawing onto the selected paper size.

Plot Stamping It is a line of text that is added to your plot. You can specify where this text is located on the plot in the plot Stamp dialog box. Turn this option on to add specified plot stamp information—including drawing name, layout name, date and time, and so on—to a drawing that is plotted to any device.

Plot Style A plot style controls how an object or layer is plotted by determining plotted properties such as lineweight, color, and fill style.

Point Light Emits radiating light beams.

Preview It is a setting in plot dialog box. It allows you to preview the drawing that you are going to plot.

Primary Units Tab The settings for primary units control the display of the dimension values, including the unit format, the numeric precision, and the decimal separator style.

Printer/Plotter Before plotting a drawing, you must select a printer or plotter. The device you select affects the printable area of the drawing.

Purge You can remove unused named objects including block definitions, dimensions, dimension styles, layers, linetypes, and text styles with the Purge command.

Q

Quick Dimension This option, QDIM, creates or edits a series of dimensions. The command is particularly useful for creating a series of baseline or continued dimensions, or for dimensioning a series of circles and arcs.

R

Radius It measures the radius of an arc or circle and displays the dimension text with the letter *R* in front of it.

Redraw This command redraws and cleans up your drawing. Any plus-shaped markers on the screen disappear and drawing entities are redrawn.

Regen This command regenerates the entire drawing and recomputes the screen coordinates for all objects in the current viewport. It also reindexes the drawing databases for optimum display and object selection performance.

Reflection It adjusts the material's reflection (highlight or specula) color. You can adjust the color using value and the controls in the color area. The swatch displays the color.

Refraction It adjusts refraction of the object. It applies to Photo Raytrace rendering only. It also affects the transparency of a material.

Render: The Render command allows you to present materials and lighting effects in the 3-D model.

Revolve It creates solids by revolving two-dimensional objects about an axis.

REVSURF Creates a revolved surface about a selected axis.

Rotate This command allows you to rotate objects in your drawing around a specified based point.

Roughness It adjusts the material's roughness and shininess. Adjusting roughness changes the size of the material's reflective highlight. The lower the level of roughness, the smaller the highlight.

RULESURF creates a ruled surface between two curves.

S

Scale/Stretch You can resize objects to make them longer or shorter in only one direction or to make them proportionally larger or smaller. You can also stretch certain objects by moving an endpoint, vertex or control point.

Scene Command Manages scenes in Model Space.

Shaded Viewport Option The options for shaded viewport plotting give you a large degree of flexibility in conveying your three-dimensional designs to others. You can convey your design intent by choosing how viewports are plotted and by specifying a resolution level.

Shell Option This option allows you to create a shell (a hollow, thin wall with a specified thickness) from your 3-D solid object.

Single face A single face aligned object appears in the drawing as a triangle.

Single Line text Used to draw text that is not in paragraph form.

Slice This command allows you to slice a set of solids with a plane.

Snap Restricts cursor movement to specified intervals.

Solid BOX Only solid box can be modified by using the fillet command and Boolean Operations.

Spelling check AutoCAD has the function to check your spelling of text in the drawing.

Sphere The command allows you to create a three-dimensional solid sphere.

Spotlight Emits light in a cone in a specified direction.

Style Name This is a general category that can be assigned any name you choose. The style name is used to distinguish fonts. You may use the same name for the style as is used for the font, or you may use a different name, single number, or letter for the style name.

Subtract This command allows you to combine selected regions or solids by way of subtraction.

Symbols & Arrows Tab You can control the arrowhead symbols in dimensions and leaders including their type, size, and visibility in the Symbols & Arrows Tab.

T

TABSURF Creates a tabulated surface from a path curve and a direction vector.

Target Point It is the location where you look at the object.

Taper Faces This command enables you to taper faces with an angle.

Text Tab You can control the text style, font, and size in text tab. You also can change the text location from text tab.

Thickness It is a property of certain objects that gives them a 3-D appearance.

3-D views Several commands are available for viewing in 3-D views, such as southeast view and northwest view.

3DORBIT It creates an interactive 3-D orbit view in the current viewport. You use the pointing device to manipulate a view of the entire model or any object in the model from different points around it.

Titleblock It is a frame to put in a drawing. It is usually an xreference attached to a drawing in Paper Space. In the titleblock, you will display all of the information about the project, design firm, and design staff.

Tools This pull-down menu contains a spell checker and a Draw Order command that allows you to place images on top of one another. The AutoCAD DesingCenter is in the Tools menu. It allows you to choose predefined symbols and graphics from the AutoCAD system and insert them into your drawings. The Tool menu also has a command for customizing menus and toolbars and activating the Options.

Torus It creates a donut-shaped solid.

Transparency it adjusts the transparency of the object. You can use value to specify how transparent the object is.

Trim Trim and Extend are paired commands. You can learn and memorize them together. You can shorten or lengthen objects to meet the edges of other objects by usingthe Trim or Extend commands.

U

UCS User Coordinate System. In 3-D modeling, UCS allows you to change the plane to any desired drawing planes.

UCSVP The UCS in each viewport is controlled by UCSVP system variable.

Union It combines selected regions or solids by way of addition.

Units Controls coordinate and angle display formats and precision.

V

View Aligned It makes the object always face the camera. This is generally a good choice for trees and other non-planned objects.

View This pull-down menu includes the commands that control the display of your drawing.

Viewport It allows you to display multiple views on the screen.

Viewport It is a rectangle created by the MVIEW command in Paper Space. It can be used for setting up appropriate scales for the drawing.

Viewres This command controls the appearance of circles, arcs, ellipses, and splines using short vectors.

W

WBLOCK Writes object or block to a new drawing file. After using the WBLOCK command, a single entity is created as a block. It can be inserted into other drawings.

WCS User Coordinate System Workspace Coordinate System

Wedge It creates a 3-D solid with a sloped face tapering along the x axis.

Window This pull-down menu is used to arrange multiple drawings when you are working on more than one drawing at the same time.

X

Xref Manager The Xref Manager dialog box makes the task of managing xrefs easier. The dialog box's diagram and button are very easy to use.

XREF It is a command to attach or detach external reference.